HUMAN POTENTIAL

THE LIMITS AND BEYOND

Wendy Cooper and Tom Smith

DAVID AND CHARLES
Newton Abbot London

To Jack and Mary, our spouses – for their proof that human patience, at least, is unlimited.

Cooper, Wendy
Human potential.
1. Self-actualization (Psychology)
I. Title II. Smith, Tom
131'.3 BF637.S4

ISBN 0 7153 7925 9

Typeset by Northern Phototypesetting Company, Bolton
and printed in Great Britain
by Redwood Burn Limited, Trowbridge and Esher
for David & Charles (Publishers) Limited
Brunel House, Newton Abbot, Devon

Contents

Introduction

Most of us are ordinary people with ordinary abilities both physical and mental. But there are others; the exceptional few who fascinate and intrigue the rest of us by their capacity to stretch themselves beyond normal limits. How do they do it? What makes it possible? Can anything be learned from them?

Like all species man has been largely shaped by his environment, evolving and functioning to a pattern within fairly closely prescribed limits, always directed toward survival.

Yet, every now and again, we hear of exceptional people who defy the rules, who, for example, survive for long periods without even the accepted essential minimum of food, drink or sleep. Others successfully endure extremes of temperature which would normally kill, or isolation which should normally disorientate and destroy. They defy torture deliberately designed to break body or spirit and defeat accidental injury or disease which by every accepted criteria should be lethal.

Then there are those who under stress perform feats of strength and agility utterly impossible by usual standards or under usual conditions. A few strive toward similar ends by special systems of physical and mental training, even achieving in some cases control over involuntary muscles and functions.

Under the spur of overwhelming reasons, there are people who manage to prolong their lives for what they conceive to be a vital extra period, against all known odds, defying the logical medical verdict of certain imminent death.

To appreciate these achievements and the significance of such strange extensions of normal human potential, it is necessary first to know the accepted limits within which most of us work and how and why they came to be proscribed in the long course of evolution. It is also relevant to consider some of the ways in which man has always sought to extend such natural limits by unnatural means, using his ingenuity and talent for improvisation, his inventiveness and scientific genius, even to the extent in modern times of recreating a complete fabricated environment to carry with him on his voyage of exploration and discovery up into space or down into the sea.

This book sets out the 'norms' of unaided human potential, the extensions achieved artificially by ordinary people and then against this background examines the abnormal achievements of extraordinary people, in terms of survival and endurance through qualities of body or mind, or some subtle interplay of both.

And it poses the intriguing question: if certain people in certain circumstances can achieve a breakthrough in potential, can others learn to do this? Can the barriers be broken at will? Or must such achievements remain isolated and sometimes inexplicable phenomena at which the rest of us can only wonder?

1
Man and His Environment

An American woman lost in the snow still lives after a lethal drop in body temperature seven degrees below the minimum for normal survival. Naked volunteers in US Air Force experiments survived 'grilling' at temperatures far above those needed to cook a steak. Sorin Crainic, a nineteen-year-old Rumanian was rescued alive after ten-and-a-half days without food or water, under earthquake rubble. The Robertson family were thirty-eight days in an overloaded open boat, living only on an impossible third of a pint of water a day. Poon Lim, a wartime Chinese sailor, survived 131 days alone on an open, fragile raft. Zoologist Murray Watson, chased by a pack of hyenas, made an impossible twelve-foot leap into a tree. Mountaineers Messner and Habeler climbed to the roof of the world without oxygen equipment. Odette, who calls herself 'ordinary', never broke faith during more than two years of torture, isolation and persistent brutality.

All these people survived conditions which should normally kill. They defeated natural laws which should naturally have defeated them, endured the unendurable and defied the limits of the very environment for which they had been made.

For above all we are the creatures of our environment. First and foremost, physically and mentally, body and brain, we have developed in response to the external conditions of gravity, sunlight, temperature, atmosphere and availability of food.

These are the basic factors which have fashioned and shaped us, confined and refined us, in a continuous process of evolution always aimed at survival.

When the early amphibians gradually adapted to spend longer and longer periods in the strange free elements of sunlight and air, structures slowly changed. Gills became lungs; fins became limbs. Then over the millennia posture too underwent a whole series of alterations. The splayed limbs of the reptile were slowly transformed to those of the balanced quadruped. The ungainly crouch of our ape-like ancestors which freed the front paws for short periods extended and finally gave way completely to the upright stance of man.

And meanwhile the increasingly used paws evolved into hands, most importantly bringing the vital opposition of thumb and fingers which produced a vast new dimension of manual dexterity and skills. It was almost certainly these which in turn stimulated the small primitive brain to expand into the larger complex brain of the first truly thinking man.

Even now the immensely complicated organism we so complacently call *Homo sapiens* (despite considerable evidence at times to the contrary) remains not fully adapted. Our spines have not completely adjusted to the vertical position and this is one reason for the almost universal complaints of backache, stiff necks and sciatica. Back-pressures within our now upright circulation help to produce haemorrhoids and varicose veins, never found in creatures remaining as they were intended to do, firmly on four legs.

The common human predisposition to feel dizzy or even to faint is only a failure to react to a change in position. Elephants don't faint, which is just as well as the problems of first aid and getting their heads between their knees might be rather tricky. But neither do cats or even giraffes, which are subject to much greater changes of posture but are clearly better adapted. However, the sad story of poor Victor, the famous Marwell Park, Hampshire giraffe who perished in the course and cause of love, suggests they occasionally have other postural problems in relation to sex, of a kind man has happily avoided.

Broadly we have arrived at a workable balance not only within the environment provided by nature but within the artificial one we have imposed on ourselves. This in the long run may be the rub. For we may have put a full stop now to any further advantageous development of our species. Any more improvement or extension of present limitations may have to be *consciously* sought. By contrast, in the past, as men spread all over the globe, adaptations and refinements were bred in by natural selection to cope with the most adverse of conditions, even those operating in what would seem totally inhospitable areas.

One of the mysteries to us today is why in an almost empty world men ever chose to live in hostile environments. Presumably it was the need to follow food or escape predators, including other men, but the human race chose to settle and survived successfully in the frozen Arctic wastes, equatorial jungle, hot and cold deserts and in the thin air of high mountains. In the process it had to adapt in a great many ingenious ways.

It seems logical that the precarious beginnings should be in an environment best suited to man's early development, and most experts agree that the common ancestors to all varieties of mankind lived in Ethiopia over three million years ago.

From there they gradually spread across the globe defeating by sheer persistence and suitable adaptations the major constraints of climate and geography. Several ice ages intervened but man still survived, adapting all the time, learning all the time and improvising on the way.

His skin colour changed in different parts of the world to balance the absorption of vital vitamin D, regulated by exposure to sunlight. Hot or cold climates led to differing fat consumption and distribution. Slit lids evolved to protect the eyes of people living where there were sand-laden winds, and the mountain dwellers even developed extra blood cells to cope with lack of oxygen. Blue eyes allowed man to see more efficiently in the poorer northern light, and those of tropical man were shielded from the sun's glare by a brown iris bred in to act as built-in sunglasses.

In all this nothing was planned, nothing was deliberate, nothing was sought. All these changes came immeasurably slowly as the favourable genes for each set of conditions most persistently survived to be reproduced and passed on again.

And in simple ways, still infinitely important, man began to modify his environment, inventing fire and clothing for warmth, building shelter from the elements, forming tribes for pooling of skills and strength, erecting stockades to keep out the enemy, making weapons and spears for battle and hunting, and eventually the plough and the wheel for the first basic agriculture.

In the vast evolutionary time scale, it has been only a short step from these simple beginnings to the complex technology of today. And despite more sophisticated modern aids and despite the natural differences that contrasting environments have produced in man, there remains as always a fundamental and common set of requirements for the support of human life. The Eskimo's average body temperature, for instance, does not differ one iota from that of the African pigmy or Australian aborigine. 98·4°F (37°C) is the body temperature for maximum human health and efficiency and each of us carries within us a built-in survival kit of body systems, designed to counter adverse external conditions and maintain the right inner environment.

But whatever our bodies can do to offset extremes of external temperature, the range within which we can operate and survive remains surprisingly narrow, set nominally between 50°F (10°C) and 77°F (25°C). The issue is complicated because technology is continually coming up with better ways of insulating us from cold and heat.

Otto Edholm, Visiting Professor at the School of Environmental Studies, University College, London, in his new book *Man – Hot and Cold* does not even try to set environmental limits. Instead he concentrates on the changes in actual body temperature that we can tolerate and these again appear to involve very narrow limits on either side of the average 98·4°F (37°C) that is optimum for health and efficiency.

On the effects of body cooling he states:

> The changes which occur as body temperature declines are first intense shivering, which diminishes gradually as body temperature falls below about 95°F (35°C), then there is some muscular weakness and incoordination, so walking becomes difficult and there are frequent stumbles and falls. The mental state is one of dulling with diminished response to the environment and difficulty of understanding the situation. Consciousness may be lost at body temperatures between 86°F (30°C) and 89·6°F (32°C); by then shivering will have stopped and further cooling can be fairly rapid.

Once the internal body temperature falls below 77°F (25°C) death is normally considered inevitable, because the chemical reactions which cause the heart muscle to contract efficiently are temperature-dependent.

On the other hand if the body temperature rockets to above 107·6°F (42°C) the result is also death. The thermostatic mechanisms of that great survivor, the human body, strive desperately to control internal temperature in the face of external temperature assaults. There is a slight flexibility between individuals as regards their normal efficient body temperature, with a variation in a few people of about one degree either way. But a swing of just one further degree over our individual norm brings all the forces into play.

We all know the signs. One degree over normal and we feel it; we flush, we sweat, we are hot and sticky to the touch and even our breath is hot. Two degrees over and we collapse. But before that the body will have sought to lose even the smallest rise in temperature by the routine cooling mechanism of evaporation. Sweat pours from the skin, overloaded by fluid from distended blood vessels and from the lungs. The higher the temperature, as in fevers or heat stroke, the more intensive the process, until the body has lost all its available fluid and the system goes out of control. If the cause is not corrected and the fluid is not replaced, the result is death.

We rely so much on sweating for our temperature control that we are super-sensitive to changes in humidity. In a moisture-laden atmosphere very little evaporation is possible and heat cannot be dissipated. This explains the much greater discomfort of humid conditions, and our ability to withstand better much hotter but more arid climates. The middle of the Sahara can seem more pleasant, though 68°F (38°C) hotter, than Durban or the Florida swamps.

The vital need for rapid evaporation to cool the body and keep down internal temperature is one possible theory for the loss of body hair in humans over the course of evolution. If our ancestors changed from mainly vegetarian tree-dwellers, as many experts believe, to become hunters on the open plain, then they needed to be capable of bursts of speed to catch fast-footed prey. Such physical exertion is accompanied by excess heat production, so more naked skin surface to permit better evaporation became an obvious advantage. This meant the abandonment of the earlier and less efficient mechanism of heat regulation. This consisted of erecting or flattening body hair to increase or diminish the thickness of the insulating layers of air next to the skin. Look closely at your goosepimples and you can still see the now sparse and delicate hairs, striving hopelessly to do their old protective work.

Of course thinking man began to improvise and still does, using artificial means over and above the automatic physiological ones to adapt to temperature and humidity. The desert Arab covers himself with loose clothing which in a sense simulates the lost body hair by trapping relatively cool air to conserve his fluids and maintain normal body temperature. He also wears white clothing to reflect the sun and prevent heat being absorbed. Once in the shade, however, with surface body heat now higher than air temperature, he changes to black clothes to allow its dispersal. In contrast inhabitants of the rain forests, where humidity is high and sweating difficult, expose their skin to allow heat to radiate away.

Limiting physical activity, discarding clothing or using loose clothing, adopting open postures with limbs extended to present the largest body surface for heat exchange, are all ways man tries to cope with heat. But sweating remains the all-important built-in method and experiments have shown that increased sweat-rate is the basis of what we call 'acclimatisation'. This is achieved by regular exposure to heat sufficient to raise the body temperature. At one time it was thought physical work had to be done too, but it has been shown to take place just as well with passive exposure, and for only as little as an hour each day.

By using impermeable plastic suits, under a specially perforated enclosing garment through which hot air can be pumped at a controlled temperature, it has been possible to carry out very refined experiments which have produced some surprising results. They have established that exposure to heat does not have to be continuous to achieve acclimatisation, and even a short period of exposure daily can enable someone used to a temperate climate to achieve eventually a *higher* heat tolerance than someone living permanently in a hot country.

Experiments in Israel with two ethnic groups in which different sweat responses might be expected, one Yemenite and the other Kurdish Jews, showed no genetic factors were involved. The mean sweat-rate of the Kurdish men was exactly the same as that of the Yemenite men, and in both cases the mean sweat-rate for the women was identical but only half that of the men.

Age, sex, obesity and physical fitness all affect sweat-rates and therefore heat tolerance. Increased body weight and thickness of subcutaneous fat decreases tolerance. Fitness and training increase it. Using what is called a Wet Bulb Globe Thermometer (WBGT) which measures the effective heat in relation to humidity and airflow, stern rules are laid down in training American Marines. Outdoor training ceases for recruits when the WBGT index reaches 89°F (31·5°C) but fully trained and fit Marines can continue until the index reaches 91·4°F (33°C).

Even under normal conditions in temperate climates we lose quite unknowingly at least one and a half litres of fluid from our bodies by evaporation each day. This can rise rapidly to two and a half litres in hot climates. The trouble with losing sweat is that in the process we also lose salt, and this can also make heat lethal.

Salt is not strictly a fuel but a chemical essential to the functioning of every cell in the body. It is the perfect balance between sodium (contained in salt) and another mineral, potassium, which permits and controls the passage of vital substances across the cell membranes . . . a legacy perhaps from that first environment, the salt oceans, which cradled the first life forms and from which all other animal life was to come.

So simply drinking water to prevent dehydration is not enough. The lost salt must be replaced too, otherwise severe painful and crippling muscular cramps can develop. In deep mines or in hot countries where hard physical work is being done, it is common to add salt to the drinking water or to take salt tablets. In drinking water at a low concentration the salt is not only acceptable but positively attractive to the taste, when sweating has deprived the body of salt. If salt and water are not replaced bizarre behaviour starts to occur, followed by severe headaches and eventually loss of consciousness and death. It is small wonder that salt has always been more prized than gold in hot countries, and that to be called 'the salt of the earth' remains a high compliment even today.

Of course that doughty fighter, the human body, tries itself to offset the effects and overcome salt loss by lowering the salt content of the urine. Normally urine is almost saturated with salt, but that of a patient with heat stroke contains none.

Despite the hazards of salt loss and dehydration, some men, either deliberately or by accident, have shown they can endure and survive heat far beyond normal temperature limits. As long ago as the eighteenth century a scientist called Blagden reported to the Royal Society results of experiments in which the subject tolerated such high temperatures that a steak exposed at the same time was cooked. This had to be dry heat, and The Guinness Book of Records under the appropriate heading of 'Human Salamanders' claims that the highest dry-air heat ever endured by naked men was 399·9°F (204·4°C). This was in the course of US Air Force experiments back in 1960, when they were presumably testing ability to withstand re-entry temperatures after space flights. There's no indication of how long the men were subjected to this 'grilling', but obviously not for long, as the heat required to cook steaks is far less at only 320°F (160°C). Heavily clothed men in the same series of experiments survived 500°F (260°C).

While these extremes were borne in the cause of science, in Finland they seem to do it for fun. It must be admitted the temperatures are not quite so high, but 284°F (140°C) is considered by some to be quite bearable in a sauna bath. The excessive sweating is deemed cleansing and healthy, while the violent contrasts of the conclusion, which involves either immersion in cold water or rolling outside in the snow, is written off as merely stimulating. No wonder such a people managed to fight both the Russians and Germans at the same time and emerge undefeated!

However it was not in the cause of science, cleanliness or health, that some have been forced to endure beyond the normal heat limits, unless you interpret health in its broadest sense of striving to stay alive.

Geoffrey Moorhouse describes in his book *The Fearful Void* his 2,000-mile journey across the Sahara, the longest ever undertaken on camel and on foot, and the terrible effect of the heat. He wrote:

> I could feel the sand burning through the soles of my sandals, and the sextant became unpleasantly hot to handle. After no more than an hour and a half in the open, my lips had dried out and the spittle had become bitter on my tongue, thick and gummy in the corners of my mouth. I could see men might die in the heat of the desert . . .
>
> [And later as his plight got worse] My feet were now swelling so that it was difficult to get into my shoes, even though these had rotted so much that normally they would have been too loose to wear. After the first hour's march every morning, I felt as if my pelvis was being

ground to powder against some ball-and-socket joint in my trunk. Perpetually my mouth burned and my throat ached with dryness. I barely noticed, except at rest, the lice that were feasting in abundance upon my scraggy flesh.

At our midday camp I had felt as though the sun were burning a hole through my skull, thickly wrapped in a headcloth though it was . . . the increase in temperatures I could only measure crudely by the amount of water I was consuming each day.

Antoine de Saint Exupéry, a French airline pilot, who crashed in the Libyan desert with his mechanic, Prévot, is another who has vividly described the effects of heat and thirst in his book *Wind, Sand and Stars*. After only three days walking under the burning sun in vain attempts to find water or rescue, both men were tortured by a mixture of mirage and hallucination. Sometimes it was water spread in a great lake, sometimes a beautiful city, always flickering just on the horizon and always retreating before them. Once it was a cross set on what was clearly a monastery, and at night Antoine saw lamps signalling out of the darkness. In the daytime he was hailed by groups of Bedouin rescuers. But the figures that had moved and even spoken to him petrified into useless rocks or fossilised tree trunks as he approached. Burned by sun and wind, dehydrated and dying, Antoine and Prévot ironically suffered intensely from cold at night.

Nineteen hours was the acknowledged limit for survival without water even by the acclimatised Bedouin, but at first an unusual wind blowing from the north-east slowed up the deadly dehydration process. And then it changed, and they knew the hot, searing blast from the familiar westerly direction signalled the end. By day they burned, by night they froze, yet still they defied the limits of endurance to survive and record their ordeal. The author described the remorseless environment:

The desert is as smooth as marble. By day it throws no shadow, by night it hands you over naked to the wind. Not a tree, not a hedge, not a rock behind which I could seek shelter. The wind was charging me like a troop of cavalry across open country. I turned and twisted to escape it: I lay down, stood up, lay down again, and still I was exposed to its freezing lash.

It seems a particular cruelty that in the same inhospitable spot, as day turns to night, extremes of heat give way to extremes of cold, both deadly to the weakened dehydrated human body. But while the changeable wind can be an ally or an executioner, the only real saviour is water, as

Antoine's story and the experience of others recorded in the next chapter show.

Man is more dependent in a hot climate on a good water supply than most other animals, simply because of the special system of adaptation to heat by sweating developed countless generations ago, when man evolved first as a tropical animal in central Africa. For this purpose we have more functional sweat glands than any other animal and consequently each individual gland is able to produce larger volumes of sweat than the glands of other species. P. F. Scholand, an eminent biologist, in describing man as a 'tropical animal' insisted the term applied across the globe – applicable even to Eskimos in its basic truth. The Yemenite and Kurdish studies suggest that he was right. As a tropical animal with a great need for water, man tends to prefer hot, moist areas and so Java and the Ganges valley are among the regions of greatest human density, while hot, dry areas tend to be underpopulated.

As a tropical animal, it also follows that man adapts better to heat than cold. Low temperatures can pose a particularly nasty set of problems for the human body and its main effort has to be toward conserving inner heat, the vital core temperature. It does this by shutting down the circulation in the skin and extremities and shunting it through the trunk and brain.

As well as its main mechanism to try and preserve its inner temperature, the body has two other familiar built-in responses to counter cold – shivering and goosepimples, both local surface reactions. Goosepimples, as we have seen, still strive pathetically and ineffectively with modern sparse hair to insulate against either heat or cold. Shivering works better and through rapid contracting and relaxing of muscles provokes all-over body exercise to raise temperature. The same mechanism is at work with shivering in high fever, but in that case it is cunningly trying to elevate the temperature even more, to a level which will kill the germs before they can kill the body.

Sadly when we need to shiver most we may not be able to do so. As we grow older our heat regulation becomes less efficient and one of the first mechanisms to be lost is shivering. Consequently the victims of hypothermia may not even be aware that they are cold and so do not attempt to compensate artificially.

Obviously if this continues too long, the skin and underlying tissues are irreversibly damaged. The type and degree of injury depends on the extent of the cold and the aggravating effects of wind and moisture. Trench foot, which we associate with World War I as the name implies, resulted from long periods of inactivity in damp, cold trenches and dugouts, often with the feet in equally cold water. Exercise might have helped to counter the worst effects, but preserving the feet from cold no doubt seemed rather less important than preserving the rest of the body from shot and shell. Trench foot, incidentally, was actually described long before the 1914 war back in Napoleonic times by no lesser doctor than Baron Larrey, Napoleon's personal army surgeon.

The familiar chilblain is a mild form of the same problem. Both are effects of cold insufficient to actually freeze the tissue. In real frostbite the water within the cells is frozen to form ice crystals, effectively dehydrating the cells and over-concentrating other substances in them. In a mild form it can be treated by thawing rapidly in hot water, but slow thawing is probably less damaging for a case which has lasted for one or more hours.

Unfortunately this sort of serious cold injury not only results in cellular damage but blockage of the blood vessels with cell debris, leading to gangrene and permanent tissue loss, sometimes involving fingers, toes and even limbs. Swelling during thawing tends to prevent circulation again and cause further damage.

Recently the use of oxygen under high pressure to saturate the injured areas in the hope of speeding repair has given encouraging results, but generally it is a difficult condition to treat, and untreated it most certainly results in death. Frostbite rarely occurs until the air temperature drops below 10·4°F (–12°C), but it can happen even at 23°F (–5°C) if there is a high wind and if clothing also becomes damp. The increased evaporation of water by the wind and conduction of heat away by wet clothing causes even more disastrous cooling effects on the body.

Nowhere is the danger from wet clothing and cold more apparent than on the hills of Northern England and Scotland. Strangely, man can work stripped to the waist in the sub-zero temperature of the dry South Pole, but may die within minutes in sodden clothing on a wet, windy Scottish hillside only yards from safety. This happened to one apparently well-equipped climber on Cairngorm in 1975. Exhausted and lost in a 'white out' blizzard, he made the standard bivouac – a simple hole in the snow facing away from the biting wind – intending to shelter there until the conditions cleared. He died, according to the medical experts who later examined his body, within two hours of entering his snow hole and never knowing he was only 400 yards away from the warmth and safety of a busy mountain-top restaurant.

Dr T. M. Stewart, medical officer to the Braemar Mountain Rescue Team, who has attended many such tragedies, emphasises that the difference between dry and wet clothing can also be the difference between life and death. He tells of a group of four Cairngorm climbers, lost in the snow, one of whom, a girl, fell into a stream. This seemingly minor incident was to prove fatal. She died within two hours from cold despite adequate shelter, while the others lived to be rescued some eight hours later.

Deaths from cold on mountains are a twentieth-century European phenomenon. The hills were as popular with the Victorians as they are with the young of today, but the heavy woollen tweeds, Norfolk jackets, plus-fours and boots, then considered compulsory wear, offered far better insulation than the casual clothing of today. It is significant that most tragedies now occur in autumn and spring, when climbers rashly venture upwards in light clothing and are overtaken by unexpectedly severe conditions.

The dangers of the combination of cold and wet have long been recognised, particularly in wartime. The Greek historian, Herodotus, as long ago as the fifth century BC gave it as the reason for many of the deaths of the sailors in a battle with the Persians. In 1792, James Currie, physician to the Liverpool Infirmary, was so concerned about naval crews dying in the sea within easy reach of land that he conducted experiments on volunteers, measuring their body temperatures after varying periods of immersion in cold water.

If heeded, Currie's work might have saved a lot of lives in this century. The *Titanic* sank in a flat calm sea, but many even in lifeboats died of cold. During World War II two-thirds of the Luftwaffe pilots who ditched in the North Sea were dead not from drowning but from cold. Others found to be alive when rescued still died later because their core temperatures continued to fall to below critical levels, a deadly mechanism emphasised by Currie 150 years before. For the same reason 200 of the 300 who were picked up alive out of the sea after the *Gneisenau* was sunk in the Battle of the Falkland Islands died on the decks and in the sick bays of the ships which rescued them. Such deaths were made the 'excuse' for the loathsome experiments on prisoners in Dachau, where it was found that death always occurred at body-core temperatures of 75°F (24°C) and was almost certain anywhere below 80°F (26·7°C).

The Allies, with their huge shipping losses, suffered in this way even more than the Germans. A Royal Naval survey during World War II showed that of 20,000 people shipwrecked in the war and reaching lifeboats or rafts, the maximum survival was ten days when surrounding sea temperatures were less than 41°F (5°C). In all, 22 per cent of those in lifeboats and 42 per cent of those in rafts died. The corresponding figures for those sunk in the warmer waters of the tropics show the vital role played by temperature – then the maximum survival was seventy-seven days and equivalent mortality rates for boats and rafts were only 5 per cent and 9 per cent respectively.

Experiments conducted by the British during the war, rather more humane than the Nazi ones, showed that the traditional abandon ship call of 'Women and children first' was logically in need of urgent revision. Women lost heat only one-fifth as fast as men, so they could survive for five times as long.

Children, however, remain a first priority. After the *Lakonia* disaster, despite the relatively warm Mediterranean sea temperature of 62·6°F (17°C), all the children who spent the night in the sea died despite being kept afloat by life-jackets. Over 100 people died that night in the water around the blazing liner in sight of land and the would-be rescue ships which tragically kept their distance until morning. Death from cold overtook all those who tried to swim ashore, and all who mistakenly stripped before they entered the water believing that their clothes would hamper them. The only survivors were adults who floated huddled together in life-jackets and made no attempts to swim.

Because it is a better conductor of heat, water soaks away the body's heat and energy faster than air. Immersion is the deadliest form of cold. Until recently it was thought that swimming, by generating heat from muscular energy, could compensate for heat loss and keep the body temperature normal. This is now known to be a fallacy. Even the most vigorous swimmer cannot maintain a heat balance if the surrounding sea temperature is less than 75·2°F (24°C), only reached in a narrow band around the equator.

The latest survival advice is to stay still, until rescued, preferably hunched to reduce exposed surface area, using as little energy as possible and retaining clothing in order to trap a layer of undisturbed body-heated water close to the skin. That this is excellent advice is proved by a considerable drop in death rates among the young members of British sailing clubs, who since the 1960s have followed this practice. Their older colleagues, who on the whole have ignored it, continue to pay the price with a higher death rate.

Neither climatic conditioning nor adaptation seem able to improve man's susceptibility in cold water. The Eskimo would survive immersion in a freezing sea no better than the Arab. The only exceptions seem to be the pearl-diving Ahma girls of Japan and Korea, whose inherited ability to resist the effects of cold clearly illustrates a genetic factor. In summer they dive naked into the northern Pacific and even in winter only wear a thin cotton shift. They have been shown to have a basal metabolic rate (a measure of their ability to convert food into energy) 25 per cent above normal. They are able to produce heat more efficiently and economically than people of other races, or even other Koreans or Japanese, and can tolerate cold much better. Tests have confirmed that they do not shiver even after three hours in water at 82·4°F (28°C) while European women shiver after the same time at 87·8°F (31°C).

Wider studies have been done in water temperatures more typical of our coastal seas, which reach 62·6°F (17°C) only briefly at the height of summer. The average survival time at this temperature is estimated at only five hours. Both laboratory and actual sea experiments have been done to find means of delaying body cooling in water. Cross-channel swimmers have been studied as they spend from twelve to twenty hours in water at temperatures of 59°–62·6°F (15–17°C). The main reasons for these swimmers being able to last four times as long as normal were found to be the intake of high-energy foods from accompanying supply boats, some heat production from fast swimming, and their thick layer of subcutaneous fat topped up by added grease. Swimmers who tired, however, swam more slowly and cooled faster. A vicious circle was set up because as they cooled muscular work became more difficult and the rate of cooling increased. Some became confused and disorientated. Coaches have sometimes reported difficulty in persuading swimmers in obvious difficulties to leave the water, as their minds are unable to grasp their situation. Others even hallucinate. The woman winner of the 1951 cross-channel swimming race told onlookers on the beach that she was chased all the way across by strange furry animals. Another competitor ate with some relish the cotton ball he requested to wipe his eyes.

It was failure to appreciate the cumulative effect of prolonged cold, wet and windy conditions that was largely responsible for the disaster that befell Captain Scott's expedition to the South Pole. Within a few days blizzards and blustering gales lowered the temperatures, increasing the risk of frostbite and sapping the strength and alertness of his team in a manner typical of hypothermia. Scott noted in his diary that their sleeping blankets and clothing were becoming steadily wetter. Unfortunately the numbness of the skin induced by frostbite allows serious freezing to occur without the normal warning pain, and in hypothermia the brain itself is also numbed as circulation slows down, so that actions and reactions are sluggish. It all sets up a vicious circle – the colder you get the slower you get and the slower you move the colder you get. Everything becomes an intolerable effort, and this shows in the weary disjointed notes of Lieutenant Bowers made near the end of the expedition and their lives. He wrote, 'Very heavy surface – ice crystals – lower temperature – Wilson's leg – Evan's fingers'.

Cold injury doesn't always pick out the weak as its first victims. On the same expedition the first man to crack was Evans, who had been a PI instructor in the Navy. He was the biggest and strongest, yet he was the first one to fall behind and was found crawling aimlessly on hands and knees, before losing consciousness and dying.

What killed Scott and his men was not the frostbite which affected skin and limbs but the fatal drop in internal body temperature.

As we have already seen, when the core temperature falls below 77°F (25°C) it is almost always lethal. Even with deliberate cooling for surgical purposes (an essential part of open heart or transplant techniques) the body is not taken below 82·4°F (28°C). At this temperature the heart still beats, albeit slowly, and natural breathing can be supplemented by artificial respiration if necessary.

The record for a survivor from this form of deliberate deep cooling was a woman cancer patient who was taken down to an amazing 48·2°F (9°C), and whose heart was at a standstill for an hour. After 'rewarming' she recovered consciousness with no signs of the brain damage that could have been expected, and only died thirty-eight weeks later from further spread of her original disease.

Another survival story, this time in extreme but accidental cold, is in some ways even more remarkable as everything would appear to have been stacked against the victim. She was not only black but an alcoholic, both factors unfavourable to her chances. Heredity would have made her genetically better adapted to heat than cold, and alcohol forces the skin to disperse heat faster, so that she should have got cold quicker and probably also been less fit to start with than a non-alcoholic. Despite all she was found alive in the snow in sub-zero temperatures with an internal body heat of only 66·2°F (19°C). Unhappily her limbs were so badly affected by frostbite that all four had to be amputated.

Confusion about the role of alcohol in countering cold or reviving victims arises from old myths such as those St Bernard dogs, famous for centuries for rescuing travellers trapped in the snows of Switzerland. They were always supposed to carry neat brandy in the little barrels slung under their collars. In fact that would have been disastrous. What they did carry was brandy super-saturated with sugar to form a brandy syrup. This allowed the alcohol to stimulate the body's metabolism while the sugar counteracted its heat-dispersing effect.

But the 66·2°F (19°C) core temperature of the unfortunate New

York alcoholic is no longer the lowest recorded for survival from accidental hypothermia. More recently a three-year-old Scandinavian child recovered from a core temperature of only 62·6°F (17°C) without any long-term ill effect.

In Britain one of the major units treating accidental hypothermia is in Glasgow. The lowest recorded core temperature for any survivor so far there is 73·4°F (23°C), and the young man of twenty-seven was only saved then by the drastic expedient of opening his chest and pouring warm fluids over the exposed surface of his heart.

Apart from evolving mechanisms to try and offset effects of temperature, the human body has also had to adapt to alterations in pressure. Surviving at all altitudes from sea level to 12,000ft (3,658m) is not strictly for the birds. Man can do it too, though less easily. Some can live healthily at heights which would be impossible for others, yet this is not built into their genes. The ability is developed as an intricate but subconscious response of the body to the lower oxygen content of the air. It takes place in anyone, given time – time is the vital factor. Damage and death only occur if we ignore the rules, changing our environment and moving from one pressure to another too rapidly.

We have all heard of mountain sickness and some have experienced it. Headache, nausea, giddiness and misery engulf half the visitors between twenty-four and forty-eight hours after rapid arrival at mountain resorts between 8,000ft (2,438m) and 10,000ft (3,048m), and *all* similar arrivals at over 12,000ft (3,658m). Even more alarmed are those who suddenly find themselves unable to breathe, with lungs filled with fluid and hearts racing as if to burst.

All these unpleasant symptoms are the result of oxygen deprivation, because the low atmospheric pressure at such heights reduces the oxygen available to the lungs. It is from the lungs that red blood cells pick up oxygen and carry it to all parts of the body. When the lungs cannot get enough neither can the red blood cells, and oxygen starvation proceeds to affect the brain and nervous system by producing the first set of symptoms, or the delicate mechanism of the lungs themselves to produce the second. Some unfortunate people suffer both.

Those who make a correct slow ascent or who always live at these levels have no trouble. Their bodies adapt by simply producing more red blood cells. Simply is perhaps not quite the right word if you stop to consider what the intricate feedback mechanism and sensory devices have to do, first in detecting the need and then in meeting it.

At sea level the average human blood sample contains 5 million red cells to each cubic millimetre. At 12,000ft (3,658m), samples from acclimatised people show 7 to 8 million red cells. So it is not surprising it takes the body's own detection and rescue services a few days to sort out the problem. Once the distress signals have been interpreted, the bone marrow has to manufacture another 2 million or more red cells and expel them into the circulation to provide more efficient transport for the limited amount of oxygen.

With these additional cells the demands of the tissues for oxygen can be met even in very rarefied air. And for the wiser slow-ascending climber, this adaptation actually takes place as he goes upward. It may not be as comfortable and convenient at the time as the speedy cable car, but it avoids the double price such luxury exacts not just in the cost of the ticket but in the cost later of physical discomfort and distress.

Although this extra cell capacity for carrying oxygen has never become a genetic adaptation, people born in mountainous regions develop it almost immediately after birth. This factor has helped athletes such as Kenyan and Ethiopian long-distance runners, who scored notable successes in the Olympics before coaches of teams from lower-lying countries recognised the value of acclimatising in advance at higher altitudes than those at which the competitions were to be held.

More recently an even simpler method of stepping up the red cell count has been found and without breaking any Olympic rules. About a litre of blood is taken from an athlete a week before his event. During that week the lost blood is replaced naturally by the body, but in addition just prior to the race, red cells obtained from the earlier withdrawn litre of the competitor's own blood are re-injected, giving extra oxygen-carrying capacity at just the right time.

There is no doubt that for fit athletes and to obtain short bursts of energy this technique is effective, but it may have dangers, as extra red cells thicken the blood, especially at low temperatures and particularly when exertion is being undertaken which can cause the daily loss of between six and eight litres of water from the lungs. In helping high-altitude mountain climbers, Dr Roman Zink of Munich University counters this by transfusing with plasma (blood from which the cells have been removed). This prevents thickening and restores the normal rate of blood flow. By this means twenty-three climbers have so far been enabled to reach heights of over 25,000ft (8,200m) without the customary oxygen equipment. Even Everest was conquered without oxygen in 1978 by two Germans, Peter Habeler and Reinhold Messner.

This was an amazing achievement. The two men joined a big expedition, but one where the rest of the party were using traditional oxygen aids. They received no encouragement for what the others clearly felt was a highly dangerous project, and indeed they were told they were going up crazed with ambition but would come down crazed in the head. If an object lesson was needed they certainly had it early on when a Sherpa porter suffered a severe stroke, leaving him paralysed down one side. Even when he was carried down and back to base camp there was no real recovery and he was finally flown out to the hospital Edmund Hillary had built in the valley.

It was a frightening incident for Messner and Habeler, because born at 10,000ft (3,048m) the Sherpas could normally cope without oxygen even at 22,000ft (6,706m) and over. It all added to the weight of rather grim mountain mythology, which hinted at a whole American expedition stricken, and members now mindless creatures hidden away in Homes for the insane. Some 30 per cent of another expedition were supposed to have suffered from burst blood vessels, brain damage, memory loss and hallucinatory experiences.

But nothing could stop the two Germans. They were highly motivated and both felt it was pointless simply repeating the ascent with oxygen in the way already achieved by so many people. They relied on the fact that they were both in peak physical condition, had climbed in partnership for many years, and most important would have acclimatised slowly in the two weeks' gradual ascent from base camp. This would be relied upon for 80 per cent acclimatisation. Even so their first try was a failure, with Habeler lost in mist and only saved by coming on a marker pole quite by chance.

Back at their camp at 18,000ft (5,486m) it took them a few days to work up confidence again. They knew the thin air was an insidious enemy that struck without warning, as it had done with the Sherpa, but if the worst happened there would be no one to carry *them* down. They actually made a pact that if an accident happened to either of them, the other would carry on and not hazard the chance of success by lingering with the disabled partner.

Their object on that second attempt was to achieve a final camp that would leave only 8,000ft (2,438m) to go for the summit. In fact they made camp at 23,000ft (7,010m) and without oxygen climbed the Lhotze face in a record four hours. Another member, Eric Jones, who adapted well to low oxygen started out with them but simply could not keep up their pace.

It was not easy and at times they almost gave up. At one point Habeler found his fingers paralysed and thought he was about to suffer the fate of the Sherpa. Unable to talk to each other he drew an arrow in the snow pointing downwards, but Messner immediately drew one pointing upwards and they struggled on, gasping for breath. Messner reached the summit first and Habeler stumbled up to him crying and actually falling over him. They were too exhausted and perhaps too disorientated to feel pride in the moment of achievement – they were just aware of being happy but hardly knew even where they were – it was just the top of some mountain somewhere in the world.

All the same they had done it. They had proved that men could reach, and for a time at any rate survive unaided on, the very roof of this world. What is more, despite getting caught in an avalanche on the descent, and damage to Messner's eyes through taking off his goggles too often, they got down safely to tell their story.

So feats believed impossible as recently as the 1960s are today being achieved by man's growing ability to manipulate his internal systems to external demands. But before we think we are too clever in beating other animals to the roof of the world, perhaps we should remember that the Bar-headed Goose has been flying in the course of regular migration 6,000ft (1,829m) higher than Everest, a height at which oxygen is so scarce that by all medical criteria the birds should be falling unconscious from the sky.

The contrasts of increased air pressure presents fewer problems. Miners, for example, are rarely affected even in the deepest mines where the pressures are twice or three times the normal. The deepest levels of mining are at Carltonville, Transvaal, where a record depth of 12,600ft (3,840m) was attained in 1975. The worst problem then was the heat with a rock temperature at this depth of 131°F (55°C). So far as oxygen goes, the body simply absorbs as much as it needs from the plentiful supply in the high-pressure air. The story is very different below the sea. The pressure only 30ft (9·1m) underneath the ocean, which is the normal limit of man's unaided survival, is over twice as great as in the deepest mine. Worse still, there is no free oxygen.

All the same some human beings such as Japanese pearl divers, invariably women, cope with these pressures in breath-held dives of up to two-and-a-half minutes, returning to the surface within that time safely and without harm, at least in the short term. Their lifelong training helps them not only to increase lung capacity to hold oxygen, but forces muscles to work under the tension imposed by the sheer pressure of water at depth and in spite of some inevitable oxygen debt.

The very latest devices used for training young swimmers emulate this system, with out-of-water machines cleverly spring loaded against the moving arms and legs of the dryland swimmer to simulate the effects of water resistance and pressure. No international swimming coach of any country can afford now to ignore this modern approach to producing successful competitors, but the full long-term effects cannot yet be known. With pearl divers the repeated assaults on lungs and circulation appear to shorten lives and they are reported to die young. Hopefully the more controlled and supervised work with young swimmers will not produce any adverse effects later.

Diving below 30ft (9·1m) normally makes the use of compressed air or some form of breathing apparatus essential. It also means the time spent under water must be carefully calculated not only because of the limit of the air supply but because with compressed air a very slow ascent is vital.

The reason for this is that oxygen only makes up one-fifth of the air we breathe. Almost all the rest is relatively insoluble nitrogen, which we cannot use and do not need and which under normal atmospheric pressure only reaches the bloodstream in insignificant and harmless amounts by diffusion. But using compressed air and with the steep rise in pressure at depth, much more nitrogen is forced into the blood and remains in solution there as long as the pressure is sustained.

If the pressure is released too rapidly by surfacing too fast, the nitrogen turns into gas again and millions of tiny bubbles appear in the blood and nerve cells, blocking the circulation and causing the painful diver's disease known as 'the bends'. The name comes from the agonised contortions of the victim; its danger comes from damage to brain and nervous system. The only answer is to re-pressurise immediately and then bring back to normal over many hours. The body can adapt given time.

Recently, a mixture in which nitrogen has been replaced by the gas helium, less soluble in blood even under pressure and non-bubble forming, has extended useful diving time by allowing faster ascent. Its advantages far outweigh the hilarious and so far unexplained Donald Duck voices it produces.

Despite the norms and rules there are some amazing diving achievements which break them. The fantastic depth of 282ft (85·9m) was reached by a Frenchman, Jacques Mayol, in a breath-held dive in 1973 made off the Isle of Elba. He lived to tell the tale despite pressure on his thorax of 136·5 psi and a pulse rate that fell to 36.

Enzo Maiorca of Italy actually beat this in 1974 with a dive of 285ft (85m) made off Sorrento, but he surfaced completely unconscious.

It is all a very dangerous business and the body does not take kindly to such abuse. Leaving aside pressure hazards of diving there are still problems for the human body in any attempts at simple immersion without breathing apparatus. Yet the records achieved are in many ways even more remarkable.

In 1959 a thirty-two-year-old electronics technician from California managed to stay under 10ft (3m) of water in a swimming pool for 13 min 42·5sec; he was helped by hyperventilating with pure oxygen for thirty minutes before his descent. The longest record without any such previous preparation was made back in 1912 by another Frenchman, Georges Pouliquin, who stayed under water for 6min 29·8sec.

The record dive with Scuba (self-contained underwater breathing apparatus) is 437ft (133m) made by John J. Gruener and R. Neal Watson, both Americans, and achieved off Freeport, Grand Bahama in 1968. A simulated dive using gas mixtures in a dry pressure chamber recorded in Marseille, France in 1972 was equivalent to 2,001ft (610m).

The deepest actual escape without any equipment was from 198ft (60·3m) and was made by Sub Lt W. Morrison, RNVR and E. R. A. Swatton from a submarine in Loch Striven, Strathclyde in 1945.

Adapted, fashioned and conditioned to living in free air, man is not finding it easy to defeat the problems of an underwater environment even with the help of ingenious training and modern technology. Yet millions of years ago other air-breathing animals, the whales, dolphins and seals, solved the problem of deep diving by a mechanism we still do not fully understand. Large whales have been known to dive from the surface to depths of more than 5,000ft (1,524m) and return in the space of minutes with no problems from pressure, and yet their ancestors too were once land mammals.

Their submersion times also put all our own diving records to shame. It is now believed that there are two separate adaptations which enable a seal to hold its breath for half-an-hour at a time. For a start the blood has a much higher oxygen-carrying capacity than ours does and, secondly, it seems that during a dive a 'shunt' mechanism alters the circulation system so that all the oxygen-carrying blood is diverted to the brain. The tissues have been adapted to cope with this temporary oxygen debt and are flushed with oxygen-rich blood again as soon as the seal re-surfaces.

The Japanese pearl divers and the success of modern training methods for swimmers show humans can improve by practice and conditioning. Exceptional underwater achievements by exceptional men such as Mayol and Foster prove some humans have special capacities or can develop them. If we are ever driven to utilise underwater resources by some overwhelming need, perhaps the human race too will prove capable eventually of better natural adaptation.

Meanwhile, however, man finds the easier answer is to take his own environment with him, oxygen, pressure and all, in the form of diving bells and submarines. The activities of the occupants are obviously limited by their necessary imprisonment within small portable worlds, and the depth at which these can be used is limited by the pressure their hulls can withstand. It is possible in the past we have not always got this right. At least one nuclear submarine, *Thresher*, was lost because, according to the most widely held theory, someone's arithmetic was wrong and the hull failed to withstand the pressures for which it had been designed.

The need to examine and maintain oil rigs has prompted some great advances for divers. Their biggest enemy has been cold and many unexplained deaths in the past are now recognised as having been due to hypothermia. Under its influence at least one cold, confused diver is known to have severed his own lifeline. Even as recently as the construction of Sealab III, the planners did not allow for the possibility of hypothermia. They gave it a pressurised atmosphere of 5 per cent oxygen and 95 per cent helium and a skin of aluminium which dissipated the occupants' heat into the surrounding water more than six times as fast as would an atmosphere of air. The deaths of its first occupants were ascribed to 'narcosis of the deep'. It was months before cold was recognised as the true cause.

Since then man has applied, some say misapplied, his ingenuity to the problem. Divers were given electrically heated suits but short circuits in the wire mesh caused burns from hot spots. It's not easy to tolerate a hole burning in your skin while you are several hundred feet below the sea and unable to change the position of your body. The diver faces the dilemma of turning off the current and chilling to death before reaching the surface, or continuing to burn during the necessarily slow ascent! Not surprisingly these suits have been abandoned in favour of hot water heating pumped from the surface through flexible tubes. Everything depends on its efficiency. If the hot water supply fails, the diver's skin temperature becomes that of the sea around him in one minute. In two he wants out – in seven, he is hypothermic. If he is quick in shutting off the now cold flow – he has a valve to do this – his maximum expected survival is 18 minutes. A neoprene suit may allow him an extra half hour. This gives time for the heat supply to be mended or for him to enter a diving bell, but not usually to reach the surface.

A much better, though much more expensive answer, is the Mantis which allows the diver to breathe normal air at normal pressure and still dive to 2,000ft (610m), controlling his speed and direction with propellers fitted to each corner, able to view well through a two-inch-thick screen and to use claw-like arms to carry out tasks such as grasping and lifting.

Going up rather than down and starting to penetrate space, man is forced to carry his familiar protective environment with him in a rather similar way. It is as simple to take normal atmosphere and pressure up into space as down into the sea, but it is another thing entirely to re-create the effects of gravity.

Although on our own earth we are unconscious of the pull of normal gravity (designated as 1g), it is still the prevailing force to which body and brain are accustomed and the means by which we have learned to orientate ourselves and keep our balance. Any disturbance of the organs of position and balance in our ears and joints, as on a fairground roundabout or with travel sickness, makes us dizzy and nauseated. The very finely tuned nerve endings in our ankles, knees and hips, and the specialised crystals in the fluid-filled canals in our inner ears normally have the steady pull of gravity as their baseline. Body movement and balance trigger a controlled signal interpretable by the brain as changes in position. Take away the gravity baseline and the reactions to positional changes become confused and chaotic.

Specialised training methods are used to try to help potential astronauts counter this. Intensive simulated space training includes use of centrifuges to set up very large forces as in take-off and loop-the-loop flights which allow the occupants to experience weightlessness if only for short periods. Although astronauts are tested early on for resistance to normal earthbound forms of motion sickness, even good natural resistance and all the pre-flight preparations are no guarantee against suffering space sickness in varying degrees. One case was reported of a crew member who suffered in this way right to the moon and back. This surely has to make the Guinness Book of Records for the longest case of travel sickness in history!

One helpful solution has been to create an artificial 'up and down' by using magnetic boots on a prepared metal floor. Away from this limited area of magnetic contact, the astronaut floats freely, which may sound fun but this condition of weightlessness can be awkward in the short term and dangerous in the long term. Alan Shepard, one of the first men in space, needed major surgery to his inner ear to relieve a permanent build-up of fluid pressure within his balance organ after his first flight. Fortunately the operation was so successful that he was able to make subsequent trouble-free space trips.

Ordinary manipulative tasks and even the simple processes of eating, drinking or excretion, are made difficult by weightlessness. Human inventiveness has overcome most of the problems with squeeze and suction devices that use pressure to replace gravity. Sleeping-bag wall attachments have been found helpful, to prevent the sleeper floating off and bumping into other walls or floating sleepers, and bags are now also made constrictive to simulate quite deliberately the tight feeling of bedclothes around the sleeper.

So in small and seemingly insignificant ways the brain and the senses crave for the normal and homely feelings of earth. Meanwhile the gallant body adapts as well as it can. The balance organs adjust usually quite quickly to the new situation, with space sickness disappearing after one or two days as mountain sickness does.

Weightlessness, however, causes the body to re-distribute fluids more evenly than on earth. Gravity normally pulls them more towards the legs and feet and this is the distribution we are accustomed to. Without the pull of gravity and the influence it exerts downwards, more fluid goes to the brain and gives rather the same feeling to the head as is experienced on earth when hanging upside down.

This fluid shift is recognised by receptors (specialised nerves) in the wall of the largest artery, the aorta, near the heart. On receiving this message from the receptors the brain sets up a chain of command which corrects the fluid balance by changing the urine output.

So once again the body finds a way to live with change but which on returning to earth has to be reversed. This takes time and there is a brief period of dizziness as the fluid returns to the distribution normal to the earthbound environment. This explains why astronauts are sometimes seen having to be helped and unobtrusively supported as they emerge from their capsules to find their land-legs again.

Such reversible changes, however, are of less concern than recently discovered permanent damage, particularly to the bony system. Bones must be subjected to the stresses of exercise to maintain their mineral content. Even when astonauts carry out their prescribed exercises they still lose bone at a rate which over a twelve-month flight would diminish their total bone mass by 10 per cent. This could cripple them when they returned to earth as bone lost in this way cannot be replaced. For this reason space flights may well have to be limited in time until a system for producing really effective artificial gravity, perhaps by centrifugal force in larger space vehicles or stations, is finally perfected.

Other minor changes during weightlessness continue to puzzle space doctors. One, for example, is the development of spikes and bumps on the normally smooth surfaces of the red blood cells. Neither their significance nor their effect on oxygen transport is yet understood, but clearly the body is trying to adapt in some way and for some reason.

Space medicine is still in its infancy and so much is yet to be learned, but the biggest problem of space flight may be none of the things yet discovered and may not be physical at all. It could be psychological. Astronauts have been noted to spend far more time than could ever have been anticipated simply gazing through the one window of their spacecraft that faces towards earth. It is thought to be a symptom of a galactic form of homesickness, an illness which, even in its more familiar earthly form, is often underestimated in its severe effects on work performance and on the normal logical processes of the mind.

It is possible that the mental adaptation to isolation in space may prove more difficult than the physical. One way to help both in long space flights of the future or in long service on space stations could be provision of that most natural of home comforts, a mixed male and female society. So far the only woman into space has been Valentina Vladimirovna Tereshkova, the Russian female cosmonaut who spent almost three days in Vostok 6 completing forty-eight orbits of the earth. The American space programme has several women, now under training, and plan to use them. Their medical experts have stated that so far all tests and simulated weightlessness suggest women will adapt to space just as well as men do. If this proves to be so, then space stations may really become home from home with one of the most unnatural aspects of isolation overcome.

Penetrating space and learning to survive in it has only been possible for man through his advanced technology and it has demanded vast spending on what is termed the 'hardware'. But it's possible the humble virus may have already beaten us to it. Astronomers Fred Hoyle and Chandra Wickramsinghe have put forward the astonishing theory that our annual winter influenza epidemics are caused by the earth moving through clouds of 'space-living' virus particles. By invading existing viruses they cause mutation so that a new virus can suddenly appear all over the surface of our globe instantaneously, without the time involved for normal spread. Such particles, they believe, may also trigger advantageous mutation in living cells.

It is obviously far more difficult for a complex organism like man with complex internal systems, but the human body has shown it can withstand many times the normal G forces for which it was fashioned. A sustained acceleration of 31G was borne for five seconds by one American R. Flanagan Gray at the US Naval Air Development Centre in

Pennsylvania. This would have made the body weight of a 13st 3lb (839kg) man seem like 2·54 tons. On a water-braked rocket sled another American took a force of 82·6g for a brief 0·4 of a second in 1958. Eli L. Beeding, of the US Air Force, needed three days in hospital afterwards but recovered.

Challenging g forces is not a pastime one would associate with primitive societies but in fact the land divers of Pentecost Island in the New Hebrides who dive off a 70ft (21·3m) high platform with liana vines attached to their ankles, to prove their manhood, are jerked to a stop (if all goes well) just short of the ground, but with a momentary g force of over 100.

So voluntarily and involuntarily, consciously and subconsciously the body strives to cope. Instruments more delicate than any on Concorde's flight control panels register changes in pressure, temperature or the composition of the air we breathe. As the sensory organs detect and the body adjusts we remain largely unaware of such reflex responses and are called upon to play no part in the vital decisions made as systems adjust or are brought into action to preserve the status quo.

In his book *The Body In Question*, Dr Jonathan Miller likens the body's automatic protective reactions to free treatment from a private physician whose personal services are available from the moment of conception. He writes:

> By inheriting the premises in which we are condemned to spend the rest of our lives, we are born into a hospital whose twenty-four-hour services are, paradoxically, designed to overcome and counteract the risks of living in such a dangerous tenement. It is a hospital staffed by its only patient, and although we take no conscious part in our own therapeutic activities, the fact that we have ourselves on call around the clock means that we can overcome most common emergencies without having to summon outside help.

But Dr Miller goes on to recognise, as we have done, that the environment around the 'tenement' can also be dangerous. He argues:

> Prevention is, of course, better than cure and ideally one would live in a world so free of risk that prevention and cure would be equally unnecessary. But it is hard to imagine what such an environment would be like. The womb is the nearest we ever come to it, and, like the womb, such a world would be so monotonous and so unchallenging that any species which grew accustomed to it would soon lose the ability to survive anywhere else. The most versatile and ambitious species are those which have evolved mechanisms capable of

recognising and facing threats before they have had a chance to inflict expensive and possibly irreparable damage.

Man has not only proved capable of that but has gone on to challenge the worst earth's environment can do to him, to explore and penetrate the dangerous depths and to even venture into the totally hostile void of outer space.

In all this, wherever the built-in body reactions cannot cope or seem to be losing the battle, man's brain comes to the rescue, with inventive genius, battling against the imposed limits our environment has tried to force upon us.

But for both body and brain to be able to react and interact efficiently they have to be supplied with the necessary energy and power. Like any machine they have to be regularly and correctly fuelled.

2
Fuelling the System

Air as part of our essential environment featured largely in the previous chapter, but it finds a vital place in this one too because the oxygen content is our major fuel. Deprived of it for as little as four minutes the rules say that survival is unlikely and brain damage certain. This is the normal estimate, but as with other so-called 'norms' throughout this book, we shall find exceptions hard to understand or explain.

Using the admittedly over-simple analogy of comparing the human body to an internal combustion engine and the motor car, then just as the spark ignites the petrol to drive the car, so oxygen burns the glucose to power the muscles and organs of our bodies. This ignition and fuel depends on carbohydrates (sugar and starch) supplying the glucose for immediate power, with the surplus converted into fat and stored together with any fats in our diet to form a reserve tank of fuel, ready for re-conversion as needed back into glucose.

The bodywork of this human vehicle is made up of protein and happily, unlike the metal or fibre-glass bodywork of that distinctly inferior mechanical contraption, the motor car, the human version is able to constantly regenerate itself.

But to do this it needs the help of tiny amounts of vitamins, which control the process, with small amounts of minerals also needed for the special parts – iron and cobalt for our red blood cells; calcium and phosphorus for our bones; zinc for our skins; iodine for our thyroid glands; and sodium, potassium and chlorine, as we have already mentioned, for cell surfaces.

Apart from air, the other most vital element for the human body is water. With a motor car water is only important as part of the cooling system, but it is far more basic to the human machine. All our bodily reactions depend one way or another on water. In fact our body weight is made up of 60 per cent water, which is what one might call a sobering thought!

So, apart from air, water dominates our needs. Without water it is normal for man to survive only about ten days even in the best circumstances. Professor Sydney Smith reported the survival of two men entombed in the wreckage of the Clydebank bombing of 1941 for seven and a half days, without food or water and with the extra disadvantage of the cold March atmosphere. But as always some humans manage to defeat the limits. A nineteen-year-old Rumanian, Sorin Crainic, survived ten and a half days without food or water, when he became entombed under a block of flats collapsed by an earthquake in Bucharest from 4 to 15 March 1977.

Obviously the need for water, like the need for air, depends to some extent on activity, climate and even age. In the average adult body there are forty litres of water, and the daily turnover under normal conditions is at least one and a half litres. Of this a minimum of half a litre is lost in the urine, four-fifths of a litre from the lungs and sweating, and the remaining fifth of a litre is used up in the fuelling process. Therefore, to maintain water balance, even at absolute rest in a comfortable temperature, we must still consume at least one and a half litres a day. Add any activity, heat and sweating to this and we need far more.

The margin of safety where water is concerned is small. Loss of one-tenth of our body water (only four litres and just the normal intake over two days) leaves us weak, disabled and unable to perform the simplest tasks. Double that loss and we die. Dehydration kills because the body is left with an *over*-concentration of salt. This is why it is only going to make things worse if victims of shipwreck, adrift at sea, succumb to the ferocious temptation to drink sea water.

The Ancient Mariner said it all when he bemoaned 'Water, water everywhere nor any drop to drink'. But he was obviously less enterprising than the Robertson family, whose epic thirty-eight-day survival in an open boat in the middle of the Pacific is described in their book *Survive the Savage Sea.* They found the temptation to drink sea water was at its worst in the first three days adrift and they would surely have died, as many sailors have before them, if they had given in. Records dating back to 1583 log the deaths within seven days of drifting mariners who did just that. But the Robertsons somehow defied the rules and managed to exist for weeks at a time on a third of a pint of fresh water per day, obtained from the rare rainfall, jealously collected and guarded, and, more ingeniously, from fish and turtles. They were perhaps fortunate that lustful turtles were deluded into trying to mate with their rubber-bottomed boat and became their main suppliers of water. Turtles, like certain species of desert frog, carry stores of pure water within them. The Robertsons were able to 'tap' these supplies just as Australian aborigines do with frogs. When they dig up the animals, dormant in retreat from extreme drought, they squeeze from them the precious drops of pure stored water, a supply which would otherwise have kept the poor creatures alive for up to five years or until the next rains came. Cacti perform the same function for the desert Indians of Arizona, though perhaps one would not recommend actually squeezing them as it might prove rather painful. But the water is there for those who know where to find it, and cultures not yet under the desensitising influence of civilisation and living in drought-ridden areas, seem to retain a strange and extraordinary ability to find water. Laurens van der Post has described the almost miraculous way in which Kalahari bushmen can detect water under the sand and suck it up through reeds. Even when shown how to do this, he was unable to emulate their ancient skill.

Two other people who beat the limits of survival without water were Antoine de Saint Exupéry and Prévot. Their classic desert ordeal began when after their plane crash they found the water tanks smashed and were left with only a pint of coffee in one battered Thermos and half a pint of white wine in another. Searching the wreckage they also found a few grapes and one orange. By all the local laws which allowed survival in that Libyan desert heat for only nineteen hours without water, both men should have died. Their meagre rations would logically have kept them going for only five hours tramping in the sun, yet they walked forty miles a day for three days. Like the ingenious Robertsons they would not give up. They spread parachute material out at night to collect dew, triumphantly pouring it next day into an empty fuel tank, only nearly to die from contamination either from magnesium in the tank or from some chemical in the silk.

Antoine described how the hammer-strokes of the sun combined with thirst produced dizziness with 'gullet hard-tongue like plaster of Paris. A rasping in the throat. A horrible taste in the mouth.' Of the nights he wrote:

> In this air devoid of moisture the soil is swift to give off its temperature. It was already very cold. I stood up and stamped about. But soon a violent fit of trembling came over me. My dehydrated blood was moving sluggishly and I was pierced by a freezing chill which was not merely the chill of night. My teeth were chattering and my whole body had begun to twitch. My hand shook so that I could not hold an electric torch. I who had never been sensitive to cold was about to die of cold. What a strange effect thirst can have!

Towards the end, if they had had food, they acknowledged they could not have masticated it – they had neither saliva nor sweat. Only three days without water, suffering intense heat and cold in turn, brought two strong men to the point of death, beyond emotion, beyond fear. But still the drops of tainted water sucked from cloth slightly damp with dew preserved them long enough to stumble into rescue. Wandering Bedouins spotted them staggering with burnt-out eyes. Gentle hands pushed them face down to the sand where they 'drank like calves with our faces in the basin'. They were carried by camel to rest in the camp while help was summoned, and by the next midnight they were in Cairo.

Unfortunately we cannot store water as some animals can; the English explorer, Wilfred Thesiger, more knowledgeable about desert life and ways than almost anyone in the West, put the absolute limit for a camel on the move at twenty waterless days. The Swiss traveller, Rene Gardi, set it at only seven, but certainly a well-watered camel has the means to survive for far longer periods than a human. Thesiger reckoned to have managed to travel for twelve days in Arabia on no more than a couple of pints a day, but others become very ill indeed on such short rations. Theodore Monod, whose whole life has revolved around the Sahara and who is one of France's great desert travellers and explorers, advised Geoffrey Moorhouse when he was setting out to cross the Sahara in 1972 that six pints of water a day would be sufficient except in the excessive heat of desert high summer when more than twice that amount might be needed.

Moorhouse tried to plan his journey as far as possible not in a straight line, but to take in whatever wells or oases offered. Even so, on his incredible journey across 2,000 miles of the most merciless desert in the world on camel and on foot, he was almost defeated by lack of water at times. He describes graphically the effects of dehydration.

> I was past the customary stages of thirst; the back of my throat was beginning to thicken, my tongue was almost completely dry, and I could sink half the contents of my water bottle, about one pint, in a single gulp. I had taken no more than three or four pints in the previous twenty-four hours and was beginning to dehydrate badly. It was this as much as the lack of sugar that had me so blindingly weary now that I could focus my mind only on immediate and necessary tasks . . . perpetually my mouth burned and my throat ached with dryness . . . I thought of refreshment and dwelt much on the memory of a waterfall which hung from the hillside behind a cottage in the Lake District, where A. and I spent the last summer holidays with my children.
>
> I was no longer walking straight, but progressed in long ellipses like a drunken man who is determined not to show it. The creeping paralysis of dehydration spread through our limbs.

There was nothing but pain in this desert, for human beings and animals alike. Life was pain. Only in death was there relief. We marched on and by that day's end I wondered how much further I could continue myself. Waves of nausea flowed through my stomach and there was a heavy ache around my kidneys. My left leg had started to drag, so that I was consciously trying to bring it forward with each step.

Normally thoughts of home and family had been his lifeline, his assurance and his insurance, but these began to fail him.

By now I could not even focus on the images of home for more than a split second. They flicked into my consciousness and were gone again and I had neither the strength nor the will to hold them to me, to retrieve them from the blankness that encircled me. Even food was irrelevant now. I could no longer identify my stomach-empty pain. Body was pain and it had no separate parts. I wanted release, nothing more. I wanted sleep, nothing beyond.

He gives a moving account of the moment they stumbled into a desert oasis and water.

Almost unconscious even of my mind, I was aware of trees somewhere ahead – then there was a tent – then a small boy running towards me, trying not to spill what was in the bowl. The water in it was the colour of diluted blood. This was the most beautiful thing in the world, more beautiful by far than the stained glass of Chartres, than a fugue by Bach, than the moment after ecstasy with the woman you loved, or the moment when your son scrambled to squeeze the breath out of you and say 'I think you're smashing, Dad'. There was nothing in the world as beautiful as this bowl of water.

I flowed in and out of sleep [he afterwards records] my only movements were to reach for my water bottle and pour the contents down. Each time within half an hour, I was conscious of my raging thirst again, but it was not an emotional need I had to satisfy; it was the dehydrated tissues of my body, gradually shrunken, that had to be slaked. In the twenty-four hours after my arrival at the well, I was to drink twenty-three pints of liquid. Not much of it emerged as urine.

It is interesting to find that like others before him, even Geoffrey Moorhouse, who had researched like the good journalist he was, made the classic mistake of believing that drinking his own urine might save him. This is a dangerous myth; for anyone already dehydrated, the urine from his own desiccated body is so concentrated with salts and toxins that it can only make matters worse.

Although the body cannot adapt to lack of water, at least people can be trained to recognise the danger signals. Sir John Hunt used this fact in training his team before the first successful ascent of Everest. With snow all around to be melted, there was no problem of availability, but there could well have been failure to recognise the need for sufficient water in cold as opposed to heat. During training this was stressed and during the climb itself the drinking of adequate water was made the first priority.

The Everest team were trained and equipped but the survivors of the Andes aircrash were neither and at first found, despite snow all around them, that melting it was quite a problem with no fuel to spare for fires. At first they tried compressing it into balls of ice and sucking it, or forcing it into bottles to be shaken until it melted. This took time which they had, but also energy which they lacked, and really all that anyone was fit enough to produce in this way was enough only for one person. In addition they needed water for the helpless wounded.

As so often in survival stories human need was met by human ingenuity. One of the group, Adolfo Strauch, noticed in the backs of the broken aircraft seats some sheets of aluminium foil, measuring about one foot by two feet. Torn out with sides bent up and one corner twisted to make an improvised spout, the bits of foil were filled with snow and tilted to face the sun on the occasions when it deigned to shine. In no time at all water began to trickle into bottles held beneath and the vital water problem was solved.

More recently and perhaps less dramatically, a young twenty-two-year-old British sailor, Ronald Gadsby, managed to stay alive in freezing temperatures without any food at all simply by eating snow. After shore leave in the port of Stavanger in Norway he missed the last bus back to his ship and with no money for a taxi looked for somewhere to shelter. He noticed the door of a railway wagon in a siding was open and jumped in, pushing the door shut accidentally. Unable to open it from the inside he was trapped for six days as the wagon travelled 300 miles across the Norwegian winter landscape. By the fourth day his throat was parched from shouting and lack of water and he could hardly make a sound. His legs were numb with cold but he managed to drag himself over to a crack he had noticed in one of the planks, and after half an hour of exhausting effort broke off a piece of wood about three feet long. Slowly a pile of snow formed on the floor of the wagon and eating it saved his life. He was finally found semi-conscious two days later when workers opened the wagon near Hoenefoss, about thirty-five miles west of Oslo.

Our better reserves of fat and protein make the need for daily food intake less vital than that for water. Like the other carnivores, we could if we wished subsist on one large meal, eaten to satiation, then wait until we were actually hungry before eating again. It's possible that at one time this was what man did, but with the advent of social living and even more with leisure and affluence, eating has gone far beyond the simple need for fuel to become one of the great pleasures of life.

Most people in the developed world not only eat too much but very often the wrong foods in the wrong balance. Taste was originally a sensory label, used partly through instinct and partly through experience, to indicate safe and suitable food. Now it has become an end in itself, so that we select and respond to a wide variety of subtle and sophisticated tastes, many of which come from the chemist's laboratory rather than natural sources even where they mimic natural flavours. The label of taste today is all too often quite inappropriate to the actual ingredients. Professor Yudkin of London University, a world expert on food and nutrition, insists we consume the labels with almost total disregard for food value. He argues this shows particularly in modern man's craving for sweet foods and he believes that sugar is not just something that rots children's teeth but may well be responsible for half the early deaths in the developed world.

Although, as we have seen, a certain level of salt is vital to survival, there is no doubt that many people in the developed world have also acquired a taste for this which goes far beyond the body's actual needs.

Professor Page of Tufts University, USA is one of the world's experts on salt, and with the unusual Christian name of 'Lot' perhaps that is not too surprising. At any rate Lot Page has not only set out to study ways in which many primitive societies adapt to lower salt intake in areas where it is difficult to obtain but has experimented to see if a modern civilised family can do the same. Far from being turned into a pillar of salt, this twentieth-century Lot's wife, together with her children, has cut salt intake from the normal six to ten grammes right down to one gramme a day. Although their food tasted dull and bland at first, they found within six weeks they had not only lost desire for salt but the flavour became positively unpleasant. Even at that level they were obviously consuming sufficient as they all kept perfectly healthy.

Modern armies in the desert, notably the Israelis, have also experimented with drastically cutting down on the extra salt rations, once thought vital for action in fierce heat. They proved it was possible to adjust to low salt needs and that this gave improved ability to withstand heat and drought as well as reducing need for water. In fact human ingenuity and strong motivation condensed into one generation the sort of adaptation that took that other desert dweller, the camel, millions of years to perfect.

Working among some twenty societies with low salt intake, Lot Page found that their blood pressure, unlike ours, remains at a healthy low level throughout life. In contrast he found where there was a very high salt intake, notably among the Kashkai nomads of South Iran, blood pressure in both sexes rose steeply with age.

Vegetarians who absorb high levels of potassium in their food need higher levels of salt to balance this and should be wary of attempting to cut down. The animal world offers an interesting lesson as in hot areas the salt licks are only patronised by plant eaters, while the carnivores just prowl around them seeking prey but never seeming to use them. Their much lower need for salt is clearly met by what is contained in the flesh they eat.

This sort of instinctive animal wisdom about what it is wise to eat seems to have been overlaid in man by the effects of civilisation, social living and jaded appetites that have to be titillated with a variety of flavours. There is no doubt our excessive salt intake helps to shorten our lives, leading to high blood pressure and related risks of strokes, heart attacks and kidney disease. American drugstores today vividly illustrate the point. Alongside shelves stocked with salted peanuts and packets of salty potato chips are ranged rows of self-service blood-pressure-measuring machines. The first such devices are also now appearing in Britain, and it is arguable we should all do better to take a lesson from the story of Lot's wife, modern version.

It has to be said, however, that doctors are by no means all agreed on what we should eat. Animal fats have also been under fire, but at least there is general agreement on a baseline of food intake balanced to maintain health. Expressed at the simplest level, purely in terms of energy units, the average young adult needs somewhere between 2,500 and 3,000 kilocalories, commonly just called calories, depending on his physical activity. The European equivalent, soon to be internationally accepted, would be 10 to 12·6 megajoules (1 KCal equals 0·004186 megajoules).

While two-thirds of the world suffer from malnutrition or hunger, in the developed world most of us tax our digestive systems and hazard our health by over-eating. It has been calculated that Americans carry food surplus round with them in the form of 2 million tons of excess fat on their bodies. In the UK where things are not much better, a typical Briton eats 3lb 5oz (1·5kg) of potatoes a week, 18½oz (524g) of sugar (plus jams, chocolate etc), 4 eggs, 2oz (57g) of sausage, 2lb 11oz (1·2 kg) of bread, 5oz (142g) of biscuits, 3oz (85g) of tea and daily high levels of fish, meat or poultry. Compare this to the rations in World War II which enforced a diet medically healthier than today's excesses. At its most severe the weekly allowance for each civilian adult was 4oz (113g) bacon or ham, 8oz (227g) sugar, 2oz (57g) tea, 8oz (227g) fat (with only 2oz (57g) butter), 2oz (57g) jam, 1oz (28g) cheese and a shillingsworth of meat. One egg a week, a very modest milk supply (with priority for children and expectant mothers) and that was your lot except for an occasional luxury able to be purchased on a 'points' system.

This certainly approaches the bottom limit for maintaining health and today even in the midst of plenty a few highly motivated people do try out a wide variety of diets, some so drastic as to be positively dangerous. Prescription slimming drugs designed to reduce appetite are also used, particularly in the US, and carried to its ultimate limit compulsive slimming can lead to a potentially lethal condition known as anorexia nervosa.

This disorder mainly affects adolescent girls and has been best described as 'wilful pursuit of thinness through self-starvation'. It starts innocently enough with dieting, either because the girl really is overweight or simply believes that she is. It then develops insidiously into a morbid fear of fatness and leads to extreme and ugly emaciation, strangely enough rarely recognised by the girl herself. For an average person, a weight loss beyond a certain point – usually 7st 5lb (47kg) – involves loss of menstruation, and often constipation and discolouration of the skin. In one recent follow-up study 4 out of 30 women with anorexia died, despite hospital treatment.

The reasons can be highly complex but anorexia nervosa cases usually fall into two types. In one the woman seems to want to negate her own sexuality – to be afraid of it; in the other, genuinely to believe that slimming will make her more attractive despite the pitiful reflection in her mirror and the brutal comments parents, friends and doctors are driven eventually to make. Sometimes it can also involve part of the whole adolescent drive towards independence or a rejection of family norms. Whatever the reason, the condition needs recognition and treatment on both psychiatric and medical levels.

This is not always easy as girls suffering from anorexia nervosa will go to extraordinary lengths to hide the fact that they are not eating. One good-looking girl of sixteen, known personally to the authors, came to resemble a survivor from Belsen in just a few months, during which time her bewildered family was fooled into believing she was having good school dinners. Not only was she never eating at school, but even at home she was managing to secrete most of the food put in front of her, smuggling it away in handkerchiefs and pockets. The background to her problem appeared to be one of sexual jealousy of an older sister becoming engaged to a boy whom she also found attractive. Hospital bed rest, high-calorie diet and psychiatric treatment eventually cured the anorexic symptoms but she went on to try to find other solutions through a secret and precipitate marriage which was utterly disastrous.

To a great extent anorexia nervosa and its opposite, the rare condition bulimia, involving a morbid desire to eat, can be considered involuntary and compulsive diseases. But there are many examples of both under-eating and over-eating which are self-inflicted forms of indulgence and for which there can be little sympathy when they go beyond the limits for healthy living. Worst of all, and totally obscene in a world where vast numbers are known to be starving, are competitions in gluttony. The man with the dishonour of holding the all-time record for this has been undefeated in eating contests since 1931. Called Edward Abraham Miller, of Oakland, California, he consumed up to 25,000 calories per day (more than eleven times the recommended level. He stood only 5ft 7½in (171·5cm) tall but weighed 20 to 21½st (127 to 139kg) with a 57in (144cm) waist.

People who get fat without over-eating have often in the past been viewed with suspicion as weak-willed secret gourmands and not been given the sympathy they deserved. They have been gawped at, usually with derision, in many a circus though at least it provided a living. Alice from Dallas was one of the most famous, weighing 685lb (310·7kg) and appearing with the Ringling Brothers and also Barnum and Bailey.

Today we are moving at last towards a better understanding of obesity and the fact that it can often be rooted merely in the victim's body possessing a special type of 'brown fat' which is not metabolised into energy. Hopefully this new knowledge may lead to better methods of treatment and diet.

But even now occasionally people like Celesta Geyer can win the battle of the bulge by discipline, and will power. She weighed 555lb (251·7kg) and was dying of heart failure when she decided to try the only thing which might save her life – a rigid diet. It took a long time but she is still alive today, over fifty years old and weighing now only 154lb (69·8kg). She has told her story in her book *Dolly Dimples*.

The secret of proper calorie intake is careful balance against likely energy expenditure, taking into account the work to be done and the extremes of climate to be faced, and where exploration and expeditions are concerned this can be not only the key to success or failure but the difference between life and death. So it proved for Scott and his men. Each of them was given a daily ration of 4,100 calories, which modern research has shown to be about 800 calories short for strenuous activity and bitter cold. Their deaths were inevitable from the day they set foot on the ice cap.

Studies of energy expenditure have shown that mountain climbing and polar trekking are very similar in their demands, involving between 400 and 600 calories per hour. Today expedition members are very careful to calculate their food requirements in relation to the work they expect to have to do in each twenty-four hours. It is not unusual for them to consume 8,000 calories a day. Also because studies have shown that the body cannot be trained or conditioned to function efficiently on a lower food or water intake, pre-expedition training involves particularly good feeding well in advance. In other words the reserve tanks are filled to capacity, so that if some disaster befalls them the members have a better chance of survival. Recognition of the value of this reserve storage may be relatively recent in relation to planned exploration, but it was long ago accepted by peoples living in drought-ridden areas. Australian aborigines and many African tribes admire obesity in women and deliberately choose fat wives. They admit this is not just because natural selection and conditioning has influenced them to 'like what they get', as it were, but also for the more practical reasons that such wives will survive famine periods far better.

At the limits of endurance, of course, survival power does not just depend on the quantity of calories we consume but on the types of food from which they come. Despite Professor Yudkin's reservations about what he feels is over-consumption of sugar, it still offers the best quick energy boost and the tennis player passing the umpire's stand during a long match can often be seen taking glucose tablets to keep his system fuelled. In the longer term proteins are essential to survival in order to keep cells healthy and regenerating, while fat is not only a more efficient provider of energy in terms of calories per gramme than sugar, it also supplies vitamins A and D.

As already mentioned tiny amounts of vitamins are essential to the chemical process of life and certainly carefully measured vitamin supplements may be appropriate for some elderly or undernourished people. For most people on a normal diet extra vitamins are rarely needed and in excess can be positively dangerous with fat-soluble vitamins such as A and D. Water-soluble ones such as vitamin C and the B group present no problem, as any excess is freely excreted in the urine.

Over-enthusiastic supporters of the present-day vitamin cult, usually ludicrous for the buyer but lucrative for the seller, might draw warning from the tragedy of Sir Douglas Mawson's Antarctic expedition where two members of his team suffered from vitamin A poisoning and one of them died.

It is a story worth telling, apart from the vitamin over-dosage accidentally consumed when they were driven by hunger to eat the livers of their husky dogs. Sir Edmund Hillary of Everest fame has described it as 'probably the greatest story of lone survival in Polar exploration' and it certainly has a place in terms of sheer courage and enterprise in any book looking at human potential.

The full story was told by Mawson himself in his own book, *The Home of the Blizzard* and re-told quite recently by Leonard Bickel in another book published in 1977 called *This Accursed Land*. The *British Medical Journal* in February 1979 carried a fascinating shorter account with all the medical evidence of the vitamin tragedy clearly presented by David Shearman, Professor of Medicine at the University of Adelaide.

It was on 10 November 1912 that Sir Douglas Mawson, then aged thirty, set out with Lieutenant Ninnis, aged twenty-three and Dr Xavier Mertz, aged twenty-eight, from their hut on Adelie land, the winter quarters of the Australian Antarctic Expedition.

The expedition Mawson was leading had the important job of making scientific observations and hopefully claiming large areas of Antarctica for the Crown. None of them could know as they started out that only two days later the bodies of Scott, Wilson and Bowers would be found, just eleven miles from One Ton Depot and the food supplies which might have saved them. Mawson's party had their own equipment and food loaded on to three sledges pulled by dogs, while the three men travelled on foot or occasionally on skis. Progress was slow because of ice-ridges, crevasses and high winds of up to 40mph, which Mawson with typical laconic understatement described as a 'breeze'. Temperatures ranged from freezing point to −5·9°F (−21·1°C). It was just as well they were all physically fit young men, as the sledges capsized on steep slopes and many times almost fell into crevasses.

Eventually, with the outward journey almost complete and hoping to extend their exploration even further, one sledge was abandoned as supplies had been consumed and the remaining food was packed on the rear sledge. Mawson reasoned this was the safest place as the leading sledge was pulled by the weaker dogs, and anyway would be the most likely to come to grief as it would be the first to encounter any concealed crevasse. In fact by ill luck it was the rear sledge pulled by the stronger team which disappeared without sound into a deep crevasse together with Lieutenant Ninnis who was walking beside it. One dog with a broken back could be seen on a ledge 150ft (46m) down but the rest, Ninnis, dogs and sledge were gone for ever. There was no hope of rescue and with them had gone almost all the food. Mawson summarised their plight in his diary entry:

> The dogs in my team were very poorly and the worst – and no feed for them – the other team comprised the picked dogs, all dog food and almost all man food. We considered it a possibility to get through to winter quarters by eating dogs – so 9 hours after the accident started back but terribly handicapped . . . May God Help Us.

They were then 315 miles away from the safety of their hut and in an appalling wasteland.

It was a question now, for sheer survival, of Mertz and Mawson pulling the sledges: weak and dying dogs were carried until they were killed and eaten. From 15 to 28 December six dogs were consumed, though some meat was stored for later use. Some parts were fried and others stewed or made into soup but there is no doubt the livers which were to prove so lethal were eaten. In fact Mawson writes 'It was a happy relief when the liver appeared, even if little else could be said in its favour, it was easily chewed and demolished'.

On 30 December, Mawson commented in his log that Mertz was 'off colour', and he also described on the next day 'keeping off dog meat for a day or two as both upset by it'. By 6 January Mertz was very weak and depressed and both men began to suffer from peeling skin and loss of hair. Skin on Mawson's ears came off in casts and both lost all the skin from their legs and genitals. On 7 January, although Mawson was desperate to move on, Mertz was too weak and declined rapidly into incontinence, fits, delirium and raving. He died on 8 January.

Mawson's condition was not much better but his will to survive was indomitable. He cut the sledge in half with a penknife and abandoned all but the bare necessities. A blizzard raged as he worked, but he made a sail for the sledge and on 11 January set out again. In his diary he noted, 'My whole body is apparently rotting from want of proper nourishment – frostbitten fingertips, festering, mucus membrane of nose gone, saliva glands of mouth refusing duty, skin coming off whole body'. His meagre rations had to be mainly dog meat; the bad weather continued, his weakness grew, yet, when on 17 January he tumbled into a crevasse supported only by the fourteen feet of rope and the weight of the sledge still stuck in the snow, he incredibly still found strength on his second attempt to climb the rope. After that he constructed a rope ladder in case the same disaster struck again. On 18 January he reduced his rations yet again and struggled on exhausted through soft snow, ice fields and blizzards that again capsized his sledge. He continued to shed skin and his hair fell out in handfuls. On 29 January, twenty-one days after Mertz's death, exactly on course, he found a food cache left by a rescue party; he reached the base camp and safety only half-alive ten days later on 8 February. By then this man, whose weight when he had set out was 15st (95kg), weighed only 8st (51kg).

In later writings, comments on his health were sparse, but clearly he continued very ill, and on 23 March he wrote, 'I find my nerves are in a very serious state and from the feeling I have in the base of my head I suspect that I may go off my rocker very soon'. Even after a further two months he recorded, 'I have a boil on left temple forming. Am quite down in general health'. On 30 July he was suffering a boil on the right side of his face.

Every symptom described for Mertz and Mawson is typical of vitamin A poisoning. A toxic dose could be contained in as little as 3½oz (100g) of husky dog liver. Mertz almost certainly died from hypervitaminosis A. Similar symptoms of vomiting, diarrhoea, weakness and convulsions have been recorded after eating seal liver, which also contains large amounts of vitamin A. Raised intracranial pressure resulting in headache and neurological symptoms occurs in chronic hypervitaminosis A and this was indicated also by Mawson's persistent skin infections and boils.

An interesting question raised by the *British Medical Journal* investigation was why one man died and the other survived. One possibility is that Mertz was almost a vegetarian under normal conditions, and the smelly dog meat may well have been very repulsive to him. So it seems possible that he found the liver slightly less offensive and struck a bargain with Mawson in dividing the food. It may have been a bargain which unwittingly saved Mawson's life. He eventually died in 1958.

Scott's and Mawson's stories are made even more poignant by contrast with that of their contemporary, Roald Amundsen. Amundsen's success depended on his deliberate policy of taking more than twice the number of huskies that others thought he needed, and to slaughter them for food on his journey. But because he was not so hard pressed for food as Mawson and Mertz, his team were able to eat only the safe meat and discard the offal. Even in the ultimate extremity Scott, whose true British grit was paralleled by true British sentiment, positively never considered eating man's best friend the dog, even though he had no compunction about eating the ponies in the earlier stages of the expedition.

In contrast survival for the Uruguayan plane crash victims in the Andes proved to be not so much a question of eating man's best friend as of eating man himself. It is easy to give way to an immediate and natural reaction of horror in the face of resort to cannibalism, but Piers Paul Read's brilliant and vivid account of the whole Andes tragedy in his book *Alive!*, leaves no doubt of the fearful struggle with instinctive repugnance and conditioned conscience each man went through before making his individual decision.

From the start their food position was hopeless. In the high, snowbound Andes there were no natural sources of food and an extensive check after the crash revealed a total supply of 8 bars of chocolate, 5 bars of nougat, a few caramels, dates and dried plums scattered in the wreckage, 2 small tins of mussels, 1 tin of salted almonds and 3 small jars of jam. The drinks in all comprised 3 bottles of wine, 1 bottle and half a hip flask of whisky, 1 bottle of cherry brandy and 1 of creme de menthe. Rigid rationing was imposed at once with a daily intake of one taste of jam or tinned fish each morning and a capful of wine and a square of chocolate at night. Initially twenty-eight survived the crash though twelve of those were to die, from wounds, accidents and starvation.

After only ten days on these totally inadequate rations not only were supplies running out but so was their strength. The survivors were mostly strong young men, members of a famous Uraguayan rugger team on their way to play a match in Chile. But on this diet they soon felt faint when they stood up, had difficulty in keeping balance, could not get warm even when the sun shone and found their skins starting to wrinkle like that of old men. Gradually and privately at first they began to face the realisation that one thing could save them all from death – the flesh of the human corpses strewn around and preserved by the intense cold.

For any so-called civilised human being there is bound to be utter revulsion at such a prospect, even in the face of terrible starvation and with all hope of rescue fading. For this group it was worse because many of them were virtually boys and they were forced to contemplate eating not just anonymous corpses but the bodies of other young men and boys, whom they knew intimately and who had been their fellow comrades and team members. Added to that were all the religious sanctions of their Catholic faith. Only when they were each so weak that it was clear they were dying did they one by one force themselves to the act.

It was one of the medical students, Roberto Canessa, who brought secret thoughts into the open and made them face the fact that the hoped-for rescue was not going to come. Their only chance was to send expeditionaries out to find help, and to keep alive in the meantime they had to eat. He emphasised how their emaciated bodies were literally consuming themselves day by day to fuel their vital systems and eventually with final inner reserves gone, they would soon be too weak even to cut up the bodies unless they acted quickly. It would be essential too for any of the boys selected to go and seek help and find a way down the mountains, to be strengthened with special feeding. At the moment they were almost all too weak to stand, let alone struggle and survive a forced march through deep snow, with heavy cushions strapped to their feet to prevent them sinking into it.

The final arguments that won the day centred round their obligation to live, not just for their own sakes but for their families', and also the fact that God must want them to live as He had given them the means to do so through the bodies of their friends. This was His gift of life and they would be wrong to reject it just because they were squeamish.

It was Gustavo Zerbino, the one other medical student, who clinched it for at least some of them. He argued that if he had died, he would have wanted his dead body to be used to help his friends to stay alive. In fact he added, 'If I do die and you don't eat me, then I'll come back from wherever I am and give you a good kick in the ass.' There and then they made a pact that if any more of them were to die, their bodies were to be used.

The first attempt at the grisly task was the worst, and four of the boys, including the two medical students, silently trooped out into the snow and watched as Canessa bared the skin and made the first cut into human flesh with a piece of broken glass. He cut twenty thin slivers the size of matchsticks and placed them on the roof of the wrecked fuselage to dry in the sun, telling the others to come out and take a piece when they wanted. No one came and poor Roberto Canessa knew he must set the example. He took a piece of the human flesh in his hand but found it would not rise towards his mouth. In the end, by superhuman effort and literally praying, his will prevailed and the hand rose, pushing the first piece into his mouth – and he swallowed.

After that, to prevent death, one by one the survivors were driven to follow suit. Longest to hold out was the one woman, a thirty-five-year-old mother, Lilina Methol. Obviously destined to die if she did not overcome her utter revulsion, she finally gave in because faced with death she found the one thing she wanted above all else was to live to be rescued and record her faith in life by having another baby. It was this that finally made her eat, but ironically and tragically she was one of the eight to die when an avalanche hit the wrecked fuselage during a night of fearful blizzards.

Given extra human flesh rations to increase their strength and with a stock of 'meat' carried in old socks, two of them finally set out on a last desperate attempt to get help before death overtook them all. Ill-equipped, with heavy cushions strapped to their boots to simulate snow shoes, wearing only layers of ordinary clothes and with a joint sleeping bag improvised from fabric from the aeroplane, Nando Parramon, who had become the leader and the inspiration of them all, together with Canessa, somehow crossed the highest mountains in the Americas and down a treacherous pass to reach a valley where they found cows grazing, an empty herdsman's hut and finally a Chilean peasant. It took them ten exhausting days and two more followed before helicopters flew to rescue the others.

The sixteen who survived endured seventy-two days, most of that time sustained by small rationed amounts of raw human flesh. Occasionally as a luxury they allowed themselves to burn a few of their dwindling supply of wooden crates and lightly brown the 'meat' to give it flavour. But they knew this diminished the vitamin content, so it was not done often. Also, towards the end, as stocks ran out they were driven to eat every part of each body, even to the brains and the often rotting intestines. Indeed it is a sign of the modern human need for flavour that some of them even chose putrid flesh because it had some taste.

The amazing thing is that despite all this, when they were examined by the doctors in hospital in Santiago, although emaciated and suffering enormous weight loss, only two were ill enough to be kept in for more than rest and tests. One of them had potassium deficiency severe enough to endanger his heart, and Javier Methol, older than the rest, had suffered during the whole time from altitude sickness.

The two heaviest, Parrado and Coche Inciarte who both weighed 14st (88·9kg) before their ordeal, had lost most weight. Parrado had lost 4st (25·4kg) and Inciarte an amazing 7st 10lb (49kg). The others, weighing between 10st (63·5kg) and 12st (76·2kg) before the accident, had lost only proportionately between 2st (12·7kg) and 3st (19kg). Tests showed all had a deficiency of fats, proteins and vitamins and all suffered from burned and blistered lips, conjunctivitis and skin infections. But it was obvious to the doctors that they had nevertheless been nourished in some way during the ten weeks they were trapped in the mountains, and so the eating of human flesh had to be reluctantly confessed.

The storm that broke until the full facts were understood hardly helped, and indeed the psychological effects of the ordeal and the measures they had been forced to take to survive were more long lasting than the physical ones. In the longer term they all felt themselves changed for the better, with their already strong belief in God reinforced and with a more serious and unselfish approach to life. In the short term the immediate reaction was total gluttony, with an irresistible desire for food and an irritable and spoiled manner with their families, whose ordeal had been at least mentally almost as great.

The solidarity of the group and their sense of comradeship remained; only time will tell now if they can go on to lead what we term normal lives. The Catholic Church exonerated them from all blame for their cannibalism, and the public, once the facts were known, accepted that any one of them would almost certainly have done the same.

The story of the Andes survivors and others in a like situation forced to a similar solution demonstrates in the most dramatic way possible how thin is the veneer of civilisation and how weak the normally strong taboos it imposes, in the face of the sheer primitive urge to survive.

In 1820, when the whaleship *Essex*, of Nantucket, was sunk – by a whale – the four survivors in one boat agreed that survival of three only was possible. One had to die to feed the others. Owen Coffin, the captain's fourteen-year-old nephew, was the unlucky one. Years later, Captain Coffin, by then something of a celebrity, was asked if he remembered the boy. The grizzled old man laughed. 'Remember him?' he said, 'Hell, I ate him!' As humour, this can only be considered very poor taste!

Geoffrey Moorhouse also found on his Sahara journey that overwhelming hunger dictates the rules and demolishes the normal limits set by conditioning both on the sort of food that is acceptable, on levels of hygiene and on methods of killing and cooking.

Initially he was appalled both by the casual and cruel slaughter of animals, in full sight of those about to devour them, by the partly cooked meat and by the dirt, contamination by flies and by lack of flavour. Time and desperate need for food changed all that. After weeks of desert travel, half-starved for much of the time, he wrote of the killing of a lamb:

> The blood spurted on to the sand in a thick jet while the limbs thrashed wildly for a moment and a rasping cough of air came out of the almost severed neck. I watched all this, the removal of the stomach and guts with only the faintest stirring of emotion, for I was much changed by

> the desert. The Englishman in me dimly acknowledged something called cruelty to animals, but the savage much more aggressively relished the prospect of meat for the first time in ten days or more. I was as greedy for it now as any man I had met since coming to the Sahara. I was hungry and I would have butchered the lamb myself if it had been necessary.

Later he described stale food he would once have spurned, but became only too grateful to eat:

> We made unsweetened tea with the last of our water and cooked a piece of meat. Eager as I was for the nourishment it offered, it tasted abominable: it had, after all, been rubbing shoulders with a camel for several days on one side and on the other it had been crawling with flies in two sandstorms. But I tore into it greedily, mouthfuls of grit and all.

Moorhouse in his desert wanderings learned to dread not only lack of food and water but the searing heat of the sun itself. Every year, despite using modern vehicles instead of camels, the newspapers record stories of people found dead because their cars have broken down and they have perished as much from exposure to too much sun as from too little sustenance.

Yet the sun is the most basic of all sources of energy, as essential to man as it is to plants and animals. Its indirect value to us, of course, is through the part it plays in the growth of crops to feed the animals, both of which in turn are part of our own food chain. Most directly it supplies not only warmth but action on our skins which produces vitamin D. This is vital to build up and maintain the correct levels of calcium and phosphorus needed to give strength and resilience to our bones.

It is possible, as with vitamin A, to have too much of a good thing. Too much vitamin D in the body leads to stones in the kidneys and deposits of bone in inappropriate places. This is one of the reasons for black protective pigment in tropical races and the pale skin common to more temperate climates where better absorption of sunshine is needed with more limited amounts available. Difficulties arise, of course, when a race adapted for one sort of climate lives in another. Indian and West Indian babies in British industrial towns can use so little of our low sunshine supplies that they are very prone to rickets, and this is one case where vitamin supplements are fully justified.

There is one other source of energy and a form of refuelling the system which deserves a chapter to itself. It becomes vital because during our waking and active life our bodies are in a sense a battleground where two opposing forces constantly skirmish for power. The sympathetic nervous system controls the fight, flight and fright brigade and the parasympathetic system commands the rest and digest troops. Each struggles to dominate. Anyone who has started to fall asleep while driving a car knows the feeling of the adrenalin surge of the fright response all too well. He is suddenly aware of his heart palpitating, his mouth dry, contractions in his gut and bladder and a cold, clammy skin. Later in describing physical limits and responses the explanation for all this will be given in more detail. For the moment, the important thing is that under these conditions or indeed any form of physical or emotional activity, the rest and digest troops and their lines of communication tend to suffer. The only way they can defeat their enemy is through sleep.

3
Sleep – the Vital Function?

The rest and digest theory to explain our regular compulsive circadian rhythm of alternate sleeping and waking is a logical one. It is not the only one and the functions of sleep seem likely to prove as varied and complex as modern methods of research have now shown sleep itself to be.

In considering any possible extension of normal sleep limits, in particular any hopes of reducing sleep time which on average takes up a third of our lives, it is important to see what the experts have learned about sleep, what they believe it does for us and what happens when we are deprived of it.

It was the development of a machine called the electroencephalograph (EEG) which supplied the means and the impetus to carry sleep research surging forward over the last two decades to penetrate some of the secrets of sleep.

By means of electrodes lightly taped to the head and eyelids, the EEG records the changing patterns of brain waves emitted as we move from the waking to the sleeping state. Very different types of brain waves soon indicated that sleep was not one amorphous whole. On the contrary, distinct and changing EEG patterns prove sleep to consist of many different layers or stages through which we constantly descend and ascend in steady cycles throughout any long sleep period. The moving pens of the EEG may cover as much as a quarter of a mile of graph paper to chart the nightly sleep journey for one person.

The first four stages of sleep have been grouped together into one type, known variously as Delta, Orthodox, Slow Wave or Synchronised sleep (S sleep). But at the bottom of each descent after the deepest form of S sleep, stage 4, brain wave patterns change quite suddenly to become similar to those of waking life. At the same time the eyes begin to make rapid, jerky, desynchronised movements, which is the signal for the onset of a totally different type of sleep called Rapid Eye Movement (REM) sleep of Desynchronised (D sleep). Woken during this sort of sleep a dream can invariably be recalled, so D sleep stands equally well for dreaming sleep and S sleep and D sleep seem the simplest and most appropriate terms. Both types of sleep occur in all higher animals including all mammals even down to the primitive opossum. If it is difficult to conceive of rats, mice and opossums dreaming in the sense that we understand it, at least the cortical activity shows a D sleep pattern. Higher up the scale, of course, anyone who has owned a dog may well accept that they probably dream rather as we do, judging by the twitches and occasional yelps of excitement strongly suggesting a chase after tantalising dream-cats.

Although there are variations between individuals within rather confined limits each animal shows a sleep pattern distinct to the species, with the amount of D sleep far less in lower animals.

Both forms of sleep have been proved essential for man if mind and body are to work at optimum efficiency. Series of sophisticated experiments have been done using the EEG machine set up in special sleep laboratories throughout the world. Some volunteers have been deprived of all sleep over many days and nights, others have been woken only when EEG patterns indicate dreaming sleep, and recently an ingenious buzzer has been found to move sleepers out of deep stage 4 or 3 sleep back to light sleep without actually waking them. From all this it is clear that on recovery nights there is a rebound effect with the type of sleep left out on experimental nights taking up more time. After total sleep loss, on the first recovery night S sleep seems to take priority, but even then D sleep is never completely eliminated. If a person is deprived of D sleep only, on recovery nights they dream 30 per cent more.

The most striking finds were that sleep deprivation in the long term, whether deliberate as in these experiments or accidental as in insomnia or illness, builds up stress, disorientates, lowers concentration and can lead in the long term to hallucinations and even death.

Modern theories about the function of sleep now usually take this into account, and strive to define and explain the separate purposes of each form of sleep. But one of the best and most convincing theories only manages an over-all explanation. Called the 'immobilisation' theory, this sees sleep as built in by evolutionary forces but with the survival value lying in the brake it applies to activity, not for digestion so much as protection. It claims sleep became a programmed part of behaviour to immobilise animals, including man, at a time when activity and food foraging would have been specially hazardous.

Before there were any artificial means of light or any effective weapons of protection, a creature like man, unable to see in the dark and poorly defended, would have had least chance of survival if he continued to be active during the night. His chance of finding food for himself would be small and he would just exhaust himself and risk his life for no purpose. Not only might he fall over cliffs or into bogs, but he might well end up food himself for some other stronger predators with better night vision.

So those humans who found relatively safe places and developed the habit of becoming inactive during the hours of darkness, were more likely to survive to produce offspring like themselves, conditioned by the family or social group to the same pattern of alternate activity and rest.

Even this begs the question of why actually sleep? Why not just stay alert, quietly hiding and awaiting the light? After all, lapsing into unconsciousness in a hostile world could well carry its own dangers.

The theory answers this by arguing that other aspects of survival demand all organisms to respond to stimuli and the waking state tends to be also essentially an active state. The immobilisation theory proposes sleep as an adaptive, protective mechanism deliberately cancelling the normal responses and inducing inactivity and rest at a time when otherwise the animal would incur danger and futile exhaustion.

Considerable support for this theory emerges from the differing sleep habits of other species. The two main pressures at work on all animals in the natural state are to obtain food and to avoid becoming food. So, grazing animals which need to crop almost constantly to obtain sufficient nourishment for survival, have developed a pattern of long active periods, sleeping only for about two hours out of twenty-four. To sleep more would mean under-nourishment and eventually non-survival. What is more the sleep is taken in brief bursts, because feeding on open plains offers no safe place of refuge. Also as part of a wandering herd, constantly having to move on to fresh pastures, long sleep periods are impossible. With food equally available day and night and with light hardly needed to locate it, no sharply fixed night pattern of sleep is necessary.

Elephants also sleep only around two hours because their enormous bulk demands vast amounts of food to sustain it. But foraging for them is slightly less efficient at night and as they are not worried by predators as cattle are, they can afford to take their two hours in one single period and at night.

The tiny shrew also has little sleep despite its safe burrow. Its high rate of metabolism requires a daily food intake equivalent to at least its own body weight if it is to stay alive, and that means food hunting almost round the clock.

In contrast an animal like the gorilla can indulge in fourteen hours' sleep out of twenty-four, because he has no predators except man and lives in forest areas where food is in constant and easy supply.

The dim and rather helpless opossum is the best example of using the defence mechanism of sleep to the full. Continuously threatened by larger species and with a good food supply on hand around him, he averages nineteen hours' sleep out of every twenty-four.

Mammals able to see and hunt at night, such as bats, sleep during the day and mid-evening in safe caves, only flying at dawn and dusk, so that their periods of activity are directly keyed to the time when their food of insects is most plentiful.

Baboons, so much nearer to us, adapt in a way very like early pre-man, retiring at sunset to the safety of nests in high trees and taking one long stretch of sleep until dawn. This leaves them free to forage efficiently and keep a look-out for predators during the daylight hours.

This adaptive immobilisation theory insists that we too inherit sleep from our distant ancestors for whom it was so protective during darkness, and that we still retain an automatic and compulsive need to lapse into a similar period of unresponsiveness and unconsciousness every twenty-four hours, preferably at night.

Other modern theories of sleep in man, distinguishing between the functions of the different types of sleep, in no way preclude the validity of the two already outlined. Sleep almost certainly serves many different purposes, by no means yet fully understood.

One school of thought even argues from the standpoint that sleep can be seen as in some ways maladaptive and even dangerous, as unconsciousness prevents response to real hazards. But they have to concede that, as experience and experiment both confirm it is still totally essential for health and even ultimate survival, we quite literally cannot live without it; it must possess overwhelmingly important functions. These are considered to be largely restorative processes, which cannot take place fully and efficiently within body systems, tissues, or the higher centres of the brain, while the organism is active and awake.

It is fascinating that even with the latest gadgets, with electronic techniques, and with chemical and hormonal methods, all helping to differentiate between the separate functions of S sleep and D sleep, we have still not moved too far from Shakespeare's innate instinctual wisdom of the seventeenth century, when he wrote 'sleep, chief nourisher of life's feast' and 'sleep, which knits the raveled sleave of care'.

That poetic language still summarises quite neatly what scientists now believe S sleep and D sleep do. Extensive studies have shown that S sleep does 'nourish life's feast' with mounting evidence of increased protein production during this form of sleep. S sleep appears most concerned with the physical aspect of refreshment, repair and even growth. More S sleep, for instance, is taken after physical exercise or physical trauma.

Boy babies after circumcision are shown to increase their S sleep. Growth hormone secretion peaks during the deep stages 3 and 4 of S sleep, and this peak has been shown to move so that it still occurs in stages 3 and 4 even when the normal night sleeper has changed to daytime sleep because of shift work.

D sleep on the other hand is more associated with the brain. Recent American research very much confirms the theory put forward some time ago by Dr Christopher Evans, a British experimental psychologist, together with Mr E. A. Newman, a computer engineer, which compared the function of dreaming sleep to the process of clearing and revising computer programmes. They pointed out that the revision and up-dating is a vital part of the 'life-cycle' of modern computers and must be done when the machine is 'off-line', uncoupled from the normal tasks it controls. In the same way, they argued, the brain is a vastly complicated adaptive computer, and will certainly require 'off-line' time for revision, sorting, confirming, rejecting or reclassifying information.

This link with memory processing has certainly now received support from many studies. It has been found for instance that the young take far more D sleep, and this is a time when 'input' and memory imprinting must be specially heavy. More D sleep also occurs in adults who are involved in learning, examinations or emotional or psychic strain. The eminent American sleep researcher, Dr Ernest Hartman, reports his own and many other people's studies confirming this particular function of D sleep in his very erudite book *Functions of Sleep*.

Other circumstantial evidence can be found in the fact that D sleep decreases in the elderly, at a period of life when there is often a fall-off in intellectual stimuli and of memory. It also decreases in the mentally ill where memory processing is also poor. Interesting experiments with perfectly healthy young subjects found that making them wear 'inverting' spectacles produced not only obvious stress but a related upsurge of D sleep during the time they were striving to adjust to an upside-down world. Another intriguing finding in recent years has been that among patients with brain damage resulting in disruption of speech, those found to be taking more D sleep were also found to learn to speak again more quickly.

Yet another conjecture links S sleep and D sleep in what is called a 'sequential' way, with S sleep leading chemically (or neurologically) into D sleep. It is believed S sleep may deplete or alter something which is then rectified by D sleep, or that S sleep produces one chemical reaction and D sleep facilitates another one further along the chain in the production of some important molecule. Equally D sleep might just utilise, activate or further the transport of some substance produced by S sleep.

All that is largely speculative, and the permutations and possibilities are endless. There *is* a chemical side to sleep and this is also being investigated. Scientists at Harvard carried out a fascinating experiment using the fluid taken from the spinal cords of sleepy goats to plunge rats and cats into immediate and natural sleep. It has been known for some time that certain brain amines such as serotonin and noradrenalin can be shown in laboratory experiments to produce sleep in cats. Tryptophan, the substance from which serotonin is derived, was not long ago hailed as a new hypnotic following its successful use in producing sleep in humans.

Some of the latest work, reported in the British newspaper for doctors, *Pulse*, concerns the role of protein chemistry in the brain in relation to sleep. Dr René Drucker Colin of Mexico believes that the increased protein output of the brain proved to exist during D sleep may be the actual trigger mechanism for that form of sleep. Recent work on other natural body chemicals such as 'endorphins' has found that they lie in parts of the brain believed to control sleep and wakefulness, and may well prove to have a role in producing sleep. They have been called the 'brain's own morphine' because they attach themselves to the same cell structures in the brain in the same way as the artificial sleep-producer, morphine, does.

Hopefully this work may extend human potential in the direction of producing or triggering sleep through use of natural sleep chemicals from the body, instead of through the vast quantities of sleeping pills, too often addictive barbiturates, which modern man consumes in his search for sleep.

Over a million sleeping pills are swallowed each night in the UK alone. Insomnia is one of the most common complaints to doctors, and pharmaceutical companies are spending thousands of pounds each year in researching for new sleep-inducing drugs.

If any proof was needed of the importance of sleep it is the fact that down the ages anyone deprived of it has been driven to relentless pursuit. Sleep seems rather like love. If you have it you tend to take it for granted. If it eludes you, the search can become a desperate business. Not long ago, a German, who had been suffering from insomnia for nearly thirty years, ever since receiving a wartime head injury, offered £7,000, all he had in the world, for just one good night's sleep.

In this anxious pursuit of sleep all sorts of strange methods have been tried out, from rhythmic rocking, soothing sounds and the monotony of counting sheep, to the eccentric magnetic theory of Charles Dickens, dictating that wherever he slept his bed must always be pointing exactly north and south.

Hop pillows, Horlicks, sexual intercourse, even the juice of a large onion (the last two not, presumably, together) have all had their devotees as sleep inducers. Now for modern man comes a somewhat dubious device, emanating originally from Russia and used widely in the Eastern block, which relies on small pulses of electricity applied to the head to induce what is termed 'electro-sleep'. Tests in this country and America have not resulted in much enthusiasm.

In considering the limits of sleep, both short and long, despite an overall average sleep pattern for each species, it is important to recognise that sleep needs (and expectations) vary from individual to individual and for the same person at different stages of life.

The average human takes between seven and eight hours' sleep in one long stretch during the night hours, but babies sleep far more. The newborn baby spends sixteen to eighteen hours asleep and at least half of that is D sleep. By twelve months of age, sleep is down to just over twelve hours but the D sleep proportion remains fairly high at over a third of the total time. The cycle length in the young is also shorter, with waking, sleeping and dreaming all condensed into fifty-to-sixty-minute sessions which gradually lengthen to ninety minutes, until the twenty-four-hour sleep–wake cycle is superimposed to conform to the adult pattern of one eight-hour overnight sleep period. Rather more time is still given to D sleep, however, though this eventually stabilises at around 25 per cent of total sleep, except when special learning or stress demands are being made.

Total sleep requirements remain fairly constant until after middle age, when D sleep often diminishes and there are more wakenings, less deep sleep and far more variations begin to show up in older people. Some take only five hours' sleep on average, even when they have been good sleepers earlier in life, while others begin to sleep for over nine and a half hours.

But sleep requirements even in the prime of life can vary enormously between individuals, with some exceptional people requiring very little sleep and yet functioning efficiently and keeping healthy. From extensive studies Dr Hartman concluded that there are two main groups of sleepers according to personality. He designated the naturally short-sleep takers (average five and a half hours) as most often efficient, energetic, ambitious, tending to work hard and keep busy. They were relatively sure of themselves, socially adept, extrovert, decisive and more satisfied with themselves and their lives than were the long sleepers.

The long sleepers (averaging over eight hours with nine hours actually in bed) were less easily definable but appeared to have more complaints, were more critical socially and politically, and some were overtly anxious and many depressed. A few of them were even aware that they sometimes used sleep as an escape when reality was unpleasant. Most of them valued sleep highly and worried if they did not obtain what they felt to be the right amount.

On the individual level, of course, there have been some very famous short sleepers, and at least superficially they would appear to fit well the group description. Edison and Napoleon were reputed to get along on four to six hours' sleep regularly and Houdini needed only two. In our own times, Lord Grade is content with four hours' sleep a night and certainly has all the virtues of energy, drive and hard work attributed to the short-sleep group. Sir Monty Finniston reckons on only three hours and Sir Winston Churchill often took only two hours, though supplemented by his now famous catnaps and an hour-long siesta after lunch. Both he and President Truman agreed on the value of this system. In his book *The Gathering Storm*, Sir Winston wrote of his wartime period, 'I always went to bed at least for one hour as early as possible in the afternoon. By this means I was able to press a day and a half's work into one. Nature had not intended mankind to work from eight in the morning to midnight without refreshment of blessed oblivion which, even if it lasts only twenty minutes, is sufficient to renew all vital forces.'

Truman (at seventy years) stated, 'If I feel tired even while in a meeting, I excuse myself, go into a nearby room, take off my shoes and take a nap, if only for five minutes.'

That most recent Tory-de-force, as someone described Margaret Thatcher, manages to tackle her heavy work load on only five or six hours' sleep and none at all if the House is having an all-night sitting. She does not even snatch forty winks or take an after-lunch nap in Winston style, but believes that anyone who seeks executive responsibility must train him or herself to cope with a longer than average day. Only once a week does she allow herself to ease up. One night at the weekend she sleeps for eight or nine hours and calls it her 'flop' night.

One sleep researcher, Dr Ray Meddis, a lecturer in psychology at Loughborough University and chief proponent of the immobilisation theory of sleep, decided to see if body rhythms could be adjusted to a forty-eight-hour, rather than the customary twenty-four-hour clock, with sleep taken only once every two nights. Meddis and his wife, Valerie, spent two months in 1969 conducting their own private sleep experiment. They found that on the nights they did sleep, they took between twelve and thirteen hours, so that there was an over-all net saving of two or three hours' sleeping time. Even at the end of two months they had not adjusted and were still feeling tired every night rather than every other night, so that obviously it could not be considered a successful system.

A greater success was achieved on the larger-scale trials carried out in Spitzbergen by Dr Mary Lobban of the British Medical Research Council. During the Norwegian summer of constant daylight, she took out groups of students, placing some on a twenty-one-hour day and others on a twenty-eight-hour day, by use of 'cheating watches', which looked ordinary but actually compressed or lengthened the day as recorded on the dials.

In most cases body temperature control became adjusted to the new rhythm within two to six weeks, but the more complex sleep chemistry took longer and in some cases failed to adjust at all.

The deeply implanted sleep patterns both of duration and distribution appear obstinately to defy change except in very minor degree. Anything above that produces a kickback of some sort. Drastic experiments in the Edinburgh sleep laboratory by Dr Ian Oswald, depriving volunteers of any kind of sleep for 108 hours, showed that on the first recovery night S sleep took priority, filling more than its usual three-quarters of the total time and confirming its essential physical restorative function.

More prolonged sleep loss has been shown to go beyond merely making the subject irritable and unable to concentrate. Ian Oswald reported paranoia and even hallucination, with a couple of his volunteers thinking they saw breadcrumbs running about the tablecloth like insects and others hearing imaginary voices.

In his harsh history, man has known only too well how to use the effects of sleeplessness. Modern brainwashing techniques have developed the *tortura insomnia* of the Inquisition into a sophisticated tool for weakening, confusing and implanting. Such methods have been used to obtain false confessions for propaganda and spy trials and to persuade the Americans captured in Korea to plead guilty to germ warfare. By such methods too, every day of the week, hapless captives of tyrant regimes are still mentally bludgeoned towards conformity.

But there are important effects of sleep loss which affect or may affect all of us, particularly in the modern world of jet travel where safe flying-time limits are vital if pilots are to maintain the alertness, efficiency and judgement on which the lives of hundreds depend.

Effects of such sleep loss could also affect the judgement of world statesmen, often flying against the clock across time zones to meetings and conferences on which the future of all of us may depend.

There are obvious dangers in continued sleep loss, and it has been found that after only forty-eight hours without sleep, the body may generate a stress chemical belonging to the LSD family. Dr Robert T. Wilkinson, in closely controlled experiments at Cambridge, U.K., showed that only thirty hours of sleep loss can significantly affect performance in tests designed to be the equivalent of a normal day's work. He demonstrated slow response, lack of vigilance and imperfect concentration.

Recent and well-designed studies, supported in part by the US Department of the Navy, Bureau of Medicine and Surgery, showed similar results over a forty-hour period. One group of volunteers was allowed ten evenly spaced periods of one hour during the forty hours in which they could nap-sleep, another group was allowed similar periods of bed rest but no actual napping, and a third group was given the same periods of stationary bicycle exercise. Apart from short breaks and meals the rest of the time was taken up with physiological, performance and mood tests. The bed-rest group were found to fare no better than the exercise group, both lots of volunteers showing significant impairment for seven of the eight measures. The 'nappers' however, showed no impairment. Given the chance the first effect of prolonged sleep loss is always to make up the loss and even short bursts of sleep seem able to compensate reasonably well.

So how far can we go in cutting down on sleep? Can we really follow the brisk recommendation of Mrs Thatcher and train ourselves to do with less sleep without our health or efficiency suffering?

The answer seems to be that given enough motivation most people can reduce sleep requirements but only with certain limitations. The same American studies, for instance, found that habitual sleep time could be reduced without deterioration in either mood or performance, providing it was done gradually by between one and two hours. By going to bed later their volunteers in California reduced sleep in thirty-minute stages, in some cases right down to only four and a half hours. After a whole year, although the very low four-and-a-half hour level could not be maintained, this was because of a continual feeling of fatigue rather than because of bizarre behaviour or significant change in ability. By taking just one more hour most of the volunteers stabilised quite happily on five to six hours' sleep.

Similar results have been obtained with other studies and while strong motivation seems to be important in continuing the habit of shorter sleep, motivation also seems to be part of the ability to tolerate sleep loss and continue to carry out tasks efficiently. One of the problems in experiments designed to test the effects of depriving people of sleep is that it is always a constant and tempting possibility. It is rather like experimenting with depriving someone of food in the presence of a tempting banquet laid out to tantalise them. The strong need to sleep and the ever present possibility of doing so is opposed to the need to stay awake and the resultant conflict may be part of the stress involved, leading to the irritability, aggressiveness and anxiety most volunteers exhibit after a few days.

Then there is the matter of attitude and expectancy. Most of us are taught to believe that sleep is good from childhood and possibly from far further back if genetic memory and conditioning down the centuries is taken into account. So we both react against sleep loss and impose on ourselves a sleep expectancy based on the notion that eight hours' sleep is normal and necessary. We also positively *enjoy* sleep, welcome the lapse into unconsciousness, the escape from problems and the recharging effect on physical and mental batteries. We also register quite clearly, even if experimental evidence does not always bear it out, the damaging effects, both of tiredness and increased irritability, if we are forced against our will to go without what we consider our normal and rightful amount of sleep.

Having admitted all that, it does seem that for some of us sleep expectations may be over-high. Given the motivation we can actually thrive on *less* sleep and train ourselves towards this by systematic sleep reduction, providing it is done gradually. However we need to be sure that what we gain in quantity of waking and activity time is not lost in general quality and enjoyment of that time, or in reduced efficiency.

Some forms of motivation and some sleep reduction can only be considered stupid and dangerous. Into that category would seem to go the futile marathon contests, which resulted in the longest recorded period for which any person has voluntarily gone without sleep. The Guinness Book of Records shows that as 449 hours (14 days 13 hours) by Mrs Maureen Weston of Peterborough, Cambridgeshire, achieved (if that is the right word) between 14 April and 2 May 1977. Though she hallucinated towards the end of this very ill-advised test, she has so far appeared to suffer no lasting ill-effects. Unless she was attached to an EEG machine (which the entry fails to note) it is more than likely that brief micro-sleeps would be taken without anyone knowing. These have been proved by EEG patterns to take place unwittingly, and are strongly suspected to be the cause of many motor accidents with sleepy drivers blanking out for what may prove a fatal second of unconsciousness.

Few people, except unfortunate insomniacs, would want to become human opossums and extend the length of sleep. This does happen, of course, in the case of narcolepsy, an unenviable and overwhelming form of compulsive sleep that can literally strike at any time. This is an illness, not really understood yet, but it appears to have no physiological basis and is possibly of psychic origin, as it is most often triggered by emotion, even laughter or love.

Narcoleptics at Edinburgh, where they were both studied and treated, complained particularly of this aspect and with reason. It must be embarrassing to say the least to suddenly slump into sleep in the middle of making love, as one victim described. Another, who suffered attacks from the age of fourteen and was known at school as the 'dormouse', found her attacks worse during pregnancy, coming once or twice a day and often at dangerous times such as when she was ironing or out on busy streets. The same mother also explained that she could never smack her children. 'As soon as I feel angry,' she confessed, 'the power goes out of my arms and my hand falls.'

This loss of muscle power, which preceded a possible attack in her case, is often involved in narcolepsy, varying from simply a 'feeling' of weakness to real sleep paralysis, that total inability to move which some people experience in the transition between sleeping and waking.

There is quite strong evidence for narcolepsy having a hereditary or genetic component, as between 20 and 50 per cent of sufferers have been reported to have other members of the family similarly affected. The attacks in 75 per cent of cases start between the ages of fifteen and twenty-five and 5 per cent before the age of ten, but onset is rare after forty.

This dramatic intrusion of sleep into waking life affects an estimated two to five persons in a thousand, but sleep research is yielding effective treatment and hope for even better control in the future. In addition to emotion, it has been found that fatigue or heavy meals, in particular certain protein-rich foods, can trigger attacks. EEG tracings have shown no connection with epilepsy, which some people feared and which shows quite different brain-wave patterns. Patterns in narcoleptics simply reveal that REM sleep occurs untypically right at the onset of their daytime compulsive sleeps, and it is likely that the problem is rooted in REM sleep dysfunction. Treatment, apart from control of diet, consists of drugs which suppress REM sleep and these are highly effective.

Playing around with extending or limiting REM sleep has led to the incredible possibility of being able to influence dreams. Already, of course, we know this can be influenced to some extent by outside stimuli. Most of us, with the sleeping brain assaulted by an insistent alarm clock, have found ourselves shifted in mid-dream to a scenario which includes a ringing telephone. Experiments with water dripped on sleepers, when the EEG machine showed they were already dreaming, resulted in their dream content changing. Woken up soon afterwards they described being under waterfalls in their dreamlife or caught in storms. The gradual identification of specific centres in the brain also opens up for some the possibility of a 'dream machine', but such a science-fiction concept of the future is already overtaken in the present with work at Harvard Medical School. There Dr Ennio Vivaldi and his team believe they have located two groups of nerve cells in the brain stem, which oppose each other to produce the cyclic recurrence of dream periods. Drugs which affect these cells have been used to either extend or shorten the periods of dreaming. The brain generator for dreaming effectively has an 'on and off' switch. When the 'on' nerve cells are stimulated dreaming sleep begins. When the 'off' nerve cells are stimulated it stops. This work obviously holds out considerable hope also for treating narcolepsy.

The real hope for the future must be not so much in extending the limits of normal sleep, or playing about with dreams, but in enabling sufferers from chronic insomnia to achieve adequate sleep. Here there seems every likelihood that the bad old sleeping pills, such as the barbiturates, which can become addictive and to which the body builds up tolerance, will be superseded by pills based on natural sleeping agents derived from the body chemicals that induce sleep. Many experiments have shown that l-tryptophan, one of the brain amino acids involved in the biochemistry of sleep, appears able to hasten and deepen sleep with use of only very small doses. The normal pattern is not changed, waking time is not altered and the whole process seems to work through the normal chemistry so that hopefully no tolerance will be built up in the long term.

It is over 200 years since Samuel Johnson first coined that marvellous description of sleep as 'The gentle tyrant'. He wrote:

> Sleep is a state in which a great part of every life is passed . . . Yet of this change, so frequent, so great, so general, and so necessary, no searcher has yet found either the efficient or final cause: or can tell by what power the mind and body are thus chained down in irresistible stupefaction: or what benefits the animal receives from this alternate suspension of its active powers . . . And, once in twenty-four hours, the gay and the gloomy, the witty and the dull, the clamorous and the silent, the busy and the idle, are all overpowered by the gentle tyrant

> and lie down in the equality of sleep . . . (The Idler, 25 November 1757)

A modern writer on sleep, Wilse B. Webb, Graduate Professor of Psychology at the University of Florida and an international authority on sleep with four books to his credit, used the title *Sleep: The Gentle Tyrant* for his latest work. In it he stresses the essential evolutionary nature of sleep, but also the adaptiveness of the system. He writes:

> We sleep as we do because we were so built over countless periods of time.
>
> Like all biological functions, sleep has its innate course of development, is lawfully sensitive to its treatment, and self-protective in its ways. At the same time it is remarkably adaptive, within limits, to man's lifestyle within his environment. When permitted and not pushed, it unfolds and proceeds to perform effectively its ordained patterns. When pushed by our real or presumed needs it yields and bends but remembers and reminds us of its nature.
>
> To live on best terms with a 'gentle tyrant' one must learn the rules by which he governs. Being gentle, he permits us certain freedoms to manifest our individual variations and differences: being a tyrant, he will not permit us to live in total freedom, and abuses carry their ultimate consequences. Although we may deplore 'benevolent dictators' in our politics, this one seems efficient, is unlikely to be overthrown, and can best be lived with in peace.

There is one way in which modern man clearly breaks the rules and fails to live in peace with the deeply ingrained rhythms of sleep – that is in shift work. The availability of twenty-four-hour light and heat, increasingly expensive plant and high production costs, continuous processing and competitive pressures, have all combined to bring about various systems of industrial shifts, and the situation is not likely to change.

So how do shift workers adapt? What is the price they have to pay? The brief answer seems to be not too well and the price is too high, at least in between 25 and 50 per cent of cases. Studies in Germany among night shift workers found this was the proportion that complained about lack of appetite and digestion difficulties. Some researchers found evidence of more severe intestinal disorders. Some 83 per cent of men on night work felt tired compared to only 4 per cent on day shift work, with poor quantity and quality of sleep the main complaints. This was no doubt reflected in the increased errors and lower production associated with night shift workers.

Many experts believe the proper 'biological' solution to these problems of shift work is a system of permanent shifts, since sleep–waking rhythms will adapt and become reorganised to a new pattern given time.

Men at sea adapt to four-hour watches reasonably well, with any trouble confined usually to switching from one set of watches to another. But at sea men carry their own microcosm of the world with them. On land social structures and pressures remain geared to daytime activity and night-time sleep. So because of the need for recreation and the demands of family life, shift workers have so far preferred to be out of biological phase periodically, rather than be out of social phase continually, despite feeling more tired and less well on this system. Industry has attempted to compensate them by incentive pay or more time off.

Experience suggests that a more 'around the clock' world, with social life, restaurants and television programmes better geared to twenty-four-hour living, would help towards more rational (and that means longer) periods on night shifts for workers who find they adapt particularly well. The present swiftly rotating shifts, or even one week out of every month, never allow time for the body and mind to fully adjust and readjust.

Other adaptations and acclimatisations show man does best and achieves most when the process is gradual. In changing, extending or reducing sleep limits, the same principle would seem to hold good. In fact sleep limits seem to require rather special respect and be particularly resistant to manipulation.

4
Physical and Functional Limits

Dr Murray Watson keeps a pair of bush shorts in his desk. They are just an ordinary pair of bush shorts, one of the many that he, as a zoologist studying the elephants in Kenya's Tsavo National Park, has to own. Except that this pair reminds him of the night that he broke the world high-jump record.

There's no need to look up the record books for Murray's name – it's not there. His world record could only have been ratified by the herd of hyenas which 'assisted' him in his jump. And the only tangible evidence of his leap is the jagged tear in the seat of the shorts made by the leading animal's teeth.

One calm, pleasant, but moonless evening in 1965, Murray was driving his Land Rover along a bush path towards his base camp. With only two miles to go, the engine stuttered and stopped, his lights went out, and all attempts to restart the vehicle failed. This left him with the choice of staying with the Rover and shivering through the night until morning, when some passer-by would doubtless stop to help, or of walking the short distance to home and a warm bed.

Being young – he was twenty-six – and relatively new to Africa – this was his second year at Tsavo – he decided on the second course. He had, of course, the respect that all Europeans have for the wild life of Africa, and would not have ventured alone into the night if there had been evidence of dangerous animals nearby. In the last few miles, however, he had seen nothing but a pack of hyenas, and their reputation as scavengers made them no threat at all. Hunger, thirst and the cold Kenyan night – and perhaps the supreme self-confidence of the young led him to chance to walk. Within 200 yards he knew he had made the wrong decision. He could only see the winding road ahead of him by looking at the branches of the trees outlined against the faint light in the sky. In another quarter of an hour the blackness would be total, and he now knew that the hyena pack was following him.

In the early 1960s little was known of the nocturnal habits of these unsavoury creatures. By day they ate carrion, following the kills of lions; even, when in large enough groups, driving away a solitary lioness from her kill. It was only in 1970 that their true character emerged. At night, they become predators in their own right. Hunting in packs, they will bring down wildebeest and other animals far larger than themselves, and humans appear to be no exception.

Dr Watson is no coward. Looking back on that night's experience, however, he admits to something close to terror. There was nothing to be seen in the total darkness near the ground, but he could hear the breathing and grunts of the pack around him. The leading animal made one brief run at him, stopping only just short, and snarling, as if taking his time before his final attack. Knowing that it would be useless to run – hyenas can outpace the swiftest of people, and that any animal will attack if the prey shows a hint of fear, our intrepid zoologist looked for a tree to climb.

The next few moments are very clear in Dr Watson's memory. The lead hyena stopped snarling and started running at him. He jumped for the lowest branch of the tree and swung himself into an upward circle in the single gymnastic movement learned at his school in Lincoln more than a decade before. It wasn't a second too soon. The teeth of the leaping animal tore out the seat of his shorts, fortunately without scratching him, while he was in mid-swing.

The rest of that night he spent in the tree, waiting for dawn and the dispersal of the hyenas. The animals stayed at its base until the full light of day, then meandered off to look for easier meat. Only then did Dr Watson attempt to climb down from his perch. To his astonishment he found that he was more than twelve feet from the ground. The drop to earth was far higher than it seemed during the night. And once down, no matter how hard he tried or how high he jumped, he could not get within four feet of repeating the previous night's leap. More than this, his research station colleagues, sceptical of his story, all failed by a similar margin to reach that bottom branch.

Dr Watson's Olympic-standard leap ranks alongside the reported weight-lifting achievement of a woman, also under enormous emotional stress at the time of her action. Her daughter had been caught under the back wheel of a reversing car, which had then stalled and could not be re-started. In a desperate effort to rescue her child from agony, the mother ran forward, grasped the rear bumper, and heaved. The car rose in the air and was held there long enough for the girl to be pulled clear. It was only afterwards that the impossibility of the whole action was brought home to her. A male world champion weightlifter of her size would have been overjoyed to have 'cleaned' and held such a weight.

How did they do it? A complete explanation is beyond us, except to recognise that we are far from understanding or reaching the true potential of the power of our bodies. Dr Watson and the car-lifting mother were both acting under extreme emotion, the one in fear of his life, the other, perhaps even more powerful, fearing for the life of a daughter. During such times our bodies switch on to one of the most primitive reactions, the fright, fight or flight mechanism. Adrenalin pours into the bloodstream, the sympathetic nervous system speeds up the rate and force of the heartbeat, opens up the airways in the lungs, the blood vessels in the muscles, and the pupils of the eyes. Consequently more oxygen is taken into the body, and is more speedily and effectively transported to the most important area of the body, the muscles that, primitively, would remove us from the threat of a predator. The dilating pupils enable us to see better, and all our nervous and muscular actions become more efficient. We react faster to circumstances, and are better able to indulge in explosive bursts of activity.

In the two cases described the reactions of these two ordinary untrained people surpassed those of trained athletes in their perfect co-ordination; perhaps for the first and only time in their lives they reached the limit of their potential. If stress can do this, perhaps athletes are still far short of their maximum possible performance.

One exception to this may have occurred in the 1968 Olympics. Mexico City is at a height of 7,400ft (2,255m) above sea level, and when it was chosen as the site for the Games the decision was described by Sir Roger Bannister, the first sub-four-minute miler, as 'foolish, astonishing, absurd'. Certainly, Sir Roger, as a miler, would have had the greatest difficulty in Mexico City. At that height the air is 25 per cent less dense than at sea level. For sprinters and jumpers, whose total oxygen needs are already within their bodies before they take part in their brief event, this is a great advantage. For the longer-distance runners, any benefit is more than counteracted by the relative lack of oxygen in the rarefied air. The winner of the Olympic 'mile', the 1,500-metre race, that year, and in record time, was Kipchoge Keino, the Kenyan, who lived and trained at an altitude similar to that of Mexico City, and whose circulation and oxygen-carrying powers were specially adapted to it. By contrast, Jim Ryun, the American favourite for the race, was second, at a speed 2·2 per cent slower than his fastest, despite having spent months beforehand acclimatising himself to the conditions.

Keino's win was, in retrospect, not surprising. Neither was the win of Bob Beaman in the long jump. But it was he who was to provide the exceptional performance. For he jumped over 29ft (8·8m) – 22in (56 cm) beyond the previous record, and a distance which some sports scientists claim will not be beaten in the next century. In 'putting it all together' in that one crucial moment, Beaman must have come very close to the superhuman, super-motivated achievements of Murray Watson and the car-shifting mother. Sport, particularly athletics, offers the most practical area for looking at physical and functional limits; even then it is that final piece of mental effort, driving on the near-perfect skill and physique, which makes world champions. Emil Zatopek, the Czech runner who stole all the headlines throughout the early 1950s, understood this completely. He trained by performing repeated squat jumps with his wife Dana sitting on his shoulders. He trained himself to hold his breath for ever longer periods until it hurt, so that his mind would not panic when his body began to run out of oxygen.

Zatopek's supreme moment was in the Helsinki Olympics of 1952. He had already won the 5,000- and 10,000-metre events when he declared himself a late entry for the marathon. Never having competed in races above ten miles, he decided to attach himself to the hot favourite, Britain's Jim Peters. He was at Peters' shoulder, the two men far ahead of the field, at the sixteenth mile post, when he became curious about how much faster they could go.

Turning to his fellow runner, the Czech said, "Excuse me, Peters, I have never run a marathon before. We go a little faster, yes?"

Peters was so affected by this he faltered and fell behind. Zatopek turned on the speed and won the race comfortably.

Man's and woman's ability to push beyond what was thought only recently to be impossible has been confirmed over and over again in the last thirty years. Shots are regularly putted over 70ft (21·3m); pole vaulters are not likely to reach an Olympic final if they cannot clear 18ft (5·5m), nor high jumpers well over 7ft (2·1m). In the ten years after Roger Bannister broke the four-minute mile in 1954, forty-four other runners also did so. Yet all these barriers were considered to be near the limits of human achievement. The mile record was held for four years at 3min 49·4sec, by John Walker, a New Zealander whose medical man, Dr Lloyd Drake, constantly monitored his heart, lungs and blood, giving him injections of extra vitamin B12 if his oxygen-carrying capacity, in the form of red blood cells, fell below the maximum. It was taken from him by Sebastian Coe in Oslo in 1979 who broke the 800 metres and mile records within two weeks, with times of 1min 42·33sec and 3min 48·95 sec respectively. In that mile race Walker was sixth, and ten men came in under 3min 55·3sec. Coe claims that he 'just runs' and is not dependent on the close medical attention given to Walker and many others. Nor is he the creature of a totalitarian state-run high-pressure training system. He is a perfect example of dedicated individualism blending innate skill with personal discipline and motivation.

Sir Roger Bannister, now an eminent London neurologist, and still very much involved in athletics, also does not approve of the ultra-scientific approach. Every athlete, he says, is physically different and needs to work out his own training routine. Much more important, according to Sir Roger, is drive and mental toughness. This quality will ensure that the vision of mechanical superstars of sport trained to slavery to a routine, with mechanically perfect actions and body characteristics altered to suit their events, is unlikely to be fulfilled in our lifetimes.

This does not mean that mental concentration and perseverance in the correct training could fit anyone for the heights. Suitability for different events depends very much on body build, and sometimes even on race. It may even depend on unalterable characteristics invisible to any but the microscopist or biochemist, such as the type of muscle fibre or the speed with which the liver and muscle cells can re-build the energy stores after their depletion. Sports research, especially in America, has become big business, and with it has developed the science of prediction of those likely to become superstars of the future.

For those who wish to torture themselves on the Olympic path, we can perhaps point you in the right direction. First, make sure that you have a physique which can be turned to the correct athletic use. This most certainly does not mean following the sort of course which leads to getting your own back on the famous muscular bully who kicked sand in your face when you were a seven-stone weakling. Indeed there are many world-beating seven-stone champions – but few, if any, with overdeveloped muscles.

William Sheldon, an American, was the first to attempt a scientific assessment of the athletic abilities of young men. After studying photographs of 4,000 students he concluded that there were three relevant aspects of body shape.

By what he called somatotyping, Sheldon grouped his students into endomorphs, mesomorphs and ectomorphs. The first had rounded bodies and heads, a heavy build and were usually fat. The second were muscular with broad shoulders, little fat and narrow hips. The third were thin, with little muscle or fat, often awkward, and with a large surface area of skin in relation to his bulk.

Sheldon believed, and many still agree with him, that these types are immutable – the fat ectomorph does not become an endomorph, nor a muscular endomorph a mesomorph. He graded people from 1 to 7 for each system, so that a score of 7, 1, 1, is an extreme endomorph and 1, 7, 1 a Mr Universe. The average man with no particular bias towards fat, muscle or skin scores 4, 4, 4.

The system very much depends on accurate measurement of various bone-to-bone prominences, of skin thicknesses and layers of fat, but it does give very closely reproducible results in the hands of many examiners. It certainly seems to work in the prediction of athletic prowess. Professor J. M. Tanner used the Sheldon technique to classify 137 male athletes at the Rome Olympics. They were all predominantly mesomorphs or ectomorphs: none had scores above 4 for endomorphy. There were even 'horses for courses'. All the shot putters were grouped closely around 4, 6, 2; the long-distance walkers around 2, 4, 4. There were sharp divisions between the 'explosive' eventers, the middle-distance runners, and the endurance-event athletes.

Anthony Smith, a zoologist, journalist and author, in his excellent book *The Body* has made a special study of body measurement techniques and their relevance to sport. He advises schoolboys keen to continue in sport to examine their shapes seriously and to give up an event if their body type is wrong for it.

Sheldon's system did not highlight one apparently vital aspect of athletic success – height. In Rome, all the shot putters were at least 6 feet 1 inch tall. All the discus men had longer than normal arms for their height. The high jumpers, too, were all six footers. As for the runners, with the exception of the shortest sprints, the longer the race, the shorter the runners. The average 400-metre man was 6ft 1in (185·4cm) tall. The 800- and 1,500-metre runners were about 5ft 11in (180·3cm) tall, and the runners in the longer-distance track events 5ft 8in (172·7cm). Marathon men averaged 5ft 7in (170cm). The 'explosive' sprinters had an average height of 5ft 10in (177·8cm).

Weight followed the same rules. The lightest 400 metres runner was 11lb (5kg) heavier than the heaviest marathon entrant, and the gap in weight between the 'throwers' and the heaviest of the runners was more than 2st (12·7kg). Anthony Smith suggests, presumably tongue in cheek, that the huge disparity in height and weight between the shot putters (the biggest of whom was 6ft 4in (193cm) tall and weighed 18st 4lb (116kg)) and marathon runners (the smallest being 5ft 5in (165cm) and 8st 4lb (52·6kg)) suggests that they are different species.

The ages, too, of the athletes, were surprisingly different. Presumably because sprinters pass their peak younger, the youngest men were running in the shortest races. The average age of the 100-metre runners was 23 years. It rose to 24, 25, 26, 27 and 30 years for the 400, 1,500, 5,000, 10,000 metres and marathon races respectively. The oldest race competitor was a 36-year-old 50-kilometre walker. In contrast, there have been several Olympic swimmers aged only 13.

The gradient of age with longer distance suggests one, or both, of two possibilities. The first is that physical stamina and endurance can only be built up to the ultimate limit slowly, over the years. The second is that the longer the race the more experience and judgement, both mental and physical are needed, and these can only come slowly.

If you are small and thin, therefore, aim for the marathon, but be prepared to wait until the end of your twenties or even early thirties before you expect to reach the heights. On the other hand, if you are built like Michelangelo's David, you must aspire to the 400-metre record. If you reach twenty-five without making the finals, then you may as well give up.

Just possessing the right build by no means guarantees success. Hard training is essential to keep the muscles efficient and stamina at its peak. The trouble is that hardly any two experts agree on its correct form, with training fashions changing as unpredictably as women's hemlines.

They have varied from interval training, involving alternate fast and slow runs, to the long, slow, distance mileage popular with athletes in the early 1970s, when the aim was to increase endurance by running more than 200 miles a week. The most discredited method is long, fast, distance training which proved damaging and consequently counterproductive.

Constant running at top speed leads inevitably to breakdown of the moving parts, not unlike fatigue fractures in metal. Knees are the most vulnerable joints, and stress fractures in the feet are a close second. One British middle-distance hurdler, a medal favourite for the Montreal Olympics and committed to a hard training schedule, insisted on continuing even after a series of pulled hamstring muscles. He went to Montreal, but as a sports commentator, not a competitor.

The arguments about the type of training could well be considered settled by the work of Edward Watt, B. A. Plotnicki and Elsworth Buskirk, who in 1972 divided university distance runners into two groups. Both groups trained each afternoon, but the members of one group ran six miles at a fast pace each morning while the others relaxed. After nine weeks there was no difference in their mile times.

It seems that the amount and intensity of the training are relatively unimportant in reaching the limit of one's athletic potential. What is important is regular exercise over many years.

Kenneth Doherty in his book *Modern Track and Field* reported his study of twenty champion runners. It took them an average of 10·4 years from the start of their athletics careers to achieving their best runs. In those years they had trained for five to six days each week for more than ten months a year.

All this training – and to stick to such schedules surely means that the runner has something obsessional in his character, and therefore the necessary mental attitude – still does not guarantee success. The champions appear to have something extra, which brings them just so much closer to the limits of human endurance. And it seems that this added factor will be found not on the track or in the mind but on the laboratory microscope slide.

Each successive Olympics since World War II has seen a rise in the political kudos gained by the countries whose athletes are forced to push beyond the limits. The production of better athletes has not yet gone as far in humans as it has in cattle, where eugenics and selective breeding is all. Hopefully that is still generations away. But research devoted entirely to the analysis and improvement of athletic achievement has mushroomed on both sides of the Iron Curtain. Sports medicine is a recognised speciality in the United Kingdom and the United States.

The Human Performance Laboratory at Indiana's Ball State University is a prime example of the changing face of scientific athletes. It is currently run by David Costill, a physiologist who is also a five-mile-a-day runner.

Under Costill's supervision scientists operate sophisticated machinery to measure the gases runners breathe in and out, their energy output, all in an enclosed chamber in which runners can exercise in highly controlled atmospheric conditions, and using a famous treadmill, where the most celebrated American runners are pushed to the limit. The results are analysed by the Institute's own computer.

One of Costill's discoveries, made in collaboration with Dr Bengt Salin, of Copenhagen, is that to be a champion runner, you need a special type of muscle fibril. Each muscle consists of many bundles of these highly specialised cells which look like hairs under the high-power lens of a miscroscope. It is contraction of each of these fibrils separately in co-ordination with all the others which produces the controlled contraction of the muscle.

With special staining and stimulation techniques Salin and Costill discovered that the fibrils teased out from samples of muscle from all subjects, whether athletes or not, fell into two types. One, which they named the FT fibre, contracted quickly in response to stimulation; the other, the ST fibre, contracted more slowly. Application of this discovery to the muscles of champion runners showed that there was a highly significant difference in their ratios, depending on their specialist event. Some 62 per cent of the fibrils in the muscles of the middle-distance runners were of the slow-acting type. This compared with 57 per cent in normal subjects and 79 per cent in the champion long-distance men.

Costill and Salin claim on this basis they can predict the limits of any athlete. They say that no one can be a champion long-distance runner unless he possesses the correct proportion of ST fibrils. This does not mean that such people should give up athletics, but that to avoid inevitable failure, they should choose another event in which they at least have a chance of excelling.

Fibril counts may even replace measurement of lung and heart capacity, previously thought to be all-important for the potential champion. Training will improve the tone of the heart muscle and the efficiency of the lungs – but nothing so far can change the vital ratio of fast- to slow-acting fibrils in our muscles.

Costill's work has reversed other old opinions, based on non-scientific data and ideas, which governed athletics practices for years. For example, until he proved otherwise, marathon runners eschewed all fluid intake throughout a race, for little other reason than that it might give rise to stomach cramps or chills. Costill showed that such fluid restrictions made runners much more susceptible to fatigue and heat stroke. Now it is well established that drinking while running improves performance and cannot harm it. This is the reason for the multiplication of drinking stations on long road runs. The proof of Costill's work can be seen in Bill Rodgers, who won the Boston Marathon in 1975 in the record time of 2hr 9min 55sec; this included four stops to drink water – he claims he cannot drink water on the run – and one to tie his shoelaces!

The Ball State group may also help to put training on a more scientific basis. Costill sees the purpose of training as the taxing of the biological systems needed for prolonged high rates of energy production. This will be of no value unless there are sufficient intermediate periods of rest to over-compensate for the stress. As the enzymes (the biological catalysts) which control the physiological activity of the muscles take three to four weeks to respond to such stress, training should be planned over a monthly period, and not week by week. This should allow for longer periods of light training.

Apart from enzymes, another essential is glycogen, the carbohydrate stored in the liver and muscles for quick conversion to glucose and therefore energy when needed. Glucose itself cannot be stored in the body. During an exhausting run, or a race, all the glycogen stores are depleted, and have to be quickly replaced by intake of more carbohydrate – usually in the form of sugar. The faster an athlete can replace his glycogen store, the sooner he can return to training or racing. Costill himself is a slow glycogen replacer, so that he recognises that he needs to train lightly for three days or more after a heavy training day, or just before a race. Fast replacers can exert themselves daily, and some may even prevent glycogen depletion by eating glucose during a long-distance running session. Almost certainly Zatopek belonged to this group. It must be admitted, however, that some doctors disagree with Costill. They claim that slow glycogen replacement is purely a sign of lack of fitness, a claim that Costill is certain to dispute hotly!

All that has been written so far has been applied to male athletes – but it can equally apply to women. The difference between the sexes in size and strength ensures that the physical performance of women will always remain behind that of their contemporary male colleagues, but they are catching up, and fast. Women athletes can outpace and out-distance males. Women's track and swimming world records today are often better than the men's records established in the early half of this century, and this is certainly not because the champions have become more manly. Women runners remain feminine, yet have started to beat the men on their own terms.

No one can deny that women swimmers, despite their hectic training schedules and their functional swimwear, still manage to look attractive. One British Olympic swimmer is said to have found this to his considerable disadvantage in one of the post-war Olympics. He was the gold-medal favourite for his two events. The story goes that he had a particularly passionate affair with a woman colleague who was expected at best to achieve a third or fourth place. As their affair developed, his times slowed and she speeded up! The end result was a bronze for the man and a gold for the girl – which should cause us all to reflect on how best to prepare for an important race!

James Fixx, who took up running in 1963 at the age of thirty-five when he weighed 16st (101·6kg), describes in his *The Complete Book of Running*, a 10½-mile mixed race in which he 'tucked in behind' a girl athlete who was running easily at a speed he thought comfortable. He reasoned that he could overtake her when she tired; but a mile from the finish it was he who tired, and was forced to watch her pulling away from him on a long, slow, uphill gradient. To Fixx the similarities between the sexes are more important than the differences. A running interview with the 1972 Boston Marathon women's division winner, Nina Kuscsik, made him so breathless that he had to stop talking until they finished the run!

Fixx does not deny that men are stronger and faster than women. Weight for weight, women have less muscle and more fat than men, their legs are shorter, their bones lighter and smaller, their shoulders are narrower. Their lower centre of gravity makes them less efficient jumpers, although it should help them in 'burst' events where they need to stand still, such as the shot put. Their hearts and lungs are smaller than men's in proportion to their bulk. Everything seems to be against them. Despite this, more and more women, particularly in the United States, are taking on men at their own races and even beating them.

The taboos women have had to face have been almost insurmountable. There are still countries which refuse to send women's teams to the Olympics, and even in the United States remnants of the taboos remain. American women have been highly successful in swimming but it is only in very recent years that they have come to the fore in running, and even then it has been black athletes who have been the spearhead.

Despite their disadvantages in size and strength, women run more fluidly and economically in terms of energy output than men. This impression was proved by Dr Richard Nelson and Christine Brooks who, in comparisons of forty-two top-class athletes, found that the women took, for their heights, longer strides than the men, had more steps to the minute, and spent less time in contact with the ground.

Naturally, on the way to the top, champion women athletes have to overcome some disadvantages. Many run too much on their toes, a fault which one woman professional blames on the wearing of high heels, and the consequent shortening of the Achilles tendon. Many shuffle, rather than run, others swing their hips too much or splay their feet out to the side. Simple training can correct these faults.

One female problem that men don't face is what to do with the breasts. The women – and the men – are still arguing. Some say there is no need to wear a bra, and indeed feel confined in one. Others recommend a firm supporting bra, particularly if the breasts are large. Bouncing breasts can disturb the runner as well as the male spectators: she waits for them to come down before taking the next step and this breaks the rhythm. One breast problem that is common to all runners is how to control the constant rubbing of the moving skin against clothing. Long distance runners of either sex can finish a race raw or even bleeding from skin flexures.

Arguments have raged about the health hazards of running, particularly for women. One critic of running, Dr J. E. Schmidt, wrote in the March 1976 issue of *Playboy* that running could result in droopy breasts, displaced wombs, slipped discs, varicose veins and hernias, not to mention 'dropping stomach', 'loosening spleens', floating kidneys, and fallen arches.

None of this has been substantiated in practice. Most women report that their breast shape is firmer because running strengthens the supporting chest muscles. Running, as far as we know, has never displaced a uterus. Indeed many women runners date their present feeling of well-being and health from the day they started the sport. Contrary to popular belief, running or training does not induce the development of unsightly muscles in women, even if it includes weight lifting. According to J. Wilmore of the United States National Athletic Health Institute, who has special interest in the limits and potential of women athletes, their power can increase by over 40 per cent without any noticeable increase in muscle mass. Most women, in fact, lose weight in the form of excess fat when they start running.

With correct training, menstruation, period pains and pre-menstrual tension need not impose limits on the physical achievements of women athletes. The Indiana University head of women's athletics, Marge Albohm, found the differences in performance due to the menstrual cycle so little as not to be noticeable, and recommended that women should take a full part in athletics at every stage of the cycle.

Pregnancy, too, does not deter women athletes. Liza Veijalainen was three months' pregnant when she won the world orienteering championship in 1976 in Darnaway Forest, in Scotland. One woman marathon runner, Sandra Davis, completed races in her fourth and eighth weeks of pregnancy. Another, Trina Hosmer, ran four miles two hours before giving birth to her son. According to James Fixx, she had not recognised that the discomfort she tried to 'run off' was the start of labour.

It took a long time for the male-dominated world of athletics to accept women in any but the short sprint events. Female field-event athletes were regarded as freaks, and any woman who aspired to running more than 800 metres was thought to be putting her health permanently at risk. Yet all the evidence suggests that the longer the distance, the more suited is the woman of normal build to run it.

The Boston Marathon is an annual American national institution. From the first race in 1897 until it began in the 1960s to be swamped by huge numbers of poorly prepared enthusiasts it was open to any male who wished to enter. The organisers then imposed a qualifying marathon time of under three hours for entrants, but women were excluded on the pretext that they could not last the distance. This changed in 1966.

Hiding in the bushes near the starting line that year was Roberta Gibb. When the race started she joined the mass of male bodies unseen by the officials, and outlasted many of the men to finish the course.

Although in the following year Kathy Switzer was the first woman who succeeded, by giving a false name, to be given an official race number, it was only in 1972 that women were allowed to compete. In that year the winner of the female section was Nina Kuscsik. She was already ahead of her rivals at the thirteen-mile stage when she had a sudden attack of diarrhoea which she could not control. Despite the embarrassment in front of huge crowds she continued to run, to win eventually by a margin of nine minutes. The first woman to finish in 1976, Kim Merritt, completed the course in 2hr 47min, and was 146th of more than 1,000 entrants, the vast majority of whom were male. Opposition to the women collapsed in that year. In the last twelve years the women's marathon world record time has fallen from 3hr 7min to 2hr 32min, the latter being faster than most top-class men marathoners have achieved. The Road Runners Clubs of England and America's standards of excellence set the target for first-class male marathoners at 2hr 35min. On present form, and assuming no real improvement in women's physiques, it would appear that the limit for women will be around 2hr 23min.

Marathons may be the longest running event in the Olympics, but they are by no means the greatest challenge to man's athletic endurance. There is a yearly race from London to Brighton, a 52½-mile run for athletes of extreme masochistic bent. At the end of the race runners feel marvellous, except for their bleeding feet, groins, nipples and other skin folds, and excruciatingly painful legs. Women have completed this race too. A similar race, the Comrades' Marathon, which takes place on the 56-mile stretch between Pietermaritzburg and Durban, attracts more than 3,000 runners.

In 1976 Park Barner, an American, completed in two successive days a 50-mile race and a 26-mile marathon. Bruce Tulloh completed the American coast-to-coast trip of 3,200 miles in sixty-five days in 1969, and had enough energy left to write a book about it called *Four Million Footsteps*. His feat was outclassed in 1978 by a religious running group, the Liberty Torch, members of which ran 8,800 miles through each of the fifty United States.

The John O'Groats to Land's End run popular with the British enthusiasts has been mirrored in New Zealand by at least one man, Don Cameron, who ran an average of almost sixty miles a day for twenty-three days to traverse the country from the south coast to the northernmost lighthouse. None of these feats of endurance, however, approached that of Pax Beale and Ken Crutchlow, two Americans who ran 145 miles in two days. The remarkable aspect of their run is that it took place in Death Valley, in which the temperature during the run reached 135 °F (57·2°C), and that it was all uphill, ending at the 14,495 ft (441·8m) summit of Mount Whitney. Beale's weight loss in those two days was 55lb (24·9kg) – of which he quickly replaced 44lb (20kg) by drinking specially prepared liquids.

In America now, marathoners who feel they have not pushed themselves far enough towards the limits of their endurance are running 100-mile races. They call them ultramarathons. One such runner, Ted Corbitt, in a discussion with James Fixx described how it feels to complete one. There are 'fatigue zones', the first of which starts at about eighteen miles, which have to be 'run through' if the runner is to retain any interest in the race. Similar zones lie in wait for the runner at various intervals. The five miles from eighty-five to ninety are the worst; only the greatest determination can see the runner through this stage. Somehow, the last ten miles are not so bad.

Why do people like Corbitt do it? They can't explain, except in terms of pushing their bodies as far as they can, to put themselves up against the greatest physical challenge of them all. Could it even be a challenge to the ultimate limit, death itself?

For some it most certainly is. Doctors qualifying in Britain and America in the 1950s and 1960s were taught that the only proper convalescence for patients with heart attacks involved complete rest, usually in bed, for six to eight weeks. Exercise was ruled out, and many relatively young men were turned prematurely into 'cardiac invalids'. Gradually the advice has changed. Patients are up and about days after their 'coronaries' and, depending on the amount of damage to the heart muscle, are encouraged to exercise, gradually increasing their activity under the supervision of their cardiologist.

Not surprisingly, the North Americans have been the most enthusiastic followers of this advice. One of the pioneers was Dr Ted Kavanagh of Toronto, a physician and athlete in his own right, who set up in the 1960s a rehabilitation centre for heart patients. He encouraged his convalescents to start long-distance running, which at first was non-competitive. The enthusiasm he kindled was hard to snuff out – he was soon faced with plans from some of his group to complete the Boston Marathon.

As Kavanagh claimed running completely rehabilitated the heart-attack patient, he could hardly oppose their attempt. Less than five years after starting his 'clinic' seven Kavanagh patients, three of whom had had two attacks, finished the marathon course, and all were fit enough at the finishing line to give him a trophy commemorating the 'Supercoach to the World's Sickest Track Club'.

Not all cardiologists go as far as Kavanagh, who describes his philosophy and experience in his book *Heart Attack? Counterattack!* Some believe that distance running for patients is potentially dangerous and arouses unrealistic hopes – and all would admit that every heart-attack patient should be treated on the basis of his own physical problem. What can be said is that those who do benefit from exercise can do so spectacularly well, even after serious damage to the heart muscle.

Undoubtedly even our world champions have not come near to the limits of their potential. World records will continue to fall for as long as can be foreseen. In the 1979 Pan American swimming games records were broken in twenty-nine of the thirty events, and women were beating records set by men only two decades before. The very rapid recent improvements have not come about in this short term by any basic change in the anatomy or physiology but in the training methods and race techniques which have improved over-all efficiency, particularly of runners and swimmers.

Historically, of course, there have been great changes in the physique of adults. The suits of armour in the Tower of London suggest that the average medieval nobleman, who presumably was the athlete of his time, was about 5ft 6in (167·6cm) tall, and anyone within three inches of six feet was a relative giant.

The improvement in physique has slowed down, and perhaps even stopped in this century. American and British children are 10 per cent taller than their counterparts of 1880. This has been reflected in the modern child's much earlier puberty.

The first menstrual period occurs in 95 per cent of girls when they reach within 4·4lb (2kg) of 7st 5lb (47kg) in weight. At the turn of this century for most girls this was around the age of seventeen. The figure dropped steadily until 1960, when it levelled off at thirteen years. There is no sign, nor does anyone believe, that it will drop further.

Countries determined to pursue glory through pushing their young people past the accepted limits have therefore concentrated until now on manipulating them biologically, chemically and even by computer. The Russians used a team of scientists and a computer monitoring system in 1970 to choose and develop Valery Borzov as their main hope for the 1972 Olympic 100-metre title. They were highly successful. In 1972 they admitted working with two- to three-year-old children, to initiate a drive towards sport in them that was 'organic' and 'beyond their control'.

East Germany has taught 90 per cent of children to swim before their fourth birthday, instituting state-run competitions where the best can be chosen for special schools to develop their abilities under the supervision not only of coaches but doctors, biochemists and psychologists.

Even such intensive care has not been considered enough in this single-minded obsession with domination in sport. Drugs were added to the scene in the 1950s. By 1960 the first Olympic drug death, that of Danish cyclist Kurt Jensen, had occurred in Rome. Tommy Simpson, Britain's only world-class road-racing cyclist died suddenly in the 1967 Tour de France from the effect of amphetamines. The Scottish World Cup Football Team lost all credibility with its own supporters in Argentina in 1978 when Willie Johnston was found to have taken drugs in the disastrous match against Iran.

The most disturbing aspect of the drug scene, however, has centred upon the 'explosive' eventers. Anabolic steroids, hormones which stimulate muscle growth, were first used in the early 1960s to improve the performance of shot putters, hammer and discus throwers, and weightlifters. They worked so well that athletes not taking them had no chance of winning events. Records tumbled like ninepins. One example was Jeff Teale, the British shot putter who won the 1970 Commonwealth Games silver medal. The drugs (and he took ten tablets a day – a huge dose) made him feel stronger, faster and more aggressive and put more than a metre on his distance.

At first, the athletes taking these drugs did not realise that there was a price to pay for them, in terms of health. They can damage the liver and kidneys, and interfere considerably with sexual function. They may produce permanent impotence, yet such was the desire to win that after these risks were known, athletes continued to abuse them. They were only stopped when it became easy to detect them in the random urine tests, now compulsory at every major athletic meeting.

The drug scene may have switched to international gymnastics. Pre-pubertal girls are much more supple than their older sisters. If they can be persuaded, biochemically, to delay their maturity for several years, they will remain small and sexually underdeveloped, but have the mental maturity to win world titles.

Rumour has it that puberty-delaying drugs have been widely used in some countries to help girl gymnasts. Whether this is true or not, the revolution in women's gymnastics in the last decade seems to point that way. Only time will tell if this has put the girls at risk, but to judge by the past behaviour of world-class athletes they will probably not complain.

Apart from drugs, there are techniques to improve performance which could be considered unethical, and certainly unsporting as they are not available to all. The transfusion of one's own blood just before a race to increase the capacity to carry oxygen, as mentioned in Chapter Two, is one. Another, surely, is the strap tied to the muscles of weightlifters at the Moscow Institute of Physical Culture. This applies electrical charges to the muscle to make it flex rhythmically, in the process apparently making it bigger and more powerful.

The Department of Exercise Science at the University of Massachusetts uses computerised analysis to help athletes. Their motion is first filmed in slow motion, then the movements of each joint are translated into mathematical symbols which the computer can express in terms of efficiency. This form of analysis helped Bill Schmidt in 1971 to change his javelin-throwing action. The computer calculated that poor left-leg action was holding him back. After altering his technique, Schmidt increased his distance by 19ft (5·8m) and he was third in the event at the Munich Olympics.

The Swedes prefer to manipulate athletes' glycogen stores. According to Dr Eric Hultman of Stockholm, athletes can increase the amount of glycogen in their muscles and liver by as much as 3·3lb (1·5kg) if they first train on a carbohydrate-free diet, then turn for three days before a vital race to a carbohydrate-rich one.

All this manipulation of the human frame to reach the ultimate may seem unfair to those to whom such facilities are not available. How much more unfair, it is therefore, to ban some competitor because of an inborn genetic abnormality which although leaving her externally female, may give her some masculine characteristics. Take the case of Ewa Klobukowska, an attractive Polish 100-metre runner disbarred from international competition by the decision of six doctors that her cells contained 'one chromosome too many'. The extra chromosome was not even one that could have been claimed in any way to produce masculine effects – indeed if anything she was a superwoman! Nevertheless she had to accept the decision, which she did in a typically female way – she burst into tears!

In contrast, such intersex can lead to unfair competition where anyone designated officially as a 'woman' has a chromosomal make-up that gives a masculine build and with it masculine power. This was the reason for the first sex tests insisted upon in Budapest in 1966 at the European Athletics Championships, when several very hefty East European 'explosive event' women disappeared from the athletics scene in that year. For them it must have been both a professional and personal tragedy. Until then they had been accepted as women and had looked upon themselves as totally female, so that it must have been a terrible shock to find themselves suddenly relegated to the emotional, sexual and legal limbo of intersex.

One athlete at least built a constructive new life after the sex tests had shown a male chromosome pattern. Erika Schinegger ten years ago was Austria's top woman ski star, the world downhill skiing champion and a member of their Winter Olympic squad. This was a case of some *physical* ambiguity which had led to wrong gender classification at birth. After the sex test revelation, surgery was used to free the hidden testicles and reconstruct the penis, and as Erik instead of Erika a new life began with his own ski school and finally happy marriage and fatherhood.

The All England Club were called upon in 1978 to rule upon a similar situation in reverse. American transexual tennis player, Renee Richards, had been competing as a woman on the US circuit, no doubt enhancing gate receipts for prurient rather than sporting reasons. This tall well-built but attractive looking 'female' was known not only to have been a male doctor, but to have fathered children, before deep-rooted transsexualism propelled him to hormone treatment and finally surgery. The male skeletal and muscular characteristics, of course, remained to confer considerable advantage in women's events, and so rightly the All England Club committee insisted on the chromosome sex test being carried out. Predictably this was refused and the entry rejected.

The suggestion has been made, no doubt tongue in cheek, that the only way to be totally fair would be to have a Chromosome Olympics. The competitors would then be classified genetically: a pair of XX chromosomes would denote the normal female category; XY would be the normal male; superwomen with XXX pattern and the extra female chromosome like Ewa Klobukowska would make another group; the supermen, the XYY type popularised in a television serial with an extra male chromosome, tall, masculine and possibly over-aggressive, would also have their own series of events. The over-aggressive aspect is still the subject of much argument amongst geneticists, but with one male in 250 being an XYY, it is thought some of the world's best male high jumpers may belong to this grouping. If this is so, why should they have the privilege of competing for world titles when the XXX super girls cannot? Presumably too the poor XO women, lacking the second female chromosome and handicapped by short stature and webbed necks, would qualify for a special Games of their own. The whole concept is patently absurd, but the problem is real enough.

Improvements in athletic performance do not depend entirely on the athletes themselves – the conditions under which they compete help to improve times. All-weather tracks and improvements in shoes and clothing shave the necessary fractions of a second off runners' times. Pool design has removed the wave problems facing swimmers, the material and design of whose trunks and swimsuits produce much less resistance to the water than before.

In many cases it is not so much a matter of faster racing, but just more accurate timing. Modern electronics separate swimmers who finish one hundredth of a second apart, and runners are now being timed in the same way. The world record for the 100 metres in 1921 was held by Charlie Paddock at 10·2sec. It has dropped by only 0·3sec to 9·9sec in the intervening six decades despite all the wonders of modern technology and training. During the same period the mile record time has fallen by 21sec. Experts predict that the limit for the mile, given no change in human physiology, will be 3min 30sec. The same experts see the 100-metre record falling by no more than 0·1sec. New record holders will have to depend on hundredths to establish their names.

To go beyond these limits, man and woman will have to turn to eugenics, not a popular subject in a world which has too recently suffered Hitler's appalling philosophy of a super race. Despite the remaining inevitable suspicions of elitism in any form, there is some evidence that 'breeding for success' may already be taking place. In some East European countries, children with athletic potential are herded into special schools where their talents can be developed to the full, and at the very least inter-athlete marriages are encouraged. Some go as far as to explain the 1970s success of East Germany's women on the track and in the pool on this basis.

Of course such marriages can happen for the right reasons and are likely to when athletes obviously meet and mix socially. Back in the 1950s for example, Tony Mottram, Britain's post-war number-one tennis player, fell in love with Joy Gannon, a beautiful leading British woman tennis star. Their offspring, Buster and Linda Mottram, as everyone knows, are now among the leading young players in the UK, proof not only of the strong influence of genetic inheritance but also of the effect of an environment which encourages inborn talent.

So far in Britain deliberate eugenics have been confined to agriculture. There it began really as far back as the eighteenth century when the fencing in of pasture land changed farming methods, allowing stock breeders to control the mating of the better bulls with cows specially chosen for quality of meat. The records at Smithfield Market show that this alone caused the weight of the average bullock to double.

Since then more sophisticated methods have followed and become almost routine, with artificial insemination from prize bulls, and fertilised eggs implanted into foster cows and sheep. But where do we go from here? Test-tube human babies are already with us and once perfected the same technique could be applied to breeding for success in any sphere. Cloning, although much further off, would be the ultimate in ensuring the duplication of the perfect athlete or for that matter the perfect brain or the perfect aggressive human fighting machine. It remains to be seen which appalling possibility is given the higher priority if any culture proves misguided enough to adopt such methods.

For most of us the thought of applying such techniques to humans, even to extend mental and physical limits, is beyond consideration. Thankfully we choose our partners on emotional and social, even perhaps on intellectual grounds, rather than for any eugenic reasons. While the human race as a whole will hopefully never allow itself to be manipulated like cattle, it remains a possibility that from some countries we may see the emergence of small groups of physically perfect specimens bred specifically for the Olympic events of the future. Already the days of the true amateur in sport are past. There are, perhaps, two exceptions. In some developing parts of the world there are people who have not yet competed in the Olympics and who have the ability to surprise everyone, even the vaunted East Germans, the Russians and the Americans.

Americans of African ancestry are already at an advantage over their colleagues of European stock in winning Olympic medals. Their achievement in winning three times as many medals as their proportion of the population would suggest, has been put down to the greater desire of an oppressed minority to excel. This is probably not the whole story. There is considerable evidence that the physique of the inhabitants of some parts of Africa is particularly well adapted to athletic ability.

Anthony Smith writes of a team of American athletes who visited Kenya recently with a treadmill device, the moving platform of which slowly rose at a rate of a degree a minute. The American champion's record on this exhausting machine – and he had six months' experience of it – was broken by two Masai men at their first attempt! And they were not even out of breath!

Even the Masai's achievements pale compared to those of the Watutsi, a tribe in East Africa, the men of whom stand an average of 6ft 5in (195·6cm) tall, and whose favourite sport is jumping. They jump over ropes slung between trees, without any of the modern aids or techniques, and many have cleared 7ft 4in (223·5cm) in this way.

Professor Ernst Jokl, of the University of Kentucky, and himself an ex-athlete of international standard, has assessed the athletic ability of the Negro to be higher than that of the Asian, who in turn is more efficient physically than the European. There are those, of course, who disagree with him, but if he is right, then all the efforts of the East Germans may be in vain – if they really wish to show off their national pride in this way, they might start by offering citizenship to the Watutsi.

The British would prefer to do it in a more sportsmanlike and, of course, less expensive way. May we suggest to the AAA that they hire a pack of hyenas to unleash on their unsuspecting high jumpers at the crucial moment? We know a zoologist in Kenya's Tsavo National Park who would be happy to provide them. He's getting tired of climbing trees to avoid them himself.

The Watutsi are at the extreme end of the scale for height. In the same continent of Africa are the pygmies at the other extreme. However, such extremes are seen in individuals of every race. The average height today for a Caucasian male is around 5ft 8in (172·7cm), but there are and have been many giant exceptions. Only the claims of those recorded during the last 100 years and subject to impartial medical supervision are really acceptable, and we must probably accept that the story of Goliath of Gath (1060 BC) at 9ft 6$\frac{1}{2}$in (290·8cm) was exaggerated in the telling, like all those fish that got away.

The tallest human being of all time, fully attested, according to the Guinness Book of Records, was the American, Robert Wadlow, at 8ft 11·1in (272cm); Britain's tallest living man is Christopher Greener at 7ft 5$\frac{1}{2}$in (227·3cm) and the tallest living Scot, George Gracie, is 7ft 3in (221cm). The tallest living Irishman, Jim Cully of Tipperary, a former boxer and wrestler is 7ft 2in (218·4cm).

Among male giants was the strange case of Jacob Earlich, born 23 June 1906 in Denver, Colorado. A weak baby, he weighed only 4lb (1·8 kg) at birth and for years was a small child. Then suddenly at ten years old he began to grow and just went on growing until he reached 8ft 6$\frac{1}{2}$in (260·3cm). The butt of his schoolmates, he eventually changed his name to Jack Earl and, like so many people doomed to exceptional stature, for fourteen years he found work in the sideshows of the famous Ringling Brothers Circus. But his temperament was not right for show business and this basically quiet and shy man finally found a happier life as a salesman for a wine company. He also became a competent painter, sculptor, poet and photographer before dying at the young age of forty-six in 1952 as the result of a car accident.

It is even more difficult for the over-tall woman to lead a normal life. Men conditioned to women looking up to them can resent the woman who looks down and in both personal and professional life it can be a handicap for a woman to be 6ft (182·9cm) and over. The average height for women today is 5ft 4in (162·6cm). Occasionally they exceed this by over 2ft (61cm). The tallest woman in medical history was Jane Bunford, born in the West Midlands, whose skeleton still stands at Birmingham University Medical School. She died aged only twenty-seven. Severe curvature of the spine meant that she measured only 6ft 6 in (198cm), but with assumed normal curvature she would have reached 7ft 11in (241·3cm). The tallest living woman, Sandy Allen, is in Indiana, America, and is so far 7ft 5½in (227·3cm) and still growing.

At the other end of the scale, while 9 feet approximates to the limit of tallness, so just under 2 feet must be considered the limit of shortness for mature dwarfs. The all-time shortest mature human for whom there is reliable medical evidence is Pauline Musters, born in Holland in 1876, who died aged nineteen of pneumonia and meningitis and a heart weakened from alcoholism, and still only 23·2in (58·9cm) tall.

The shortest adult male dwarf was Calvin Phillips, an American, only 26½in (67cm) tall, who died aged twenty-one from progeria (a rare disease characterised by dwarfism and premature senility). Alive now are Mihaly Meszaros of Budapest, reported to be 2ft 9in (83·8cm) high and weighing only 25lb (11·3kg), and an Indian, Nruturam, only 28in (71cm) tall. But while few people have heard of any of these, everyone is familiar with the name of General Tom Thumb. His real name was Charles S. Strattan and although only 3ft 4in (101·6cm) tall he achieved fame and fortune with his talent for singing, dancing and telling jokes. He was fêted by President and Mrs Lincoln, entertained Queen Victoria, and when he married Lavina Warren (also a midget) in 1863, their grand wedding at Grace Church, New York swept news of the Civil War from the front pages of the newspapers of the day.

Tom Thumb clearly overcame his physical limitation to make for himself a successful and exciting life – perhaps too exciting, for he suffered a stroke and died at the age of only forty-five. Lavina, his widow, married another midget and lived to the age of seventy-eight.

Physical limits, large and small, have always fascinated the human race and often been cruelly exploited. Dwarfs abound in literature and legend and were much in demand throughout history at the courts of kings and emperors. A few even achieved real greatness and influence, among them Bishop Gregory of Tours and Jeffery Hudon, the King of England's spy.

In recent years a group of midgets called The Dancing Dolls became known to millions when they played the Munchkins in *The Wizard of Oz*, and their successful career extended from the 1920s to the 1940s. They were born in Germany with the family name of Schneider and there were four other children of quite normal size. But Harry was only

42in (106·7cm), Tony 40in (101·6cm), Grace 44in (111·7cm) and Daisy, the tallest by a further inch, was known as the 'midget Mae West'. After they went to America, when Harry was only twelve, they began their career dancing in a sideshow on Coney Island and then after changing their name to Doll they joined the Ringling Brothers. Again they showed human adaptability and a large degree of pragmatism by using their disadvantages to advantage and to provide a living. These living Dolls also managed reasonably normal lives in a specially constructed house, with Daisy driving the adapted family car and Harry becoming a keen sportsman.

It is doubtful if genetic or drug-induced limits to human potential would really have a place in this chapter, if it were not for the inspiring way in which such victims often cope with what to most of us would seem total tragedy.

Siamese twins, Chang and Eng, married and raised twenty-one children despite being joined at the breastbone. Charles Tripp, born without arms in 1855 in Canada, used his feet so well as hands that he could shave himself with a cut-throat razor and became a skilled cabinet maker. He married at seventy and lived to eighty-four.

Eli Bowen was the only abnormal child in a family of nine brothers and sisters. He had feet which grew from his hips but still managed to walk by using them combined with his hands. He married at twenty and his wife bore him a fine healthy family.

In our own age the victims of the thalidomide tragedy are just reaching their own most testing time and coming through with flying colours, showing again that the human spirit can overcome one way or another almost every physical limitation, though a little human ingenuity can help as well. One outstanding example is seventeen-year-old Ronnie West, born without arms. He has learned to compensate with such skill that he drives a specially adapted Mini with his feet (passing the stringent British driving test first time), is a swimming and high diving champion able to perform 1½ somersaults off a 30-metre board, plays football for the instrument firm where he works, and in his spare time goes mountaineering, canoeing and runs a discotheque business.

Another young boy, Paul Taylor, severely disabled when a coach rammed the back of the family car, took nine years to learn to walk. He managed by hanging on to walls and chairs, refusing all help. He still cannot run but, mad on football, has won a place in the school side as goalkeeper. He has also won a Spastic Society International Year of the Child Special Award.

The story of Sir Douglas Bader's return to flying after the loss of both legs, his achievements as a wartime Ace and in peacetime on the golf course are well known, but there is also Norman Croucher whose name may be less familiar.

He was just nineteen when he lost both legs below the knee in a railway accident. A keen outdoor type he determined that the tragedy would not turn him into a vegetable. On false legs he has since climbed the Jungfrau, Mont Blanc, the Eiger and the Matterhorn, and in discussing the difficulties of climbing such peaks all over the world (he was recently involved in an Andean expedition) will quickly point out that his shorter circulatory system allows him to stay warmer than his companions, and at higher altitudes also protects him to some degree from the symptoms of anoxia. 'There are not many advantages,' he says, 'in having metal legs except that I can't get frost-bitten feet.' He is the first physically handicapped person to be appointed a member of the Sports Council and is also continually becoming involved in schemes to provide outdoor pursuits for other physically handicapped people.

It may never be entirely possible to eliminate flying, traffic or industrial accidents, but drug-induced abnormalities can at least be reduced with the better understanding we now have of the vulnerability of the foetus.

Meanwhile hormonally based problems are finding solutions too. Few of these tragic people are normal in the sense that they are genetically programmed for their positions at either end of the human growth distribution curve. Most, as their early deaths suggest, were *abnormal*, usually due to hormonal problems.

Today modern medicines can restrain growth in the potentially over-tall girl or extend it in the potentially stunted boy. This is frequently achieved by delaying or advancing puberty, the time when bones stop growing, or by giving growth hormone, a natural chemical which stimulates growth in those who are deficient and will respond to it.

Such controls may eventually ensure that there will be fewer unhappy 'misfits' for size, and it is one case of human potential where medical science should properly be used to reduce rather than increase the numbers going beyond the limits.

Any evaluation of functional and physical limits in humans must also embrace fertility and sexuality, as we are the most sexual of all animals, constantly instead of only periodically 'on heat'. The average age of puberty, and therefore of possible conception, is thirteen years, but unhappily cases of pregnancy and birth have been recorded in many ten-year-olds, including at least one pair of twins in 1979. Indeed girls with precocious puberty have been found to be pregnant at the age of six, but these pregnancies, of course, were terminated. Overt puberty, indeed, is not essential before a girl becomes fertile. One thirteen-year-old girl seen at the Royal Women's Hospital, Melbourne, is known to have conceived *before* the appearance of her first period.

Fatherhood in the very young, obviously, is more difficult to determine. It is awkward to prove fertility in young boys: the normal methods of obtaining sperm samples from ejaculation or needles in the testicle are, of course, ruled out. The next best thing is to look for sperms in the urine. This was done as long ago as 1928 by B. T. Baldwin. Of 123 boys aged between nine and seventeen, the youngest with sperm in the urine was eleven years and three months. One twelve-year-old and five thirteen-year-olds were also producing sperm, and one had none of the pubic or armpit hair which normally pre-dates sexual maturity. Boys are therefore potentially fertile at the very beginning of puberty. The *Sunday Mirror* in 1979 printed the story of Espaquito and Judith, Parisian children who were aged eleven and fourteen when their child was conceived. Espaquito's reaction was to 'find it fantastic that I was able to make a baby at the age of eleven'. He was annoyed with Judith, however, because she did not consult him about baby Daniel's name. Daniel, who is being brought up by Judith's parents, was 4lb 13oz (2·2kg) at birth.

Much better documented is fertility at the other end of life. There have been stories of women having babies in their seventies, but these are either based on unsubstantiated age records or used as blinds to conceal the illegitimacy of grandchildren. The oldest mother for whom there is fully documented evidence is Ruth Alice Kistler whose daughter Susan was born in Los Angeles in 1956 when her mother was 57 years 129 days old. Probably the oldest English mother was Mrs Elizabeth Pearce who gave birth to a son when aged 54 years and 40 days.

Facts on older fathers are suspect for many reasons, not the least cuckolding by younger men. The most famous case in English history was that of Thomas Parr born in Shropshire in 1483, nine years before Columbus discovered America. As a young man he was considered a rake, and in fact did not marry until the age of eighty. This did not stop his affairs, for when he was 100 years old he was forced to do public penance at the door of a church, wearing a white sheet, having been found guilty of adultery.

He still went on to marry again at the age of 120 and had children by both marriages. On his death at the purported age of 152, his wife stated that he had intercourse with her 'after the manner of other husbands with their wives, nor until about twelve years back had he ceased to embrace her frequently'.

John Gilley (1690–1813) who married an eighteen-year-old girl at the age of seventy-five, not only had eight children, but according to his wife continued virile until three years before his death at the age of 123. He may have been the original model for one of the oldest doctor–patient jokes. The old man, asking advice about his intended marriage to a young girl, is told by the doctor that 'it could be fatal'. 'Ah well,' he replies, 'if she dies, she dies.'

There are many authenticated cases in this century of men in their eighties and nineties fathering children, including one reported in the *Journal of the American Medical Association* in 1935 of a man of ninety-four.

While fertility is cut short in women by the menopause, it can clearly continue far into old age in men. The greatest number of children born to one woman is supposedly sixty-nine, to the wife of a Russian peasant, Fyoda Vassilet. Mrs Vassilet was so renowned for this achievement that she was presented at the court of Tsar Alexander II. Her present-day rival is probably Madalena Carnaubra of Brazil, with thirty-two children, reported to have held her achievement 'very ordinary' and to have declared 'I don't know why people make such a fuss.'

The highest British figure is twenty-four, born to Mrs Emily Jane Lucas of Tonbridge, Kent, who died in July 1967.

The greatest number fathered (and acknowledged) by one man would seem to be 888, to the highly polygamous Emperor of Morocco, Moulay Ismail (1672–1727) – small wonder that he died at forty-five! He was also known as 'the bloodthirsty!'

Are these limits to male and female fertility capable of further extension? There is some evidence that the length of fertile life in women has already stretched at both ends, but it is unthinkable in today's social climate, not to mention in the light of medical knowledge, linking increasing abnormalities in offspring to parental age, that many people will choose to use the extended opportunity to have more children. And it is even less likely, with the improved status of women in Muslim countries, that the Moroccan Moulay's feat will ever be surpassed.

One interesting possibility for men, however, lies in the freezing and banking of sperm, which theoretically could allow a man to father from a distance in time and space, thousands, even millions of offspring.

The creator of the internationally famous 'Love Is' cartoons, after being widowed, elected to bear a child conceived by sperm taken from her dying husband and stored for just this purpose.

Hundreds of thousands of men have had vasectomies, and increasing numbers are choosing, as an insurance, to store samples of sperm in the same way, in case reversal is unsuccessful and for any reason they desperately desire more children.

In both sexes there is no automatic cut-off point for sex. Some begin to enjoy sex only in later years. Bernard Berenson, the art critic, who died at the age of ninety-four, in his posthumously published diaries, wrote 'Only in what might be called my old age have I become aware of sex and the animal in women.'

One doctor records a woman patient who had been frigid with two husbands over a period of thirty years, yet at the age of seventy-two she began to have passionate extramarital affairs. For the first time in her life she had excellent sexual response and reached orgasm.

Alfred Kinsey's research established among the 126 men over sixty that he studied, that the oldest, aged eighty-eight, married to a ninety-year-old wife, was still sexually active. Another aged seventy still averaged seven ejaculations a week, and of the females studied the Kinsey investigators found little evidence of any flagging of sexual interest with age. This tends to confirm the comment of Madame de Stael who when asked at the age of eighty at what age women lost interest in sex replied "You will have to ask someone older than me!"

Other recent studies have shown that 75 per cent of men of seventy years and over still have a desire for sex, and 55 per cent still have sexual capability.

Of 149 persons in the Piedmont area of North Carolina, aged between sixty and ninety-three years and still living with their spouses (or perhaps it should be spice!) 54 per cent were found to be sexually active with frequency varying from once every other month to three times weekly. Nevertheless, Dr Freeman of Philadelphia found only 17 per cent of men still enjoying sexual relations by the age of eighty.

One factor to emerge in every study is that sexual activity in old age is closely related to the strength of the sex urge in youth.

Sexuality has been considered, by many, not the least Freud, to be the most dominant of the senses, and this is true of its importance in the continuance of the human race. But all the senses have played their part in man's survival, and the next chapter looks at how we use these and if they too are capable of extension.

5
The Senses

In November 1978, Mike Tetley, a forty-nine-year-old British physiotherapist, telephoned Frank McCready, who was in the process of organising a 'walk-in' to Base Camp Everest. The expedition would take twenty days from Katmandu and the members would climb, on the '200 mile advanced obstacle course' a total of 64,000ft (19,507m), twice the height of Everest. The aim of the expedition was to reach a 'small' hill, 19,800ft (6,035m) from sea level, overlooking the Base Camp. The path was rough and narrow, so that for almost all the way the walkers would travel in single file. They would cross deep ravines on narrow tree trunks, or rivers on suspension bridges with no sides, or use rocks as stepping stones. They would cross glacial moraines.

There would still be nothing particularly unusual in the trip, but for one thing. Mike Tetley is totally blind, without even the ability to perceive a glimmer of light. Despite this, his qualifications for the journey were impressive. He had climbed the 19,340ft (5,895m) of Kilimanjaro, ridden 500 miles across Kenya on a tandem in four days, and wandered round the edge of the Amazon basin. Frank McCready accepted him.

Mike completed his walk without incident. 'I held on to straps attached to the back of my guide's haversack,' he wrote in *The Remedial Therapist* in March 1980, 'and I followed directly behind him like a leech, and there were plenty of those in the rivers.'

Mike obviously kept his sense of humour. He gratefully acknowledges the 'superb guiding' of Reg Denny, a thirty-seven-year-old London policeman and Brian Higgins, a twenty-one-year-old waiter from Claridge's who helped him. Without sight, he was still able to 'feel' the splendour of Everest. When the others finally saw the summit at sunset, he knew exactly 'in his mind's eye' what they were seeing from the many photographs he remembered of the scene.

The most important and dominant of the five physical senses in man is undoubtedly sight. Our two eyes set well forward and able to see the same object at the same time help us to determine distance and assess speed. This must have been valuable even in primate forest days, but still more so once our ancestors emerged on to the open plains and needed to scan long distances, standing upright and searching with their eyes for both prey and predators, to plan the hunt or avoid being the hunted.

Sight remains the sense we are convinced we need most, rely upon most, value most and whose impairment or loss we dread most. Although severe deafness imposes far greater isolation, it is still the prospect of total blindness which inspires the greatest fear.

Inevitably the type of sight each species finally evolves is that best suited to its own particular needs and there is wide variation, so that other animals' perception of the world can be quite different from our own. For example, because presumably there was little survival value in distinguishing colours for a lot of the vertebrates, many of them, such as lemurs, racoons, hamsters, rats, mice and marsupials see only in black and white. Scientists have also shown that dogs, cats, rabbits and probably bulls have little or no colour sense. They insist that the old adage equating provocation with 'showing a red rag to a bull' is a nonsense, and that any rag, flag or cloak waved around would similarly frighten and enrage, as it is the movement not the colour which the bull perceives and resents. It must be admitted Spanish bullfighters remain entirely unmoved by such proof as the experts can offer!

Convincing experiments have been devised to test animal sensitivity to colour, using different-coloured cards, codes and trap doors associated with reward or punishment in the form of food or light electric shocks. Much has been learned including the fact that some animals only respond to some colours – the red-backed vole, for instance, only senses yellow and red, the small civet cat only red and green, while aphids are sensitive to and attracted to only the special yellowy-green of young shoots. Cunning rose growers have learned to exploit this fact by painting the bottoms of bowls of water with this particular shade to lure the deluded greenfly to a watery grave.

Horses, red deer, sheep, giraffes, guinea pigs and polecats have proved to register a far wider section of the spectrum, while monkeys begin to approach the range of man, and the chimpanzee, our nearest relative, actually has a colour sense at least as good as ours.

Man's normal potential for colour appreciation is much vaster than most of us probably realise. In the human eye, as part of the light-sensitive layers of the retina, there are approximately 125,000,000 special cells called rods and another 7,000,000 called cones. Information from these millions of receptor cells is passed to the brain via the optic nerve.

If the precise working of rods and cones is still not fully understood, at least we know that rods are connected with night vision, able to detect only shades of grey, while cones are for day vision and can sort out colours. Nocturnal birds have fewer cones than those active in daytime, and nocturnal bats also have more rods than cones.

The mechanics of sight and the interplay of these receptors with the brain and nervous system are incredibly complicated, but in man the result is ability to perceive 17,000 variations of colour across the spectrum from red at one end to violet at the other, and 300 shades of grey between white and black.

While our colour range is broader than that of most other animals and insects, their sight can include abilities we are quite unable to match and some we cannot even begin to comprehend. Keenness of vision is determined by the density of the visual cells in the vital area (the fovea centralis). A lion, with a density similar to man's, can see its prey at a distance of just under a mile, but elephants and rhinoceroses with far fewer visual cells see only their immediate surroundings as blurred, and over 100ft (30·5m) away can hardly make out even quite large objects. At the other extreme, great density of cells allows the hawk to see what man could only discern with binoculars that magnify eight times, while the golden eagle can spot a small hare around 18in (46cm) long from a distance of almost two miles. Nocturnal birds show similar superiority over man, with the barn owl, for example, having night vision between fifty and a hundred times as powerful as ours.

The bee's eyes can do even more incredible things. For a start its world is dominated by sensitivity to ultraviolet light, which we are unable to see at all. So for the bee red appears as black, and white flowers shine with strange iridescent colours. It is the navigational function of the bee's compound eyes which man might envy most. The 15,000 eye facets, all set at different angles, divide the sky into a screen of squares, with one special lens always electing to register the sun. From this input of visual signals, the bee's tiny brain automatically and continuously calculates the required angle of flight, the homing course and even its flying speed.

Man's own eye equipment by purely optical standards does not even offer the retina a particularly good image, but, as with the bee, the brain works its own magic, making the required corrections and conversions to produce in the end an almost flawless picture in our *minds*, which is the important thing. Our nervous system eliminates the blurred effect which we would otherwise get round the edges of our vision, and brain and imagination combine to reverse the upside-down picture received by the retina, so that we perceive the world the right way up.

Fascinating work to confirm this amazing ability of the brain to correct distorted images and even to check how far such potential can extend has been done by Dr Anton Hajos of the Institute of Experimental

Psychology at Innsbruck University. He supplied volunteer students with spectacles fitted with severely distorting prism lenses, so that angles were altered, sharp outlines became fringed with colours, straight lines appeared curved and objects seemed to move about as the wearers themselves moved. It all added up to a frightening and grotesque new world, yet within only a few days the conjuring tricks of the nervous system brought it back to normal. When the prism glasses were removed, however, for a time everything was seen again as if in a distorting mirror, until once more the brain reversed the process and imposed what we accept as normal perception. Similar mental magic underlay the experiments described in the chapter on sleep, where the brain reversed the images seen through 'upside-down' spectacles.

Sight, vision and perception is clearly not just a matter of optics, but of brain, mind and imagination working to interpret, convert and correct towards some semblance of reality, or what we believe to be reality which perhaps comes to the same thing.

The process is too complicated to describe in full detail, but at the simplest level light waves enter the eye by passing through the transparent cornea, then through the fluid-filled anterior chamber and pupil gap, on via the lens and another fluid-filled posterior chamber, finally to reach the light-sensitive retina.

The pupil is able to contract or dilate in response to the amount of light, and as the focal distance of the lens changes to keep the brightness of the picture constant. Unlike the pupils of cats, which change shape as they close down to become sinister slits, the human pupil even in the brightest light still remains circular though much smaller. It dilates not only in poor light but also under the influence of fear and emotion. Anthony Smith in his book *The Body* reports the fascinating if frivolous fact that men's pupils dilate by some 30 per cent at the sight of a pretty girl. Emotion presumably rather than fear in that case! It is even less relevant perhaps but equally interesting to note that we are attracted to dilated pupils and in the past belladonna (literally translated as beautiful woman) was used to achieve just that effect. Arguably the secret of the universal appeal of the Mona Lisa was perhaps not so much in her smile as in those large open pupils. Maybe *she* was attracted to Leonardo da Vinci and her pupils were dilated with emotion, which could have been rather frustrating in view of his well-known homosexual proclivities.

All the light entering the eye is focused by the joint action of cornea and lens, but while the cornea is static in its function the lens is more flexible and makes the final adjustments. It is for this reason that as the lens grows flatter, yellower and harder with age, becoming less flexible, we are unable to focus correctly without the artificial aid of spectacles. There is a common misconception that it is weakening of the eye muscles with age which causes sight to deteriorate. In fact it is the changes in the lens and its greater rigidity, so specialist practices based on the theory of exercising eye muscles to preserve good sight are not likely to be very effective, except in preserving the doctor's bank balance.

Fortunately, however, modern optical knowledge today involves many techniques that can be used to extend and maintain normal sight throughout life, preventing the diminishing vision which otherwise comes with age, and counteracting the effect of much eye disease.

Men have always tried to augment poor eyesight and Nero is reported to have used an enormous emerald to magnify objects. Primitive spectacles were invented by monks as early as the fourteenth century, but these days modern methods of grinding lenses to exact requirements together with accurate ways of testing and assessing vision have enormously improved the situation. Contact lenses even offer the chance of doing away with external attachments.

More recently a technique has been developed for actually grinding away part of the cornea to flatten the curvature and help to correct shortsight. Increasing the curvature to help long sight, a common defect with ageing, is a more complex procedure but has been done. Although these new skills are still in the pioneering stage, they are obviously going to offer new means in suitable cases for maintaining normal sight beyond the present limit, without external artificial aids.

The main disease of the lens, cataract (again very common with age), is already most successfully treated, with the opaque, diseased lens peeled away and replaced by a new artificial lens. There are also people whose normal sight is threatened by disease of the cornea. In developed countries this may occur after virus infection of the eye or after damage which leaves scar tissue. In the underdeveloped tropical countries hundreds of millions of people are blinded by a bacterial infection of the cornea called trachoma. If caught early with penicillin it can be cured, but this is rarely available and in any case medical services are almost non-existent. Itinerant healers peel off the diseased corneas with their thumbs, but unfortunately scar tissue forming within days causes the blindness to recur. The miracle of Christ curing the blind, as described in the Bible, bears a striking resemblance to this method still commonly used today.

The modern medical answer to these problems is corneal replacement, and for years this has been successfully done by graft from the freshly dead, who have had the compassion to donate their eyes for the purpose. Even so there has always been a shortage of such corneas even in the developed countries, and no such facilities at all in the poorer countries where they are most needed.

In recent years corneal cells have been grown in cultures, which have enabled surgeons to do without donated tissue. But the real advance will come when medical laboratories are created in space. When tissue cultures can be grown without the influence of gravity, it is calculated that sheets of cells of perfect shape will be produced, and this should overcome the present problem of distortion of vision which can occur with some of this grafted tissue.

So even more than extending the time limit for good sight, we are today preventing or controlling diseases which in the past restricted or destroyed normal sight. Glaucoma for instance can now be treated with good results, again providing it is diagnosed early and supervision maintained. Both the chronic type known as 'creeping blindness' and the rarer acute form are caused basically by a build-up of the fluid in the eye. The outcome at one time was first a diminishing field of sight, then tunnel vision and finally blindness. The disease affects roughly 1 in every 100 people, accounting for 1 in 10 of those on the Blind Register in the UK. Modern treatment combined with comprehensive screening could reduce the problem considerably and many doctors believe that all opticians should be equipped and trained to do at least the preliminary test which can reveal signs of incipient glaucoma, whenever they are carrying out normal routine testing for glasses.

Individually too we can be alert to detect the early warning signs of eye disease. Floaters, those apparently fibrous specks often seen by the healthy eye moving against a white background, can denote the first sign of cataract when they appear to be stationary. Glaucoma is signalled by a reduced field of vision, and Dr Eric Trimmer, editor of the *British Journal of Sexual Medicine*, a medical educator and an active GP, described to the authors how he first discovered his early glaucoma when teeing up on the golf course. 'I found I was losing sight of the ball before I'd even hit it,' he explained.

Many of us given to the grievous golfing error of lifting our heads might say the same, but Dr Trimmer recognised the reduced field of vision, and early discovery and treatment means that years later he is still able to do his many and varied medical jobs as well as enjoy golf.

Detached retina, which can result from a blow or sometimes just from spontaneous haemorrhage within the eye, can today be repaired with the laser, literally fused back into place.

As with all vital organs and systems, the body itself does provide a certain amount of built-in protection. Those 200 eyelashes we all possess, although constantly falling out, are just as constantly replaced and help to filter out unwelcome dust and other invaders. The eyelid provides instant reflex action to screen the vulnerable eyeball if anything heads towards it, and tears yield a constant sterile wash. It is interesting that medical history records that the active anti-bacterial agent in tears and nasal mucus, which is called lysozyme, was discovered by Sir Alexander Fleming as accidentally as he was to find penicillin six years later. This earlier, and it must be confessed less world-shattering, find came about when a nose drip from a heavy cold fell into a dish where bacteria were being cultured. To Fleming's surprise, where the drip had landed the bacteria died. So tears serve a practical physical purpose with lysozyme helping to guard eyes, nose and mouth against unwelcome bacteria, and providing the lubrication the eye must have, as well as the emotional outlet just as necessary at times.

In all this progress towards pushing back the limits age and disease impose on sight, it would be unforgivably complacent to forget the very different situation in poorer tropical parts of the world. The victims of fly- and virus-borne eye diseases, over a quarter of the world's blind population (getting on for 5 million) live in India alone. The medical knowledge exists to prevent or cure much of this if only conscience, will and resources were sufficiently applied. World Health Organisation figures indicate that 1 in every 175 people in the world is without adequate sight. In Britain it is 1 in every 480 and only 1 in a 1,000 without any useful vision at all. Of those on the Blind Register more than half are over seventy and only a quarter less than sixty years old.

There seems to be no real evidence of people possessing exceptional sight. What is termed 20:20 vision in America or 6:6 vision in Britain represents average sight, the one expressed in feet and the other in metres, and both describing the ability to read letters of standardised sizes on a card twenty feet or six metres away.

There are many people with better than average sight, of course, and this means reading smaller than the standard-size letters from the same distance; what is termed in the UK then as 6:4 vision is still considered within the normal range.

A case was reported at the end of the last century by two French scientists concerning a boy who appeared able to guess correctly every time the page numbers on a book held by another person standing opposite him, in a position where he could not possibly see them in the normal way. His 'guess work' turned out to be the unusual ability to read the numbers from the tiny back-to-front reflections on the cornea of the other person's eye. These were only a tenth of a millimetre high and such a sense of sight must be rare indeed. This seems a reasonably well-documented case but modern records fail to confirm similar exceptional vision.

It is impossible to put a norm on long vision because atmospheric conditions vary so much. One criteria in the UK might be the safety test applied to motorists, which requires them to be able to read the number plate on a car at 75ft (22·8m).

The normal visual field (without turning the head) is 210 degrees, but again facial contours, deep-set eyes and size of nose can influence this. Someone like poor Cyrano de Bergerac for instance must have had a decidedly restricted sideways view.

A phenomenon which until recently was given considerable credence even among reputable scientists and doctors was what is termed 'eyeless sight', that is blind people who could apparently see or at least detect colours through some other part of their body or some other sense. In Italy, the neurologist Cesare Lombroso was supposed to have discovered a blind girl who could 'see' with the tip of her nose and the lobe of her left ear. When a bright light was shone on that ear she winced. In 1965, according to Lyall Watson's book *Supernature*, a blind schoolboy in Scotland was taught to differentiate between coloured lights and learned to pick out bright objects several feet away, while in 1960 he records a medical board examining a girl in Virginia, who despite wads of bandage taped over her eyes could still distinguish colours and read short sections of large print.

Unfortunately, fascinating as all this is, the case of Rosa Kuleshova who claimed to be able to see with her fingers has now thrown doubt on all such cases. Rosa herself was not blind but grew up in a family of blind people and learned to read Braille to help them. At the end of 1962 she began to become a celebrity on the basis of her strange powers, and it was all so convincing that exhaustive tests were supposed to have been carried out by leading Soviet scientists with the girl securely blindfolded and even with her arms stuck through a screen, when she was still supposed to be able to differentiate colours. It started an absolute cult in Russia with special surveys carried out and reports that about 1 in 6 people could learn to recognise the difference between two colours in a similar way after only an hour's training. Soon students were attending classes in 'eyeless sight'. Colours were credited with different textures; yellow as slippery, red as sticky and violet with a braking effect on the fingers. Watson can hardly be blamed for falling for it all like the highly qualified men who accepted the Soviet Academy of Science reports. In his book Mr Watson even hazarded that if light affects the chemistry of a simple polyp like the hydra, so that it is inspired to move towards it, then equally it may affect the body fluids of man, enabling blind children to 'see' with ears, tongues, tips of noses and tips of toes.

It was all good stuff, but unfortunately both Rosa and her testing commission have since been exposed as frauds with the girl squinting past her eye bandages. It was all a great pity, because in the animal world there are certainly plenty of examples of light sensitivity of the skin and a faculty for registering light without eyes. No doubt it was this which made scientists take it all seriously. With such an apparently well-investigated case finally proving a hoax, it must obviously make other similar claims also highly suspect.

While researching this chapter an unusual case was given wide publicity which further confirms the ease with which illusions of seeing through bandages can be created. A well-known professional illusionist, whose stage name is Romark, found himself in court accused of reckless driving, a not surprising charge considering he crashed into the back of a Black Maria (the vehicle used by the British police to convey prisoners to court or prison) while driving a car blindfolded. Before judge, jury and counsel, in aid of his own defence he placed lumps of dough over his eyes and put 10p pieces on top. Then he asked a prison officer to tie a black velvet blindfold round his eyes. Still wearing this he correctly identified which jurors were holding up their arms. He told the jury 'It is a trade secret of illusionists but it is very simple. Our eyelids are stronger than the material over them so if we tilt our heads up and open our eyes the dough and 10p pieces flip up and we can see out through the bottom of the blindfold.' An optician's test gave him 20:20 vision even while wearing the blindfold.

For the moment, however, reluctantly it looks as though extending sight can only be done through artificial aids, and we must be glad that man's ingenuity in producing better and better means and more and more powerful binoculars and telescopes, increasingly allows human eyes to see over distances no other animal can scan and reveal planets and stars whose existence only a few decades ago was not even suspected. Periscopes allow us to see round corners and from beneath the sea, while modern electron microscopes can magnify hundreds of thousands of times. Already they are revealing the very secrets of life itself, as they probe molecules, allow the human eye to study stretches of DNA, and scientists to identify chromosomes and examine their genetic make-up.

Using fine electrodes to measure the brain's response to different visual stimuli, scientists are able to identify the different cells in the brain's surface which specifically respond to lines, dots, or to particular colours. They have also found other cells which do not register either to shape or colour but react to direction of movement or speed of movement. Perhaps the future for extending, improving or even restoring sight will lie in this more precise mapping of just where and how the action takes place in the brain to interpret the wide variety of visual signals and form them into the mosaic we call sight, allowing us our human perception of the moving world.

It may also lie, according to some experts, in what they term the 'living superchips', which may provide the basis not only for robot superbrains, computers literally able to think, but are already being used in America to produce artificial eyes and ears.

After sight, the next most important sense for man is hearing, though again it is only poorly developed compared to that of many other animals. Bats have the most acute hearing of any land animals, being able to detect sound at a high pitch we cannot register at all. During flight they both transmit and receive continuous signals in this ultrasonic range (vampire and fruit bats at 150,000 cycles per second) giving them an incredibly accurate echo-location system similar in principle to the sonar used in submarines, which of course works within our own human hearing range.

The human ear has the ability to detect frequencies from 20 to 20,000 cycles per second, beaten at the upper end not only by the bat but many other animals including the dog, with the bottle-nosed dolphin holding the record and able to hear 153,000 cycles per second. At the lower end we are also beaten by something as seemingly insignificant as the grasshopper.

A few people do report being able to hear sound within the supersonic range, particularly the radar squeaks of bats which they sometimes also sense merely as a vibration in their own throat. Interestingly the majority reporting this unusual ability are also asthmatic.

The human ear was probably not initially much concerned with hearing and detection of sound waves, but with the vital sense of balance and orientation, briefly already touched on when considering man's ventures into space and his adaptation to weightlessness.

The fluid in the three semi-circular canals, which are all set in different planes in the inner ear, reacts by accelerating and decelerating to register all head movement. In addition a combination of hair cells and chalky particles called otholiths respond to gravity, so that we can tell which way up we are. Our eyes obviously can also help to some extent in this sort of spatial location, but they cannot really compensate for damage to this delicate mechanism, which can doom the victim to live in a constantly reeling world. Anyone who has suffered even temporarily from severe vertigo can at least comprehend what this permanent loss of equilibrium must be like.

If hearing was in some ways originally a secondary function of the ear, man has certainly learned to put it to good use in conjunction with the brain, not only to help in location of sounds important to him, such as running water or movements made by other men or animals, but in developing from the first basic sounds of simple communication the later infinitely precious system of language. It is speech with its multiplicity and vast permutations of sounds, which has allowed man to convey precise information and instruction, pass on learning, frame abstract thoughts and stimulate other minds. From such sounds written symbols evolved to give permanence and build such knowledge down the generations. And all this depended on hearing.

The essential link between hearing and speech seems obvious, yet it is only in recent years that it has been recognised that people are not born 'deaf-mutes', a term and concept commonly used in the past. Deaf children become mute simply because they cannot hear and, therefore, cannot mimic and learn speech. Today the importance of deafness being diagnosed in children as early as possible is accepted, and a new machine recently developed in Canada is reputed to allow detection within a week of birth. Some experts believe deaf children can be helped as early as eight months old with special exercises to simulate the preparatory stages of sounds heard and emitted by normal children before they go to actual speech. A child who is not speaking by the age of two is usually either backward or deaf, though there have apparently been some notable exceptions, including Einstein, who did not speak until the age of four.

The Canadian machine also discovered that newborn babies have some temporary deafness from a residue of amniotic fluid in their ears. This soon disperses and they will then react strongly to any sharp sound, which after the muffling effect of the fluid and the even earlier insulation offered by the relative quiet of the womb, probably seems frighteningly loud. Again, they adapt quite quickly, clearly enjoying familiar sounds and being curious about others, until the ear and brain of the adult can eventually assess 1,600 different frequencies between the highest and lowest, and some 350 different intensities between the quietest and the loudest.

Noise level is measured in decibels. Most people associate the name of Alexander Bell only with the telephone, but it was also he who applied the term 'bel' to units of loudness, with a sound only just audible registered as 0 bels, and a whisper calculated at a thousand times more powerful as 3 bels. This is because intensity of noise is measured logarithmically, and a thousand is 10^3. Conversation another thousand times louder than a whisper (10^6) rates 6 bels, a shout 9 bels and 12 bels is about the top limit of noise which can be endured without distress. Noise of more than 16·5 bels can be lethal. To simplify the whole system decibels equal to one-tenth of a bel are more commonly used, so 165 decibels is the lethal level.

Although modern technology is being used to correct hearing defects with increasingly sophisticated aids, we now also know that modern living in some ways, far from extending our potential for hearing, can hazard it. Jet engines a few metres away reach 40 decibels, riveting hammers 130, a pneumatic drill heard from five metres 100, and 110 is the height from a typical disco. There is definite evidence now of the harmful effects of this sort of exposure to noise directly on hearing, and indirectly on the nervous system and on sleep. Reports have shown admission to mental hospitals in West London to be far higher in areas affected by aircraft noise, and as our world grows noisier our tolerance appears to decrease. Recent figures have shown that complaints about noise in the UK increased by 10,000 in 1977 to 37,871 and they did not all come from industrial areas.

Mr James Robinson, an ear, nose and throat consultant at the Royal Gloucester Hospital, found increasing numbers of patients from his largely agricultural community turning up with noise-induced hearing defects. He was so intrigued by this that he researched and found that intense noise levels came from squealing pigs at feeding time, noisy chain saws and milking parlours, not to mention gunshot reports. A Suffolk farmer, Peter Raven, even insisted that the noise of a giant bulldozer working on the A45 near his farm, was putting his pigs off sex and that takes some doing! During the time it was operating 120 of his sows had rejected the advances of the boars, so perhaps we are hazarding even more than our hearing!

In all an estimated half million British workers are considered at risk from sound levels sufficiently high to cause permanent damage to hearing. Discos, sometimes reaching 120 decibels, assault the ears of young people even though the permitted level for noise is 90. In Denmark, half of all children are estimated by audiologists to have suffered impaired hearing from the large scale firework celebrations held every 31 December. Just as too intense a light can damage the eyes, so can too intense a noise damage normal hearing potential.

The need to counteract these adverse effects of exposure to high noise levels has resulted in the UK in a special commission to report on the problem, but meanwhile one bright inventor has come up with a special noise neutraliser, featured on BBC's 'Tomorrow's World'. This machine, based on the principle that one sound wave can be, as it were, complementary to another, neutralising the unwanted oscillations, produces a form of 'white sound' which considerably reduces the irritating noise from drills, circular saws and other machinery on the factory floor.

The mechanism of hearing is almost as complicated as that of sight and just as ingenious. Where hearing is concerned, the ear has three main functions: to collect sound; to amplify it; and to translate it into nerve impulses for the brain to interpret.

The outer ear (the part we hang our spectacles and earrings on) is the collector. It is not a particularly efficient one, but better than a simple hole in the head. The sound passes along the ear canal to the outer ear drum, dividing the outer from the middle ear. To the other side of this drum is attached the first of a chain of three small bones, the joints and pivots of which are arranged so as to amplify the vibrations over 100 times. These bones are located in an air-filled chamber, called the middle ear, and the last of them, the stirrup, has its footplate attached to the inner ear drum. Behind this is the inner ear, sensitive to these amplified vibrations and able to translate them into nerve impulses, which are then passed to the brain to be re-interpreted as sound.

A good normal ear is so sensitive, even in humans, that it can pick up sounds which deflect the membrane as little as one ten-millionth of a millimetre. But as with sight, it is the analysing and transforming of the nerve signals by the brain into sense impressions which constitutes the real miracle. In the case of hearing the range of sounds is vast, covering everything from grunts and bumps and bangs to complex music and language.

Like failing sight limitations on hearing are most often associated with ageing, but deafness whenever it occurs falls into two main types and again extension of limits and potential lies largely in better methods of dealing with such problems. Conductive deafness, where the trouble stems from the middle ear bones or drum, can usually be helped by simply amplifying sounds artificially. The other type, perceptive deafness, is caused by problems with the receptor system and simply making sounds louder can sometimes just add to the confusion.

Old-fashioned hearing aids such as ear trumpets simply added about 20 decibels, but the latest modern aids, powered by transistors, can really extend hearing potential. They can be tailored to individual needs, designed with 'cut-off' mechanisms to respond to either high- or low-frequency sound depending on the range of hearing loss, which can be determined by special machines.

The original bulky wired pocket aids have given way these days to bone and air conduction models, worn imperceptibly on the body or head, built into spectacle frames or simply concealed in the ear in the form of individually moulded fittings, complete with tiny batteries. The silicon chip revolution promises even further improvements and refinements, and the same applies to radio hearing aids and speech training units used to train deaf children to talk. Amplified telephone hand sets and radio and television adaptors which allow the deaf to listen while keeping the volume normal for other listeners are also preserving the 'norms' of hearing and living, albeit again artificially.

Extending normal hearing potential like extending normal sight by what might be termed natural means is not really possible, but what can be achieved is fuller use of our normal potential and this applies to all our senses. Most of us simply do not realise or use our full capacity for seeing, hearing, touching or smelling. This is made very clear by people deprived of one sense and able to compensate for the loss by much better use of the others. The blind vividly demonstrate latent human ability to interpret shape and form by touch, to locate position by sound, and even to use alteration in echos rather like a simple form of sonar. Blind men make excellent physiotherapists and osteopaths because they develop special sensitivity of touch, and they also excel as piano tuners by sharpening up the human potential for differentiating pitch. In a comparable way the deaf learn to use their eyes more acutely than most of us to distinguish mouth movement for lip reading and vibration for a degree of musical appreciation. At least one leading ballerina in Europe, twenty-four-year-old Nina Falaise, is so deaf that she can only just hear the bass notes. She compensates by accurately sensing the musical vibrations through the floor boards and does it well enough to have danced top roles in Rome, Germany and Switzerland.

The great human gift of adaptability was very well demonstrated by one blind man well known to one of the authors. Jack Bradley Hoskisson took a BSc, managing the practical examinations with minimal help from a sighted assistant. He then became a noted osteopath with a Harley Street practice where he ministered to the members of the Royal Ballet, and he also ran a country practice at weekends in Warwickshire. He carried out original studies on sleep, at Oxford University, because sleep and relaxation were very much part of the picture in dealing with back injuries often aggravated or induced by stress. He became the first blind man to win a Churchill Travelling Scholarship to continue his sleep studies abroad, and could have looked forward to a brilliant future if he had not been tragically killed when a car struck the horse he was riding on a narrow country lane. Even without sight he was one of the most complete and alive human beings it would be possible to meet. He appreciated music, enjoyed plays and even wrote them. He used his gifts also to invent special back supports and special braille printing systems. He was larger than life, a zestful, life-loving extrovert, and the loss of one sense simply inspired him to use all the others to the fullest.

Although man invariably loses out on the keenness of some particular sense when compared to other species, it is the sum of his over-all ability and adaptability, his very non-specialisation which has made him in general terms the most powerful and efficient creature of all.

Certainly if the sense of *smell* was paramount to success and survival man would not have done very well. It would be the dog who was our master instead of the other way round, for a dog's nose can be over a million times as sensitive as a man's. For this reason dogs are used to detect victims buried beneath avalanches or to track escaped prisoners. They are able to distinguish so precisely between individual people that after just being allowed to sniff some article of clothing they can pick up the trail of the owner, sorting out the right footprints even from a confusion of others. What is more they can tell the direction taken, by the minute difference in freshness of scent between the prints. Considering that this special human smell has to penetrate and leak through layers of leather, rubber or plastic that go to make up shoes, it indicates an incredible sensitivity. With special training dogs can also learn to sniff out gas leaks, barking at the spot where a pipe has burst often feet below a paved street. They can equally be trained to locate contraband such as opium and heroin; and just as usefully today in our terrorist-ridden world, to sniff out explosives which the human nose cannot register at all.

The difference in smell sensitivity between man and dog lies in the greater number of olfactory cells and types of receptor dogs possess. The German sheepdog for example, with the most acute sense of smell in the canine world, has 220 million olfactory cells. Man has only 5 million with only fourteen different types of receptor.

For our purposes and the way we have evolved these serve us reasonably well, but there is no doubt the sense of smell is one which with training and practice we could learn to use far better than we do. An ordinary person can learn to distinguish as many as 10,000 different smells, but one perfume manufacturer worked out that a real expert in his line of business could eventually register 30,000 nuances of scent.

Even with training and practice, however, the human nose still cannot normally smell other people (which is perhaps just as well) or pinpoint individual smells as a dog can, though there is evidence that some people are sensitive to different racial odours. The Japanese are said to find European body odour strong but often sexually stimulating. Food and lifestyle may well affect what the advertisements once so coyly called BO, and certainly in our culture the modern fashion is to obliterate natural body odours with anti-perspirants and perfumes. Ironically these scents are most often based on 'musk' from the scent glands of animals so that we are replacing our own built-in attractant with an animal one.

There is no doubt the sense of smell does play a big part in the sexual context. The stories may be apocryphal but both Napoleon and Nelson were supposed to have found body odour attractive in the opposite sex. Napoleon is reputed to have sent a message to Josephine from the battlefield 'Home in three days. Do not wash.' Nelson sent a similar message to Lady Hamilton by fast frigate before he was due home with the Fleet.

Smell is even more important in the animal world, with the scent from sex glands being used to mark territory as well as for sexual stimulation. Female mice have been shown to be so sensitive to the odour of individual males that the mere presence of a strange male deliberately placed near pregnant females was shown in well-documented experiments to cause the majority of them to abort.

In the human world recent experiments with human babies show that at least at that age they swiftly learn to distinguish the special smell of their own mothers. Twenty newborn babies aged two to seven days were presented with a breast pad on each side of their faces, close to the nose and touching their cheeks. One breast pad had been up against the mother's breast for three and a half hours, and the other pad was clean. Each baby had two minutes to smell the pads, and they were reversed halfway through the experiment. But each time the babies turned significantly more towards their mother's breast pad. They seemed to know the smell and turned towards it perhaps in the hope it would be associated with food.

The experiment was repeated with thirty-two other babies in a similar manner but on one side was hung a breast pad that had been in contact with their own mother's breast and on the other side a breast pad from a strange mother. At two days of age babies turned about the same amount to each pad, but when tested at six days significantly more babies spent more time with their noses buried in their own mother's pad and this effect was even stronger at ten days old. So it was a learned sensitivity reinforced by longer association, but was it the smell of the milk or of the mother? Twenty further babies were tested just with milk expressed on to pads, but in this case there was no discrimination between the two, which confirmed it was the mother's own smell that registered – a good argument perhaps for young mothers giving up deodorants for a time while their babies get to know them.

As adults we appear to lose any such ability to respond to a particular individual's body smell at least on the conscious level, but recent research has shown that the human male, quite apart from butyric acid, which is the smelly constituent of sweat common to both sexes, and the more intimate male musk-like genital scent observable on occasions, also produces a pheromone, termed androsterone, in his sweat and urine. By definition pheromones are smells which are not consciously recognised by the brain but which affect the behaviour of others. The same pheromone rather unflatteringly is also found in male pigs, and under the name Boarmate has been found by vets to bring on 'difficult' sows. Before eager males rush out to see if it has a similar effect on 'difficult' women, the female co-author of this book hastens to advise that at an experimental testing (at least in the concentration used) she found it totally revolting. The same reaction, but perhaps more understandable, occurred with samples of 'copulins', the female pheromones apparently attractive to men. According to Dr Alex Comfort these are put out particularly by blondes and redheads, which presumably helps to explain why gentlemen are supposed to prefer blondes, and redheads are so often considered sexy.

Experiments have been carried out where these normally undetectable substances were sprayed on theatre seats and telephones and were shown to possess a powerful attractant effect. It was all somewhat unscientific and although the opposite sex appeared to show preference for seats and telephones which had been treated, nature probably knows best in letting it all operate at an unconscious level.

An interesting and far more scientifically proven observation during recent medical research into the menopause, has been the discovery that prior to ovarian failure women are far more sensitive to the scent of musk than men are. The smell has to be a thousand times stronger for a man to notice it than for a woman to detect it. But if a woman has her ovaries removed or they cease to function after the climacteric, then the scent of musk becomes as faint for her as for a man. If she is given hormone therapy so that the hormones the ovaries no longer produce are replaced, then the scent again becomes vivid. This effect was shown by the work of the well-known British zoologist, Professor John Ebling, and bears out other indications that once the reproductive years are over evolution loses interest as it were. Certainly in the human female, once her sex hormones fail there is not just loss of this particular response to male sex scent but accelerated ageing with brittling of bones, loss of muscle tone and very often some loss of sexual interest and responses. By the rather brutal laws of nature there is little purpose in the infertile women being attracted or attractive, as there can be no beneficial outcome in terms of progeny and survival of the species, which is the dominant force at work.

It seems likely that the sense of smell more than any other sense may well have been attenuated in man by what we call civilisation, by social living, cultural habits and acquired or enforced standards of hygiene. Elsewhere in the animal world it remains a vital sense for recognition, mating, marking territory, homing, warning and even possibly control of breeding numbers. It is, for example, the special scent of the queen bee which inhibits development of ovaries in her worker bees. It is the scent of what might be termed 'togetherness', a sort of mob smell, which turns relatively harmless small locusts into ravaging and super-fertile swarms of enormous, large, long-winged migratory invaders. In other creatures mass scent acts as a contraceptive that inhibits fertility, as with the flour beetle – a dreaded pest in the world's flour stores. Their own excrement has been found to contain a chemical scent substance which reduces fertility, prolongs the development time of the larva and triggers egg cannibalism, a very effective way of controlling numbers.

By comparison, even with training and practice, our use of the sense of smell is very limited and so is our knowledge of how it works. Animal and human studies have not so far revealed much beyond the fact that it all operates right down at the molecular level. Some scientists have suggested that the different scent receptors have different tiny holes keyed to different-shaped molecules, representing the basic smells from which others are mixed, as are colours from the primary ones. They believe in this way that some receptors are specialised to receive only certain smells, while others may be more generalised. All of them must then pass on the scent signals to the brain rather as visual or sound signals are passed, but far less is understood about the process.

Apart from improving our keenness of smell by practice and usage, there is little that can be done at the moment artificially or technically to extend potential, although a complicated apparatus has been devised to act as an 'artificial nose', though only in the sense of analysing and defining scents by acting as a sort of gas chromatograph. Secretions from the human body passed through this artificial nose revealed twenty-four different fractions, and even if the real human nose cannot distinguish individual human body odours, this strange machine was claimed to be able to do so as accurately and personally as a fingerprint or photograph could do, offering a new form of identification by scent index and register.

The inventor of the artificial nose, Dr Andrew Dravniek, reported in the *New Scientist* in 1965 both his results to date and his hopes that improved versions of the machine might not only be useful to the police, with criminals virtually leaving scent visiting cards at the scene of the crime, but that it might be developed medically too, as diseases may well be accompanied by characteristic body secretions, so that a scent analysis could provide early reliable diagnosis.

Most people tend to associate the sense of smell and taste, often insisting that a heavy cold which blocks our ability to smell also reduces taste sensation. Personal observation would certainly confirm the idea but scientifically, at least, there is no evidence for this, with a complete division of receptors. While smell can be perceived from some distance, taste can only register by direct contact, and before we can experience the faintest taste, 25,000 times as many molecules have to affect our tongue as would be necessary to stimulate the nose.

Our sense of taste is very poor and crude with the 3,000 taste buds on the tongue registering the four basic sensations of sweet, salty, sour and bitter. The more subtle appreciation of delicacies does rely on the scents arising from the mouth cavity to the nose, and so in that way there is a link, with both taste and smell working together to savour the full delights of food, but with the mechanisms themselves quite separate.

The pig, which most of us would regard as greedy rather than discriminating in its approach to food, has twice as many taste buds as man. Some fish have taste buds extending the whole length of their bodies, but in our case although they do report taste signals received to the brain, our taste buds are almost more concerned with a reflex action by which they carry out control of the saliva. In this way, depending on the kind of food in our mouth, our taste nerves can vary the production of the salivary glands to digest it.

Presumably early man used his sense of taste to distinguish harmful plants and foods, and bitterness which is often an indication of danger can still be sensed at a far greater dilution, as little as 1 part in 2,000,000 using special taste buds raised on long nodules at the back of the tongue. By comparison sourness can only be detected with a dilution of 1 in 130,000, saltness 1 in 400 and sweetness 1 in 200. Smells need dilutions of only 1 part in a 1,000,000,000 or more, so poor as it is our sense of smell is far more sensitive than our sense of taste. It is also probably less subject to cultural influences. Really pleasant smells are appreciated by most races and societies and really unpleasant ones rejected, but food tastes can be cultivated and acquired – the widespread use of garlic in France and Spain is one example, the variation in use of salt in differing societies which we have already noted is another, while the absolute addiction to sugar and sweet things is quite a recent phenomenon in the affluent developed world.

There is no doubt that our sense of taste *is* capable of development as the skill of the professional wine taster well illustrates, and indeed it is the one sense which the increasing sophistication of modern living may gradually extend. Once the level of affluence allows food to be chosen for pleasure rather than mere survival, subtle and varying flavours will play a more and more important part and our taste buds may well learn finer appreciation of gourmet delights.

And so to the sense of touch. In his book *The Stages of Human Life* J. Lionel Taylor wrote 'The greatest sense in our body is our touch sense. It is probably the chief sense in the processes of sleeping and waking; it gives us our knowledge of depth or thickness and form; we feel, we love and hate, are touchy and are touched, through the touch corpuscles of our skin.'

Touch is certainly the earliest sensory system to become operational in all species, and in the evolutionary sense too it was the one which developed first to become differentiated later into the others. So, it has appropriately been called 'the mother of the senses'.

For all that, it is a sense we take very much for granted, hardly realising that it is through touch that we constantly relate to our environment and our place in it. Bertrand Russell, philosopher and mathematician made this point well when he wrote, 'Not only our whole geometry and our physics, but our whole conception of what exists outside us, is based upon the sense of touch.'

Like most of our senses, touch is both under used and under-valued, except perhaps by those deprived of sight who quickly realise its potential, finding the extreme sensitivity of finger tips in reading braille or tracing the contours of a face to comprehend how people look, a true form of 'seeing with the fingers'. The sensitivity of normal finger tips is such that a vibration with a movement of only 0·02 of a micron can be detected.

Our whole skin is an organ of touch with some areas more sensitive because they contain a greater number of nerve endings to register feeling. Contact, pressure, pain, heat and cold are all touch reactions with different types of receptors involved. In addition to finger tips, the tip of the penis, the clitoris, lips and tongue are the most sensitive and reactive, though hairy parts of the body have the additional factor of hair-pull or movement.

The importance of touch as a form of communication and reassurance between people, and particularly perhaps between parent and child, is only just being realised as a result of recent studies. It is rather surprising that it has taken us so long to understand this, because we have seen it at work in animals with all their licking, nuzzling and grooming. For animal mothers and their young, it not only helps to establish the bond of familiar feel and smell, but to maintain in mammals good lactation and in birds to provoke regurgitation of food for nestlings. In many species the licking and touch stimulation of genital and anal areas in the young is the trigger for essential urination and defecation. At one time it was not realised why so often hand-reared young animals failed to survive despite every care. Now the missing mother's touch is simulated with gentle stroking with damp cotton wool or even the human finger to help the orphans begin the process of waste elimination.

In his well-researched book *Touching*, Ashley Montague offers chapter and verse of the many experiments with animals showing how gentle handling and touching helps them to thrive and survive. Rats that had been 'gentled' over several generations not only bred better and had offspring with higher weight at weaning, but were able to survive trauma far better. In one experiment the thyroid and parathyroid glands were removed from contrasting colonies of rats, one 'gentled' and one given cursory treatment. The 'ungentled' rats were nervy and irritable and 79 per cent of them died. Only 13 per cent of the 'gentled' rats died.

A great deal of evidence is also quoted from special studies and observations showing the same sort of effect on children deprived of touch, cuddling and loving contact. In their case it led not only to unstable and withdrawn behaviour in their early life but to disturbed behaviour in adult life, when they often failed to develop emotionally, were afraid to touch or be touched and seemed unable to relate to others. Some adults retain this fear throughout life and interestingly George Washington is reputed to have fallen into this category.

Touching in the sexual context as part of love-making can be immensely enjoyable, not only to arousal but in the subtle intimacy of skin-to-skin contact. Awareness of the part tactile sensation can play offers an extension of touch potential which for some can open up new dimensions of experience.

There is no doubt that we can, if we wish, extend touch potential also in more mundane ways. There has long been a popular party game in which everyone is blindfolded in turn, while quite ordinary objects are passed round to be identified merely by touch. No one is usually very good at it and it is surprising with the eyes covered what subtle differences of shape and texture become apparent to puzzle and confuse. In a way this demonstrates how much we are dominated by sight, so that normally we hardly bother with touch. Sight also imposes what Ashley Montague terms 'censorship' of the senses. He argues that vision acts as an arbiter of behaviour and an inhibitor, while touch is free and without prejudice. Experiments showed that students shut in a darkened room freely touched each other with normal inhibitions relaxed, but once the lights went up the usual reservations and shyness barriers operated again.

Both men and women use self-touch gestures to relieve tension. Men rub their chins, tug the lobes of their ears or rub the forehead, while women put a finger on their front teeth or under the chin. In alarm or grief we wring our hands, and playing with smooth pebbles or worry beads is a common way of using touch to tranquillise. The latest modern equivalent is small bits of polished wood called 'Feelies'.

So touch is physically useful but psychologically vital. Montague and many other experts now, including followers of the Leboyer ideas on childbirth, believe tactile stimulation is fundamental to healthy behavioural development of the individual, with failure to receive it in infancy resulting in stunted emotional growth.

Not being touched presents one sort of danger; not possessing the ability to feel, actually lacking the sense of touch, presents quite another. In fact the real value of this particular sense can only be fully appreciated when you meet the unfortunate few who for some reason do not have it. Take the case of a young seventeen-year-old farm worker, a patient of one of the authors. While hitching a lift on the back of a tractor his left foot slipped into the wheel. Both bones in the lower leg were broken and the main nerve to the foot torn from its origins. Over the next few months his bones and muscles healed and he was able to walk. Nerves, however, take much longer to recover. One evening, while the family sat around the fire, the room was filled with a smell as of roasting meat. The meal had been over for hours, the kitchen empty, the cooker off. It took several seconds for them to realise that the smell was coming from David's injured foot. A cinder from the fire had lodged between his great toe and the second and they were being 'done to a turn'. The burned tissue took much longer to heal than the broken bones.

The results of loss of touch and pain sensation are taken to extremes in the case of leprosy. Everyone recoils from the thought of this mutilating disease – the ugly stumps of fingerless hands, toeless feet and noseless faces have filled people with horror since biblical times – yet these ravages of the body are not directly the result of the germ which causes leprosy. The bacteria specifically attack the nerves of sensation: as with young David, the damage is done by failure to withdraw the exposed area of the body from danger.

If it is difficult where the senses are concerned to find examples of people with more than average natural ability, and only a few who by practice and deliberate effort even manage to utilise their full sensory potential, at least there are some outstanding cases of coping magnificently with almost total sensory deprivation.

One shining example, known the world over, is Helen Keller. An illness in infancy robbed her of all sight and hearing. Most people in such circumstances would also end up dumb and doomed, existing without means of communication, shut away in a dark, silent, lonely and limited world.

For a time it seemed that might be the fate of the young Helen. She was subject only to a few primitive basic emotions and desires and with no words to make them known. She was described at that time as a little savage 'perverse and destructive, a rebel locked within prison walls'.

A dedicated teacher, Anne Sullivan, once blind herself, managed to unlock the prison doors. She bore the tantrums, tears and even violence of the cruelly deprived child, until she won her trust and then together they began the years of struggle. First she taught Helen finger language, and that objects she could feel all had names. That abstract things and movement had special words too and that all these could be strung together by fast-moving finger talk, tapped into a hand, to make sentences. Helen's marvellous memory, colossal determination, courage and curiosity about life soon took over. She not only learned braille but the ordinary alphabet so that she could type. Against all odds finally she learned to talk, perfecting speech in a way that even the sighted deaf rarely manage, to the point where she was in demand all over the world to give talks, as part of her campaign to help the blind which raised over a quarter of a million pounds.

Not only did Helen Keller learn to talk herself, she learned to lip read the speech of others, not by sight as most deaf people do but by using her fingers to distinguish the different shapes the lips form for different sounds and to interpret these and the varying vibrations into living speech. In a very similar way she registered vibrations, enabling her to enjoy and value music, without ever actually hearing a single note.

Even more amazing, without ever being able to hear a human voice or see a word of printed text Helen Keller not only learned to write and speak English but several other languages, including French and some German. She coped with Latin and Greek for University entrance, translated the Odes of Horace and took a BA degree at Harvard, where every obstacle had initially been raised against her acceptance.

In her meagre spare time she rode on horseback, became a very good swimmer and travelled widely. She achieved far more than most people with five fully functioning senses and showed graphically how mind and will can overcome the most insuperable handicaps.

Another example of zest for life, splendid curiosity and sheer courage overcoming sensory deprivation was illustrated by the case of Hilary Pole. A spirited, talented and pretty girl, just in her twenties and starting her career teaching among other subjects dancing and gymnastics, Hilary contracted a severe and rare disease called myasthenia gravis. This involves a failure in the connection between the nerve endings and the muscle fibres. Within a few years she was reduced from a lively sports-loving girl to a body unable to support itself, unable to turn even in bed, unable to breathe without a ventilator, unable to see because her eyelids could not be held open, unable to speak and unable to take food or drink except by tube because her jaws would not work and the swallow mechanism had gone. In the end the only movement left to Hilary Pole was in one big toe. Most people would have sunk into some sort of escapist torpor and welcomed the death that threatened so often when ventilators broke down or generators failed. But not Hilary. She not only fought to survive but to really *live*, which in her terms meant continuing to be involved with everything and everyone. Life remained, even in this limited form, something to be grasped and experienced. As long as she could, she watched her sports on television, was even taken complete with ventilator to the county grounds at Edgbaston to watch test matches, and when watching became impossible she savoured all she could on the radio. Speech was lost quite early in the grim progress of the disease, but Hilary soon devised her own method of communication, tracing each letter to outline words and sentences on the sheet of her bed. Sometimes briefly she could hold a pen, but eventually neither this nor sheet writing was possible and then she had to rely on a bell attached to the one toe that she could still move. One ring indicated the letter she wanted was in the first half of the alphabet, no ring meant it was in the second half. Then as the first or second half was recited through to her, she rang the bell at the right letter. Surprisingly swift communication could be made with nurses and friends used to the systems, and always Hilary's sense of humour surfaced if given half a chance. In her book simply called *Hilary*, Dorothy Clarke Wilson records a typical instance where a nurse had been struggling to straighten her nightdress. 'Might have been doing the twist,' Hilary scrawled in her sheet writing, 'should have sat that one out.'

In her last few years the POSM (Patient Operated Selector Mechanism) Foundation developed a special unit for her, worked by a micro-switch so sensitive it would respond to the one-sixteenth of an inch movement left in Hilary's big toe. There was no other movement to utilise, and to make this operate at all and serve a whole lot of uses provided them with their biggest challenge ever. But after some teething troubles they produced a 'Possum' that gave Hilary the independence her spirit longed for. The basis was an intricate code which she managed to master in just two days. With this she could control and use an electric typewriter, reaching forty words per minute despite the involved code. Possum also enabled her to operate her radio and tape recorder, but best of all it provided at last a safe alarm system with a loud bell for an urgent SOS and a buzzer for normal aid. This took the mental anguish out of a situation which Hilary had had to bear for years, knowing that her life depended on rapid attention when her support systems failed as they occasionally did.

The renewed ability to communicate which Possum gave to Hilary triggered an even stronger compulsion to live, because now she was able to realise her primary purpose of giving moral and practical support to others, struggling to adapt to crippling disabilities. Hilary claimed she needed a thirty-hour day for all she wanted to do – there were articles for 'Possibility', the magazine of the Possum Users Association, letters to other members and to friends, and her regular output of witty poems.

When Hilary died only a few years ago, her deep concern and interest in life was undimmed, her spirit quite unbroken. Her brother Ian's words describing how he felt after a visit, sum up the effect she had on everyone. 'It just doesn't occur to me that she isn't 100 per cent physically,' he explained, 'mentally she is so alive. You don't even seem to notice she is bedridden, her personality so oozes all over the room. I think she must have decided early in her illness that she wasn't going to dwell on what she had lost, but on what she had left. Thinking, hearing, feeling. She can learn. She can listen. She can teach and help others. That's Hilary!'

Both the foregoing stories illustrate yet again how the ingenuity, determination and courage that can be summoned up by the human mind can overcome physical limitations.

As we have seen in considering each of our physical senses, many of them play a part in what we term our sexual sense. Although the physical and functional aspects of sexual and reproductive potential quite properly belonged to Chapter 4, sex as a sense finds a place in this chapter too because it is both served by the other senses and yet dominates them, since it is the one absolutely fundamental in initiating the process which leads to survival of the species.

Sight would seem to play the major part in the human species in arousing preliminary sexual interest, particularly in the male, with response to the female face and figure not only 'in the flesh', as it were, but also in pictures. Men can respond strongly to the sight of erotic pictures, often to the point of erection and even orgasm.

Women are rather less strongly stimulated by male physical appearance. While clearly able to appreciate the good-looking male or well-made male body, perhaps because their basic need at least in the past has been for security and protection, they tend to be wary of dangerous good looks which may offer neither. Instead there seems to be response to a quality which may not be linked to physical appearance but which suggests a degree of male dominance and aggression. The wiser woman looks also for consideration and tenderness sensed by the mind rather than the eyes and through experience rather than first impressions.

Touch is the next most important component of the over-all sexual sense and there women are just as responsive as men. Finger tips and tongue are the super-sensitive agents in sexual arousal while the skin itself provides a whole responsive playground, with certain highly erogenous zones heightening pleasure as intimacy progresses.

Smell, as we have seen, can have both a conscious and subconscious influence. At the conscious level it is a highly individual matter and by no means all humans appreciate natural body odour as Napoleon and Nelson were reputed to do. Artificial perfumes can certainly titillate the senses as the widespread use of body lotions, after–shave, spray colognes, scents and talcs, all with delicate or heady perfumes indicate. Resistance of the traditional British male who felt there was something slightly unmanly in all this has gradually been overcome. But however strange it may seem to some of us, sex books make it clear that sweat and genital odour remain a 'turn on' for some people.

The place of sound is at once more subtle but more universal. Legends down the ages of music and siren voices luring men (usually it must be admitted to their doom) are common in many cultures. These almost universally apply to women's voices singing, whether it be mermaids or the famous Lorelei. In more practical and mundane terms few would deny that a woman's voice full of charm and allure can promise much and stir the male senses. Equally, although there are no legends about them, male voices can attract women with timbre and tone. But of course it is the words of love which form the most powerful aphrodisiac. Where a woman is concerned words that confirm she is desirable and desired can set the pulse and hormones racing.

For at the most basic level the sexual sense is rooted in our sex hormones. If for any reason the levels drop too low or if castration before puberty eliminates them entirely, the sexual sense and response is diminished or lost completely.

As with the other senses, the organs and hormones directly involved do not operate in a vacuum. They closely interact with the mind, controlled in the case of sexual arousal and response by that oldest part of the brain, the hypothalamus, which directs the master gland, the pituitary. This orchestrates all other glands including the sex glands (or gonads), regulating hormone levels and surges, which in women involves the regular ebb and flow of oestrogen and progesterone which result in the monthly cycle and ovulation. In the male the levels of male hormones, the androgens, stimulate continuous production of sperm and sexual desire.

This inter-dependence and interaction of brain and hormones through a complicated feed-back system works both ways. The emotions and mental state can influence hormone levels and sexual and reproductive behaviour, while hormone levels, if out of balance, can exert an equally strong effect on the mental state. In women this is clearly seen with post-natal blues, pre-menstrual tension and menopausal depression and confusion, all the results of disturbed hormone levels.

Influence in the other direction is clearly illustrated in the disruption of periods in young women when they come under stress or anxiety. It shows particularly at the time they first leave home for university or job training. A quarter of girls first entering university are reported to miss up to three periods just as a result of excitement and stress. Perhaps the strangest example of the influence of mental state on sex hormone levels is 'phantom pregnancy'. The obsessional craving for a child can lead to the raised hormone levels and normal symptoms of a real pregnancy. Recently, Patricia, a girl of thirty still childless after five years of marriage (and well known to one of the authors), began attending an infertility clinic for full investigation of herself and her husband. No functional reasons for failure to conceive were found and after a few months everyone was delighted when she declared herself pregnant. She had no periods, suffered morning sickness and her breasts became swollen and tender. The only trouble was that repeated pregnancy tests showed negative, but Pat told no-one about this and utterly refused to accept the results. In her own mind she *was* pregnant and her body responded. For between four and five months she fooled everyone, until the fact of her pregnancy was by chance mentioned to the gynaecologist who had been treating her. Only then, with a firm talk in the presence of her husband, was the delusion finally dispelled and a course of clomiphene started to prod the ovaries back into action and at least provide a chance of real pregnancy.

In some cases phantom pregnancy can even proceed to pseudo–labour, obviously with no end product except bitter disappointment. This may seem something of a diversion but it illustrates graphically the interaction between mind and body in this instance affecting hormone levels to influence and mimic a state of pregnancy. Mental factors can just as effectively influence the preliminary stages of sexual arousal and response, blunting or heightening the sexual sense. Again this particularly applies to women, so that the girl involved in hurried, unloving intercourse under stressful conditions, will often find it hard to generate real sexual feeling or reach orgasm. The human male, it must be confessed, appears rather different in this respect, responding far more easily to straightforward physical stimulus. The fact that he can also respond to erotic pictures shows that the mind can also play a part in his case too. In many cases just talking about sex or thinking about it can set up sexual fantasies which rouse the sexual sense. Equally men under stress, worry or depression find they suffer loss of libido, temporary impotence and then more depression and loss of confidence, thus setting up a truly vicious circle.

So for humans it can be a complicated mixture of mental and physical factors that together form our sexual sense. Down the ages many methods have been tried to expand and extend this highly prized sense through what are termed 'aphrodisiacs', a word derived from Aphrodite, the goddess of love. Orthodox medical opinion is highly sceptical about most of them which range from powdered rhinoceros horn, widely favoured by the Chinese, to asafetida – a resin with a very pungent odour, derived from an Asian plant and much prized in the East. Ginseng has also been used for thousands of years by the Chinese and is currently in vogue here too via the health food fanatics. Pollen, fennel, liquorice, hops, mandrake root, yohimbine and vitamin E all have their supporters. Those which work at all may well do so by acting as general stimulants, though yohimbine is actually incorporated in one preparation which many doctors in this country do prescribe for patients with loss of libido. The best one can say is that most of them at least do no harm, and as so much is in the mind and in 'confidence', to that extent they may even help. The one substance which should be completely barred is Spanish fly. This is made from small beetles, native to France and Spain, called *Lytta vesicatoria.* The chemical extracted from them specifically irritates the bladder and stimulates sexual arousal but at fearful cost, including the risk of convulsions. The Marquis de Sade was accused of trying to poison prostitutes by feeding them with this highly dangerous substance.

Fortunately today modern endocrinology can help to improve failing sexual sense. The most important male sex hormone produced in the body is testosterone, and in both men and women sexual desire is dependent on it. It is only obtainable on prescription and use of this for women must be limited to short periods, as it can cause unwanted facial hair growth and a deepening voice if too freely used. All the same it does have a place with proper supervision, and implants of testosterone are a particularly effective way of using it.

Perhaps the single most inhibiting factor which so often prevents our sexual sense reaching full potential is guilt. This can be inculcated in us as children, when well-meaning parents striving to protect adolescents make them feel that sex is wrong or dirty. This attitude, often reinforced by religious taboos, can wreck adult experience and blunt the sexual sense. Wise counselling to remove guilt and restore confidence can be a major factor in freeing the mind so that the sexual sense can be used responsibly but fully.

Finally, over and above the five physical senses and better use of these, and beyond the subtle blend of these which together with hormonal and mental factors go to form our sexual sense, is there yet another? Is there, as many have suggested, also a sixth sense, a form of instinctive reaction or behaviour? This is very tenuous speculation and has had to be seriously considered only because there is no other way of explaining at the moment some of the odd happenings – the disturbed behaviour of animals shown at a time of imminent death or disaster. The ability shown by dogs and cats to find places or people over routes they have never travelled and sometimes hundreds of miles away. Even their highly developed sense of smell can in no way account for some such feats.

Only recently in the UK a cat called Micky, living near Tamworth, Staffordshire, made national headlines. He was a country cat and when his family had to move for business reasons to a busy built-up area in

Hampstead, London, they thought it kinder to leave him with relatives near his own home. But Micky had other ideas. After a few days in which he was clearly moping, he disappeared, only to turn up six weeks later at the new house in Hampstead which he had never seen. He was exhausted, half–starved and with the claws of one paw missing, but somehow he had found his way across 107 miles of strange country to a place he had never been and located his special family among the teeming millions of London. On the face of it it sounds utterly impossible and there is no logical explanation.

If man ever had this particular ability he has certainly lost it now. Even with the aid of maps and road signs he sometimes has difficulty finding his way in wilderness or urban sprawl, though some people retain what we call a 'bump of direction' which others totally lack and which enables them again without any clear reasoning to know roughly the way they should go. But that is the best we can do. Some people also seem to have occasional premonitions of danger or disaster as animals do – they withdraw from aircraft flights, for instance, which later unhappily crash, but often feel too foolish to even mention their reasons. A study across the world of plane and train crashes recently revealed an interesting point – statistically there were fewer people aboard the ill–fated craft than would have been expected, suggesting some people at least changed their travel plans, perhaps not consciously even knowing why.

It is all very unscientific but it could be that some old animal instinct which senses danger still lingers, buried deep in genetic memory, surfacing in a few people just now and again to help them avoid accidents or sometimes even to foresee them for others. One woman in America claimed to have foreseen the entire Kennedy assassination, but how does one prove this sort of thing? Easier to establish is the rare form of 'second sight' or 'instinct' exercised sometimes on behalf of the police. One well–documented case was that of Gerard Croiset of Utrecht, a Dutchman known to have clairvoyant powers, consulted by the police in 1964 to help solve the murder of three civil rights workers in Mississippi. He proved able to give accurate information and descriptions of the area in which the bodies were eventually found and to implicate, correctly as it turned out, certain local policemen in the killings.

Another Dutchman, Peter Hurkos, fell from a ladder in 1943 fracturing his skull and losing his powers of concentration. But he found he had gained a strange new power, a form of second sight. Asked to assist the police at The Hague and given the coat of a dead man to hold, he was able to describe the man's murderer in detail. When the police admitted they already had just such a man under arrest, Hurkos went on to tell them exactly where to find the murder weapon.

So is there a sixth sense, a special power we have lost the art of using or which has been attenuated by the artificial living imposed on the primitive animal instincts by our civilisation? Or is there an explanation lying somewhere in the intricate working of the brain, which we are only beginning to understand?

Certainly the range of the normal mind and brain, the occasional extensions of these into the realms of genius, the ability, often entirely divorced from other signs of extreme intelligence, to make lightning calculations, all make consideration of the limits of the human mind the most fascinating prospect of all.

6
Mental Limits

Defining the limits and exploring the potential of the human body is difficult enough. To try to do the same for the human mind is almost impossible. One way or another mind and brain are involved, consciously or subconsciously, in our every action or reaction, physical as well as mental.

The brain serves as the central clearing house for the vast stream of information constantly flooding in through our senses and nervous system, acting as receiver, processor and storage department. It sorts, reacts, directs, compares, calculates, rejects, discards and at times off-loads into deeper recesses information too painful for us to bear.

Over recent years neurologists have begun to understand a little more about how all this is achieved and locate the areas of the brain performing certain tasks or reacting to certain stimuli. In doing so, many of the cherished beliefs of doctors of previous generations have been destroyed. Scientists assumed that because the human brain was particularly well developed in the frontal areas – the reason for our domed foreheads – this was where our intelligence lay. Super-intelligent people were eggheads: the popular image of scientists, at least as portrayed in films and television, necessitated an actor whose looks reflected Einstein. It was a convenient but quite erroneous theory, probably arising from modern man's wish to separate himself from his low-browed ape-like ancestors.

The size or weight of the brain has little or nothing to do with intellect except, of course, where the brain is small because of disease or a disorder in development. The average adult brain weighs 3lb 2oz (1,410g) which admittedly compares well with the 1lb 6oz (567g) of an average gorilla.

The brains of brilliant men have often been dissected – after death of course – in an attempt to discover the reason for their brilliance. This exercise has been totally unsuccessful: only two, Oliver Cromwell and Lord Byron, appear to have possessed exceptionally big brains and although many research laboratories throughout the world received pieces of Albert Einstein's brain, none have found anything which could explain its exceptional ability. Parts of it are still around in bottles, inspiring curiosity but no new knowledge.

Indeed the heaviest brain ever reported by medical journals weighed 4lb 8oz (2,049g) and had belonged to an ordinary fifty-year-old Florida man. In Britain the record is held by an Edinburgh man, who died aged seventy-five in 1890. His brain weight of 4lb $\frac{1}{2}$oz (1,829g) was apparently no asset as he died in a hospital for the insane.

It is obvious that weighing an organ such as the brain is a method far too crude to give any idea of its potential, particularly as it has to be done when it is dead! A good analogy to this idea would be to weigh the pulverised remains of a crushed used car of unknown horse-power, and from that estimate its powers of acceleration and braking. Much more relevant is to study the function of the brain cells when they are alive and well.

When the twin sciences of neuroanatomy (the study of the structure of the nerve cells) and neurophysiology (the study of their function) had progressed far enough to allow detailed research in healthy volunteers, the results were truly astonishing. The cells in the brain number about 100 thousand million (100 billion American) and of these about 7 thousand million (7 billion American) are arranged in orderly layers in the thin grey-matter outer covering. This surface of grey-matter cells is the key. If any tissue can be associated with thought and logic it is this one.

In 1964, J. Z. Young, an eminent British zoologist, showed that the average nerve cell would make 5,000 different connections with its neighbours; the largest ones, typical of the grey-matter layer, made many more. The surface of one single grey-matter cell is in direct contact with electrical and chemical terminals from several hundred other cells, and a massive network of communications exist in which most of the cells connect either directly or indirectly with every area of the brain. The mathematical implications of such a system are quite impossible to comprehend. Charles Herrick, an American neuroanatomist, calculated in 1956 that there must be 10 to the power of 2·78 million connecting pathways between the grey-matter cells throughout the brain. Just to print this number would fill more than two thousand pages of a book like this.

Some of these connections will, of course, be used regularly, like those involved in receiving, interpreting and co-ordinating messages from the senses and passing on instructions to our muscles and glands. Others, it is assumed, are used rarely – they are involved in abstract and logical thought. By far the great majority perhaps may never be used in a lifetime. We don't yet know how many cell signals are used in forming a single thought. It would appear that thought and logic are to be found not in the structure of the cells but in the energy that flows between them.

So our intelligence and our consciousness depends not on the absolute number of cells in any particular part of the brain, but on fast, reliable, repeatable communication between them and on the network of connections remaining intact. Remove the connections and thought and consciousness disappear: this is the cause of prolonged coma after head injuries following a road accident. At the moment of impact, the softer cell-containing grey matter slips over the tougher nerve fibre containing white matter, severing the connections between grey-matter cells and stimuli from the outside world. The sufferer is 'locked in', unable to receive or transmit any communication. Whether thought is still possible in a 'locked in' state may never be known. Is coma just the absence of communication or does it include the absence of thought itself?

Occasionally people recover from coma even after months. It is assumed that some of their communicating fibres have not been severed, and the brain builds on what is left to re-establish a new network of communication which finally breaks through the barrier to consciousness.

Of course certain areas of the brain are responsible for particular functions of the body. This is why we are right- or left-handed. The brain is formed of two half spheres, one of which is dominant over the other. The left hemisphere appreciates sensation from and controls movements of the right limbs and vice versa. In the right-handed person, therefore, the left hemisphere is dominant. One hemisphere, usually the left, is responsible for the production of speech. This is why a right-sided stroke, which stems from brain damage to the left hemisphere, so often carries with it loss of speech, a hardship which rarely accompanies paralysis of the left arm or leg.

The brain is remarkably resilient, as the re-training of stroke patients shows. Within a year, many patients with perseverance and skilled treatment have learned to speak again. This is not because the damaged cells have recovered, but almost certainly because the second hemisphere has taken over the job, setting up new circuits. The recovery of actress Patricia Neal and her return to her professional career is a supreme example of the brain's ability, given the impetus of tremendous courage and motivation, to overcome disastrous damage.

Consider, too, the case of Mr Takacs, the Hungarian pistol shooting champion in the 1930s. He represented his country at the Olympics in 1936, then in 1938 lost his shooting arm in an accident. In months he had taught himself to shoot with his left hand, and by 1939 was world champion. He won the Olympic gold medals in 1948 and 1953, surely the only naturally right-handed man to do so with his left hand.

The damage to Takacs' nervous system, of course, was outside his brain. By training, he taught his right brain hemisphere to become as efficient as his left. This is by no means as complicated as repairing damage to the specialised cells within the brain itself. Until 1979, all neurologists thought that this was irreversible: that recovery was only possible by finding new pathways to circumvent the diseased area. Even then complete recovery was very rare. In these days of transplants, however, what seemed impossible now may become feasible.

Already, brain-cell transplants have 'taken' and are functioning well in mice. Admittedly, they are not surface grey-matter cells, but cells taken from an area deep in the centre of the brain called the basal ganglia. This is the area affected in the crippling and distressing Parkinson's disease in humans. Mark Perlow and his research team in Washington's National Institute of Mental Health found that basal ganglia cells taken from mouse embryos and placed in the same area of the brain of mice whose basal ganglia had been destroyed by injection, not only survived and multiplied, but stopped the symptoms. The rejection problem so well known in other organ transplants did not occur, because there is a barrier between the bloodstream and the brain cells which prevents the rejection-inducing white blood cells and proteins from reaching the transplant site.

The technique has not yet been applied to humans but it is a pointer to the future, and not just for Parkinson's disease. Many other brain diseases may respond to such treatment. The technical expertise is surely already within the grasp of competent neurosurgeons, but there are ethical problems as the only possible source of donor cells would appear to be aborted human foetuses. Also such transfer of living materials into the human brain may prove dangerous. However, if the results justify the risks and the ethical reservations are overcome the future may hold both promise and peril. Cells from the areas of brain to do with the reception of vision and hearing might be transplanted to help the blind see and the deaf hear. Cells from the surface of the hemispheres could be used perhaps to repair the damage done by strokes. Even further in the future, could the transplant of cells into the brain improve the intelligence of the subnormal, or boost the failing intellect of the aged? The dream could easily become a nightmare because it contains the seeds of mind manipulation not necessarily for the patient's good.

For the moment at least we should be happy to work with the intelligence we have. It offers the one form of mental capacity and ability which can be measured, albeit somewhat crudely. The methods used can only measure those aspects of what we term intelligence which lend themselves to formal testing and that usually means judgement, comprehension and reasoning. The sort of intelligence involved in works of great creative imagination or deep philosphical thought can be recognised, admired or criticised subjectively, but can rarely be assessed in any comparative objective way.

Even the one accepted method of gauging intelligence, the IQ (Intelligence Quotient) test, is somewhat controversial, as it is a guide to mental capacity at the *time* of testing, only applicable to someone from the culture on which the questions are based. But although experts such as Professor H. J. Eysenck frankly admit these limitations and the fact that there is no firm scientific basis for the methods used in testing IQs, they still argue for their validity and their correlation with later achievement.

The special reservations Professor Eysenck makes are that tests must be carried out several times to eliminate any advantage to those already familiar with the type of questions, and he also insists it is not enough to test a child at six or even ten. Six is the earliest age at which he considers the test useful, but it needs to be done again at about fifteen when the IQ usually reaches a peak. After that age it levels out and there is not much change until later in life when it begins to decline.

It is interesting to note from graphs plotting the growth and decline of mental ability against age for three categories, the bright, the average and the dull, that there is a fairly rapid growth from birth to twelve years or so in all groups, but then it slows down reaching its peak at around fifteen and remaining reasonably level for a while before beginning a slow decline. This decline comes later in the bright group and is only very slight, while in the average group it comes earlier and declines faster. For the low intelligence group, growth ceases earlier, declines earlier and the final drop is far more precipitous.

The methods of testing, if not scientific, are at least fairly logical. Questions are grouped into sets which can normally be answered correctly at a given specific age. So for children of six, the questions are all drawn from those which extensive testing has proved can be answered by average children of that age. A child of six able to answer these but *not* able to go on to answer those applied to a seven-year-old is confirmed as having the expected mental age of six. If the six-year-old can also answer the questions normally put to seven-year-old children, then the mental age of that child is gauged as seven. To get the IQ, mental age is put over chronological age and multiplied by 100 to get rid of the decimal point – thus, mental age of 6 and chronological age of 6 give an IQ of 100, which is the average. But mental age of 7 over chronological age of 6 gives a higher than average IQ of around 116. In contrast a six-year-old who can only answer correctly questions normally directed to a five-year-old, has a mental age of 5, with 5 over 5 times 100 giving a lower than average IQ of around 83.

On this basis, 50 per cent of our population prove to have IQs between 90 and 110, 25 per cent score above this and 25 per cent below. Of the 25 per cent above average, 14·5 have IQs of 110 to 120, 7 per cent between 120 and 130, 3 per cent between 130 and 140 and only half a per cent go above 140. Roughly you would expect grammar-school places under the old selective system to go to children with IQs above 115 or thereabouts, with university students averaging about 125. To get a first-class degree (or some equivalent distinction) a student would probably have an IQ of 135 or 140 at least, but there can be no hard and fast rules as social environment and motivation can be strong qualifying factors.

An IQ of 150 is considered 'genius' level, and although indices above 200 are sometimes considered immeasurable, a figure of 210 has been attributed to Kim Ung-Yong of Seoul, South Korea. The Guinness Book of Records notes that he was born in March 1963, and composed poetry, spoke four languages – Korean, English, German and Japanese, and performed integral calculus at the age of four years eight months on television in Tokyo in November 1967.

We may not be able to quite rival that in the West, but exceptional youngsters are constantly turning up; even while researching this book, British papers have reported young Grahame Burke of Sydenham, London, able to read fluently at the age of two and choosing to study French and German for relaxation. In between he dips into encyclopedias and beats his father at chess. When his IQ can be calculated perhaps Kim Ung-Yong's record will be challenged.

While IQs were obviously not employed at the time, on their known performance a figure of over 200 is estimated for John Stuart Mill (1806–73) who began to learn Ancient Greek at the age of three. A similar rating is attributed to Goethe (1749–1832) and Swedenborg (1688–1772). In our age more than 20 per cent of the 22,000 members of the International Mensa Society have an IQ of 142 or above.

Below average IQ level there is a similar distribution pattern, with 14·5 per cent having IQs between 80 and 90, 7 per cent between 70 and 80 and the rest below that level. The old text books rather cruelly and arbitrarily classify those below 70 as feeble-minded, with more precise sub-distinction into morons with IQs between 50 and 70, imbeciles between 25 and 50, and idiots below 25. The moron is considered able to learn useful tasks and adjust under supervision; the imbecile has to live in an institution but can care for simple personal wants and avoid simple dangers, while the idiot cannot even do this. These denigrating names have now been deleted in favour of less hurtful terms, such as subnormal and severely subnormal. In any case, mental deficiency in its legal aspects is only perfunctorily related to intelligence, with much more comprehensive criteria applied before classifying. This is just as well, as some people in hospitals for the subnormal have proved exceptions and been found to have IQs as high as 125.

Because our mental age remains more or less a constant after fifteen, while the chronological age increases, the same ratio system cannot be applied in calculating an IQ for adults. So instead of using a set form of intelligence test, the average number of correct answers or mean response for the group is identified as an IQ of 100, and the other scores are related to this average. Clearly this can only be accurate in wider terms if all the separate groups are random, comparable and reasonably large. But within the group itself it seems to work. For instance, among the battery of tests given to candidates for pilot selection and officer training, intelligence test results correlate particularly well with later success in gaining commissions. Scores of 140 IQ or over on the Army General Classification Test used in the United States during the last war were followed by 90 per cent success. Of those with scores under 110, only 50 per cent received commissions.

Happily there are always plenty of people who defy the norms, disprove the rules, make nonsense of examination results. Life would be all the more dull without them. Winston Churchill is perhaps the best-known example of someone who was hopeless at school, but he went on to succeed as a brilliant war correspondent, politician, wartime leader and later as an outstanding author and historian. Yet his Latin examination paper for Harrow contained nothing but the figure one in brackets, two smudges and a blot!

Churchill was accepted by the headmaster of Harrow only because he could not believe Lord Randolph's son could really be so stupid. Winston did little, however, to justify his faith in hereditary intelligence, remaining throughout his Harrow days perpetually at the bottom of the class, with his one and only prize awarded for his recital of 1,200 lines of Macaulay's 'Lays of Ancient Rome'. But as soon as his interest was fired and motivation came into the picture, everything changed. He galloped away into the Boer War to file riveting, colourful copy as a war correspondent; in politics he became the outstanding orator of our age, and later an inspired and inspiring leader when Britain was fighting for her life against Hitler. If it could be argued none of these achievements are necessarily linked with intellect, at least the same cannot be said of his books including his unique *History of the English Speaking Peoples*.

History bristles with similar examples. Sir Isaac Newton for a long time was bottom of the lowest form at Grantham Grammar School. Jean de la Fontaine was described as a 'hopeless dunce' and so was Clive of India. Oliver Goldsmith according to his masters was a 'stupid heavy blockhead, little better than a fool', Jonathan Swift was 'dull and inefficient'. Sheridan's parents wrote him off as 'a most impenetrable dunce', Balzac's teachers reported him 'in a state of intellectual coma'. This latter comment may well be the true answer to many of the cases of apparent late development. In some it was just boredom with the subjects they were forced to study and it seems equally to apply to others succeeding after a bad start in various spheres.

Johann Heinrich Pestalozzi, later to give his name to revolutionary methods of teaching which put the emphasis on motivation, as a schoolboy was himself poor at writing, bad at spelling and with no head for arithmetic. His teachers predicted he would be a failure and his fellow pupils nicknamed him 'Harry Queer of Foolstown', not it should be emphasised with the modern connotation of 'queer' in mind, but simply because he was very odd and awkward.

Lord Alfred Tennyson, due to become Poet Laureate in later years, is reputed not to have spoken a single word of any sort by the age of four and then it was only sharp physical pain and shock which got him talking. It seems his devoted Nanny accidentally splashed the little boy with very hot water. While she was distractedly running round striving to soothe him and find salve at the same time, she was stopped in her tracks by hearing what must surely be the most amazing first utterance of all time – 'The pain has now abated,' young Alfred announced, 'you may desist from your efforts.'

Dr Alexander Murray, the son of a shepherd near Kirkcudbright, was thought by his father to be stupid and lazy, incapable even of driving the sheep and cattle home and quite unworthy of formal education at all. His father taught him the alphabet and that was all. Yet by the age of fifteen the boy had taught himself Latin, Greek, French and Hebrew. Soon after, he was reading Caesar, Ovid and Livy, and after leaving home went on to master German, Anglo-Saxon, Abyssinian, Visigothic, Welsh and all the European languages. He researched the strange dialects of the East, becoming at thirty the most accomplished linguist of his age and at thirty-six Professor of Oriental Lanaguages in Edinburgh.

Successful women too defied early verdicts on them. Beatrice Webb was described by her mother as 'the only one of my children who is below the general level of intelligence' and Margaret Murray, to become a famous Egyptologist and one of the first woman dons, wrote, 'I never got through any examination in my life until I took the full doctorate.'

Scientists seem to have been particularly poor at school. Apart from Newton already mentioned, James Watt was described as 'dull and inept', and Darwin admitted, 'I was considered by all my masters and by my father as a very ordinary boy, rather below the common standard of intellect'. Edison was always bottom of his class and his father thought him stupid. After hearing one of his teachers describe his mind as 'addled', Edison left school and refused to return. Taught by his mother, who would not accept their verdict, he soon showed his real talent. Einstein was called by his teacher 'Herr Langwill', translated as 'Mr Dullard'. Roentgen, who discovered X-rays, was not a bright pupil and had nothing to point to future genius except an aptitude for mechanical contrivances. It is interesting that in our own time, Dr Godfrey Hounsfield – joint winner of the 1979 Nobel Prize for medicine, awarded for his Head and Body Scanner with its rotating source of X-rays and crystal receptors revolutionising diagnostic medicine – was also totally undistinguished at school, where he was only interested in and any good at mathematics. But in practical matters it was different and there his potential genius showed – at five he understood the principles of the steam engine, at six he had mastered the petrol engine, while at ten he was taking motor bikes apart and more importantly putting them together again in working order. Despite all the doctorates and fellowships showered upon him later, including Fellow of the Royal Society in the steps of Newton and Faraday, Hounsfield never went to university and his only formal training was in radar and electronics at RAF Cranwell.

In their fascinating book *Lessons From Childhood*, from which many of these examples are drawn, R. S. and C. M. Illingworth, both experts in child health at the University of Sheffield, conclude that lack of success at school and in examinations may be due to slow maturation or misjudgement by teachers in the face of their pupil's disinterest in the syllabus. Sometimes it can also result from physical or sensory defects such as poor vision or hearing or difficulties with reading, which can give the impression of mental slowness. They list Berzelius, Darwin, Faraday, Fresnel, Newton and Gladstone among the slow starters.

They also emphasise that a poor home can retard progress. As well as material and intellectual poverty this can include emotional poverty, in the sense of insecurity, unhappiness, friction and general lack of love.

The real reason in most cases for early under-achieving is seen by them as lack of interest in the subjects taught, with success coming only when strong motivation breaks down previous apathy and innate ability surfaces under the spur of real desire to learn, create and achieve.

The child who is a dreamer such as Hans Andersen or Einstein may also appear infuriatingly dull; children totally absorbed in their special interests such as da Vinci in nature or Marconi in mechanical matters will neglect all other subjects. The great weakness, perhaps, of our present educational straitjacket is that it makes too few concessions to the single-minded student exceptionally gifted in just one direction.

How far training, environment and a more flexible education can extend mental ability also depends on how far this is rooted in environment and how far in heredity; how much intelligence is innate and how much acquired.

There is no doubt that children tend to follow their parents to a great extent, not just in physical characteristics but in mental traits such as intelligence or exceptional mathematical or musical talent. These can still be due to or at least be enhanced by the shared environment, reflecting the parents' intelligence and interests.

Where IQs are taken for groups of parents in various social strata and compared with groups of children from the same social strata, it is interesting to find there is similarity but also a tendency for regression towards the average. The fact that this regression works for some physical as well as mental traits confirms a strong hereditary factor applying to both. The children of very tall parents, for instance, are taller than average but not on the whole as tall as their parents. Children of short parents are shorter than average but again not as short as their parents. It is the same with IQs. The children of bright parents are not quite as bright on the whole and the children of dull parents not quite as dull.

The best way of determining the relative influence of heredity and environment is through studies of identical twins. Coming from one egg these have the same genes and womb environment and usually the same upbringing. In such cases the IQs tend to be very close together although seldom exactly alike. The difference between them averages little more than 5 points as compared to ordinary twins where the difference averages 8·5 points, and ordinary siblings where it can be as much as 10 to 14 points.

However, if identical twins are reared apart the difference in IQs tends to be greater but still less than for ordinary twins or siblings reared together. Not surprisingly the brain-wave patterns of identical twins are also shown by electroencephalograph to be almost the same.

The influence of environment can be seen even more strongly in final achievement than in IQs. This was shown very much with a pair of identical twins, sons of an Oxford tutor who died just before they were born. The mother was able to keep one child and gave the other for adoption. The twin, George, who remained with his mother had a brilliant academic career. One day a former teacher seeing a man he thought was George called out a greeting, only to be answered in a strong uncultured Welsh accent. In this way, totally by chance, the twin brother was discovered. Reared by his adoptive parents on an isolated farm in Wales, he was backward in reading and verbal performance, but his IQ on testing was found to be 137, as good as that of his educated twin.

In a deliberate study of identical twin girls, two Yale experts (the late Dr Arnold Gesell and Dr Helen Thompson) tried giving one of the three-and-a-half-year-old girls intensive special training for a long period. But when this ceased, the advance she had shown also ceased and before long their performance had levelled out to be much the same.

Perhaps the experiment with intensive stimulation of one of the pair of identical twins should have been carried out for a longer period. At any rate there is growing support in the US, Canada and more recently in Europe for the notion that the difference between an exceptionally bright child and an ordinary child may just lie in the amount of time and effort parents put into teaching and stimulating the baby from a very young age.

One couple using such methods certainly achieved their aim. Soon after their daughter was born, Aaron Stern, a New York scientist, called a press conference at the Brooklyn hospital, showed reporters the child and affirmed he was going to make her a genius.

After that he and his wife set out quite deliberately to stimulate the baby every waking moment, talking incessantly to her and always providing a background of classical music. There was no baby talk, and letters and number cards were her constant companions. Despite a period of rebellion when the child was old enough to realise she was not having a childhood like other children around her, they persevered and by the age of six she was reading two books and a newspaper daily. By fifteen she was already taking her degree at Michigan State University and teaching mathematics at the same time. The final outcome was an IQ of 200 (50 points over genius level) and a woman who became a brilliant teacher herself, publicly declaring she could never thank her parents enough for all their efforts.

It is a convincing success story on the one level. Aaron Stern proved that his forcing-house system, at least with the right subject, could produce early mental development and full final growth. But there is more to life than learning, and relationships are as important as the three 'R's. So judgement must be reserved until Miss Stern's life is seen as a whole. Has such concentration on mental growth stunted emotional growth? If not and she proves to be essentially a whole and happy person, able to relate to others and give out love as well as lessons, then there may be valuable guidelines for parents with sufficient motivation and time to want to foster young genius in this way.

American twin studies have yielded some fascinating cases, such as Millan and George, identical twins born in Salt Lake City and separated almost immediately after birth to be brought up by foster parents of different types under quite different conditions. When they came together again at the age of nineteen, they were found to be alike not only in looks but also in temperament, intelligence and achievement. Both had won amateur boxing championships, both had artistic talent, one at music and the other in drawing. Sadly at a later date while serving in the Army but far apart, both developed simultaneously, though perhaps not unexpectedly, the same hereditary disease of the spine, ankylosing spondylitis.

Louise and Lola were identical twins, but brought up by different foster parents and bearing different surnames. Reunited as young women of eighteen through a chance meeting at Baylor University, Texas, where both again by chance happened to be studying, their amazing similarity made them instantly recognisable to each other. Even after years of separation, testing showed closely matching IQs, common artistic ability and similar personality traits.

Another significant case was that of two male identical twins, given the names of Tony Milasi and Roger Brooks, after their separation as babies and adoption in one case by an Italian couple living in New York State and in the other by a Jewish couple in Florida. They only found out about each other through another case of mistaken identity, meeting up once more at the age of twenty-three. Tests done then by Dr Sybil Marquit of Miami showed that the two men, reared in such different cultures, still had nearly the same IQs and basic aptitudes.

Ability in mathematics, science and music seem particularly strongly inherited. Families like the Huxleys and Darwins still produce outstanding scientists, and in music there are many examples such as the Strauss's and Menuhin's. Of Toscanini's three children, only Wanda inherited her father's musical talent, but when she married another musician, Vladimir Horowitz, bringing two sets of musical genes together, their child displayed musical talent as early as three and a half and by sixteen was a talented pianist.

What is the conclusion on the relative influence of nature and nurture. Different environments clearly have some influence and where siblings or twins are reared apart then variations in IQ appear to be the greatest. The general conclusion based on a whole array of such studies is that where mental ability and traits are concerned, heredity accounts for about four-fifths and environment about one-fifth. As we can have no say in choosing our parents, any hopes of improving our mental capacity and achievement must lie in environmental factors, motivation and within limits some benefit from training.

This is particularly true where memory is concerned. This is clearly an important constituent of most forms of exceptional mental ability or achievement and is certainly involved in what to most of us appears an almost uncanny gift – the ability to make lightning mental calculations.

The norm for short-term memory, usually estimated by ability to remember a random sequence of single numbers read out at a rate of one per second, is 7 items in the mid-teens. This is about 1·5 items lower than for university students. After the age of thirty this memory span begins to decline, but still only drops to about 6 items in the mid-fifties. There is strong correlation between above-average short recall in above-average intellectual ability, and very low recall in subnormal people. Adults can increase short memory span to some extent by practice and by the trick of breaking down the digits into groups. Fatigue, distractions, alcohol and even smoking have been found to diminish recall.

The genius calculators, people able to pluck square roots apparently out of the air or add, multiply or divide long sequences of numbers in their heads, rely both on good short-term memory and an acquired knowledge of numerical facts, short-cut methods and what might almost be described as calculating tricks. A simple example would be that to multiply anything by 25, the short cut is to first multiply by 100 and then divide by 4. The sort of numerical language needed for rapid mental calculation is quite different from that taught in school and this explains why the talent can often be possessed by people who have not had much schooling or did not particularly shine in the little they had. George Park Bidder, for example, was a calculating genius who later became a distinguished engineer. At six he could neither read nor write, did not understand written numbers, yet he could do complicated calculations, even though the term multiply had to be explained to him as 'something times something'.

Professor Alexander Craig Aitken, who died in 1967, is often cited as the greatest ever genius in mental calculation, in his case combined with outstanding intellect and an amazing capacity for memory of all kinds. He could not only recall a vast array of facts about numbers, calculative methods and mathematical short cuts, but play the violin recalling most of the music by heart, quote extensively from English literature and recite tracts of Latin and English verse. He could also recall details of events he had witnessed so accurately that committees consulted him as an unofficial minute book.

Ian Hunter, head of the Psychology Department at the University of Keele and the leading expert on memory in this country, was a great friend and admirer of Aitken and made a special study of him. In the *British Journal of Psychology* in 1977 he analysed Aitken's own words of an experience in the trenches in July 1916. Under bombardment Aitken was obviously still registering the conversation around him and could summon up memory so accurately that when he heard a discussion about a missing roll-book urgently required by Platoon 10 (his own platoon), he was able to conjure up a mental picture of it and dictate all the details of full names, regimental numbers and the rest of the information needed.

One of his pupils remembers Aitken amusing them in class by demonstrating how he could associate line numbers in Virgil with the words in the line or conversely recite the words in any line a boy might specify. As a young teacher, a single reading of the names and initials of a new class of thirty-five boys enabled him never to need to consult the lists again.

This amazing ability, however, does not amount to total recall, which Professor Hunter insists is a mythical concept.

> If we really could recall absolutely everything we had ever experienced, such an ability would be impossible to support and would end in madness. We have to be able to be selective. Even as it is, the increasingly crowded mass of information stored by the time we are older adversely affects our ability to learn and remember. It is rather like trying to retrieve a book from a very large library. It is obviously much simpler and quicker from a smaller one. Instant recall is easier for the young. And it is particularly noticeable with mathematical type questions that students with less information packed into their mental libraries can retrieve what they do know far more readily. On the television programme 'Ask The Family', for instance, with this type of question it is always the boy or girl of fourteen or fifteen who comes up with the answer first rather than their parents. With the young the little they know they know very well.

Both Professor Hunter and Professor Aitken were convinced that motivation and interest in a subject are the vital spur to memory even in people with high ability. Of Aitken, Hunter writes:

> The ease with which he learned and remembered anything, and indeed whether he learnt and remembered it at all, depended squarely on the meaning and interest it had for him. Thus, whenever something interested him deeply, he was typically able later to recall many details of it despite his having had not the slightest conscious intention of committing anything to memory. Again, if he were given material that for him had little meaning (say, a random string of digits) he typically pronounced it 'uninteresting' or even 'repellent'. If asked to commit such material to memory, he might oblige if he thought some psychological value might emerge from the exercise, but usually remarked that the exercise was 'unnatural' and 'went against the grain'.

One of Aitken's subterfuges in his memory feats was not concentration, as normally understood, but relaxation and 'assimilation by interest'.

Although Aitken had something approaching photographic memory, judging from his account of summoning up an image of the missing roll-book, in his words as if it were 'floating' before him, there is no evidence of this form of memory being totally accurate. In his Pelican paperback, simply called *Memory*, Professor Hunter states:

> What approximates most closely to the popular notion of 'photographic memory' is a remarkable form of visual imaging which has been estimated to occur in something like 1 to 10 per cent of the adult population and 50 to 60 per cent of children under the age of twelve years.
>
> This image is never localised within the head as ordinary memory images so often are, but is outside the person projected onto a wall or some other surface. If the surface is folded or bent, the picture appears folded or bent, but is so strong that it tends to obscure the background otherwise. It is something like a negative after-image, but whereas that occurs only after prolonged gazing at a relatively simple object, the memory image occurs after letting the eyes rove over complex detail for only a short time and can be revived at will often hours, weeks or even months later.

Details from such images, according to Ian Hunter, can include even the number of buttons on the jacket of a passer-by, the number of whiskers on a cat's lip, and even in some experiments done with British children quite unable to speak or understand German, they could still see with what approximates presumably to the 'mind's eye' and therefore remember most of the letters from German wording written above the door of an inn. With this form of memory, properly termed 'eidetic', there is a tendency to omit uninteresting detail and occasional distortion so that it cannot be described as truly photographic.

Some mental-calculating experts use a similar power of visual imagery in exercising their amazing skills. One such was Salo Finkelstein, a Polish genius in this field. He was even hired by an American broadcasting company to tally the returns of the 1932 Presidential election because he was faster than any of the calculating machines of the time. He saw his numbers as if written with chalk on a freshly washed blackboard and always in his own handwriting, regardless of how they had been presented.

Like other forms of memory, it seems that ability for visual imaging declines in most people sharply after about eleven, the age which Professor Hunter believes marks the point at which what we call 'logical' thinking emerges. Only a few exceptional individuals seem able to retain the ability into adult life. The Russian, Shereshevski, was one, and carefully controlled tests established he could recall lists of a hundred or more digits, words, nonsense syllables, words in unknown languages, lengthy formulae, musical motifs, and repeat sequences of items either in the given order or in reverse. What is more, he could recall these lists years later as though he was reliving or re-seeing the original event and re-reading the material rather than reproducing it. A. R. Luria, the distinguished Russian psychologist who tested him, described Shereshevski as acting 'as though the list was present in front of him'.

Apart from these famous and authenticated cases of real Memory Men there are the music-hall versions, justified in terms of entertainment but usually relying on ingenious forms of conjuring tricks to simulate apparently miraculous memory feats. We can learn little from them, but from the real memory experts we can borrow mnemonic systems involving visual imagery or word association. The successive comparison depends on vivid relationship between successive words, relating the first word to the second, the second to the third and so on. The important thing is that at no point is it necessary to be concerned with more than two words – each relationship works in pairs.

Visual imagery can be applied even to numbers by some people. A Cambridge man, Henry Herdson, as far back as the mid-seventeenth century employed images of the numbers themselves – 1 was a candle or any elongated object, 2 a swan, 3 a trident, 4 a dice or some object with four parts, 5 a hand or some object with five parts, 6 a tobacco pipe, 7 an open razor, 8 spectacles and so on. Much depends on whether your mind works visually or verbally, and to both authors of this book such a system would lead to utter confusion!

There seems no question that undertaking learning enables us to learn *how* to learn. Memorising itself does not necessarily improve ability to memorise. What it may do is enable you to discover the best ways for *you* to memorise things; what tricks and short cuts you can best employ.

Rhymes are one old memory aid and most of us have used the familiar jingles of childhood to help us remember the number of days in the month or the order of succession of British kings. In other parts of the world they use other methods. Knuckle counting is used in Greece, Finland, Russia, China, Tibet and most of South America, using knuckles and hollows for long and short months for instance.

This type of tally principle is ancient and is reflected in the use of notched sticks to keep track of events. In fact the word tally comes from the Latin *talea* meaning a rod or stick. For centuries the English treasury used notched sticks to keep official records of state finances.

Australian aborigines also used what were called message sticks, pieces of wood bearing incised markings. Most of the message would be in the head of the carrier, but the message stick acted as a guide to recall.

Ancient Peruvians used pieces of string in which knots were tied for similar purpose, while prayer beads of the Mohammedans and rosary beads of the Roman Catholics also employ the tally principle. In Africa the rhythm of the drums serves as a mnemonic aid, since words and phrases can be transported into the drum code in all languages, and it is easier to remember the rhythms than the phrases or tonal melodies. The history of the royal house of Dagomba and that of the Akon States have been largely preserved by drum code.

Special remembrancers, called Griots, have been used down the ages to remember and pass on history orally in cultures where no written language was in use. Certain individuals were charged with remembering certain sections and for teaching their individual successors.

Written language obviously offered a gigantic step forward in the storing and retrieving of knowledge, but new memory aids and storage methods are being added all the time. The more complicated our world and the more there is to know, the more we need such help in both learning and remembering. Professor Hunter, discussing this with us, made the point that human ingenuity would always come to the rescue of human physical or mental limitations, inventing aids which at least enable the brain's own incredible computer to be used more efficiently. 'Just as we have used inventions and aids for the senses, as with spectacles, microscopes and hearing aids,' he pointed out, 'and compensated limited muscle power with power tools and fork lift trucks, so for the mind we have employed language, writing, lists and moved from the simple abacus to modern computers.'

In addition today we have tape recorders, microfilm and massive television and film archives so that there is a verbal and visual library on which to draw for total and accurate storage of information and events. In the future history will not be a matter of recall but of replay.

Regarding the much-advertised memory training courses, Professor Hunter had reservations about their value.

> They don't actually defy the Trades Description Act and they do show you how to go about learning and memorising some kinds of material using imagery and linking. In general the more you study anything the more links you find and the easier it is to hold it and recall it. My own feeling is that where they go wrong is that they reinforce the idea that the only kind of memory you need is to be able to recall disconnected items – the shopping list kind of operation. Nearly all the exercises are of this meaningless kind. I wouldn't recommend people to spend money on them.

Disconnected learning can be the most difficult. In plays, for instance, where there is meaning, characterisation, interaction and continuity in the dialogue, many actors never need to sit down and learn their parts word by word. They absorb the lines by a sort of verbal osmosis through interest in the action and in their role.

Inability to recall on the spot or remember the immediate past is very much a feature of ageing. In contrast events from the more distant past become increasingly vivid as current and recent facts fail to imprint in the memory. It is as though the early input was absorbed deeply into the fresh clean surface, which later became so heavily scored with messages that in old age there was neither room nor ability to absorb left. A more accurate analogy perhaps is the contrast between open clear telephone lines receiving and transmitting messages, and heavily used lines with no open circuits left to allow further messages through.

There is the story of a famous Indian Chief, renowned for his exceptional memory. After a group of investigators had questioned him for hours, one joker suddenly asked him what he had had for breakfast that morning and the Chief replied, 'Eggs'. Chancing on the same Chief some forty years later, the same questioner gave the proverbial Indian greeting 'How!' The Chief replied 'Scrambled'. Maybe if he had asked the now old Indian what he had had for breakfast that morning, he would not have remembered.

Hunter recalls an old lady taken to revisit the village where she had been born. Asked next day about the place, the old lady vouched she could remember it just as if she had seen it yesterday. Indeed she had but didn't remember the fact at all, though she gave a vivid account of the village as it had been in her childhood days.

Memory and intelligence are, of course, only two of the functions of the brain and both are involved in thinking. We think only because we receive input from the senses, which we act upon after processing the data through the brain's computer. Obviously some brains' computers appear to function better than others, given the same input: but do we all have the same input? Our senses seem complete enough to enable us to survive in our environment, with our unique ability to think logically, and to communicate ideas through language and actions. Yet are they complete?

For none of our senses – at least those we are conscious of – explain such phenomena as extrasensory perception (ESP), the apparent control of one mind over another in hypnosis, or the mind-over-matter control which allows Indian fakirs to walk over red-hot stones and yoga adepts to control their heart rates and blood pressure. Have we other senses whose messages reach the subconscious levels of our brain, and upon whose reception we act, unknowingly? There is plenty of evidence that other so-called 'lower' animals have.

The radar of bats is one example. They can detect and avoid cotton threads hanging in totally darkened rooms. The explanation, of course, is that a bat's mechanism for producing sound and interpreting its reflections are infinitely better than our own. Although hardly believable in its complexity, and in the speed with which the bat can take avoiding action, the mechanism is understandable in human terms. The nerve pathways and the specialised brain cells which control the bat's acrobatic skills have been mapped and understood by biologists. They differ only in some details, but not in principle, from many of the mechanisms in our own brains, and can hardly be called a mystery. And just to prove that they are fallible, it has been known for bats to collide with each other in flight! Blind persons, in fact, do appear to 'switch on' to a form of echo location which enables them to avoid obstacles. The tapping of a blind man's stick is not just to feel the obstacles in front of him but to create an echo the shape of which serves as a warning. For the same reason the blind often whistle quietly. The success of the system depends, of course, on good hearing.

It is less easy to explain the ability of animals in the wild to 'home in' on breeding grounds or to travel along migratory routes often never before seen by those individuals. Young swallows from Western Europe, for example, fly for the first time to Africa, much of the journey by night, weeks after the last of their experienced fellows have gone. Pacific seals return year after year across 6,000 miles without landmarks to the human eye, to reach the same small, featureless islands. A flock of birds will turn and wheel as one, with no hint of a sign from a leader. Tales of dogs and cats journeying miles to former homes after family removals abound.

None of this applies to humans. Let an average Briton loose in the countryside and ask him to set off in the correct direction for home and he wouldn't know how to start. And as for the other abilities of animals, such as the vital one of recognising which foods are valuable and which are likely to poison them, our high death rates from the over-eating diseases and our consumption of tobacco and alcohol prove conclusively that this is another area in which we are a poor second to the animal kingdom. It is only when stressed by overcrowding or competition, for example, that cats will choose to drink alcohol-laced milk in preference to the usual stuff. This may say much about the human condition today.

There is no hard evidence, therefore, that we humans possess a special power of the brain, whether it be called a sense or an intellect, outside those provided by the recognised senses. Such evidence abounds in the rest of the animal kingdom. The homing and migratory senses of birds, for example, are almost certainly guided by a collection of cells in the brain which respond to minute changes in the strength and direction of the earth's magnetic lines of force. Cover a pigeon's eyes with an opaque filter which not only blurs its vision but prevents it navigating by the direction of the sun, and it will still fly home. Leave it free to see, but place small magnets on either side of its head, and it will be completely lost.

Humans feel nothing when exposed to radioactivity. If they did, perhaps the stars of the John Wayne film made in the Utah desert shortly after the bomb tests in the 1950s would still be alive now, instead of dead from various cancers. Yet, with hindsight, they could have known, when crawling around the radioactive desert sands, that something was seriously wrong, from the snails. Snails react to radioactivity by drawing in their horns. Rats, apparently, can smell it, and don't like what they smell.

Like pigeons, worms and snails respond to magnetic fields, and there are microscopic single-celled creatures that line up in parallel rows at right angles to the lines of force.

Most remarkable of all, perhaps, is the possibility of inheriting the memories of others by eating them. It is said to be one of the reasons for the old New Guinea custom of eating the brains of one's recently deceased relatives. Of course no one in the sciences believes that such a transference is possible – in humans. They have to accept it in lower life forms, however. For the humble flatworm, planaria, is said to remember the painful and pleasurable stimuli heaped on one of its colleagues, and react accordingly, after it has eaten the unfortunate colleague, minced.

These examples have often been used to support and explain ESP, hypnosis and the 'feedback' success of the yogi and fakirs. It is suggested that they are all rather crude remnants of functions of the brain which with civilisation became dormant while the part which controlled reasoning became dominant.

Human ESP, some say, is only a very limited and inadequate expression of the vast mental communication so obvious in the flock behaviour of birds. The perception by animals of radiations of which we are totally unaware leads ESP buffs to believe that 'thought waves' may, whatever they are, be transmitted and perceived in the same way. If we could unlock the door and open up our present very limited experience what a difference this would make! Once expert in ESP we could cheerfully disconnect our telephones. Think of the saving at today's prices.

At least one set of twins believes it can be done. Dr Louis Keith of Northwestern University School of Medicine in Evanston, Illinois, is an expert on twins. He is also one himself, and his twin brother, Lieutenant Colonel Donald Keith, a retired US Army officer, is currently executive director of the Center for the Study of Multiple Gestation.

Both men are convinced from the many cases they have studied that telepathy often takes place between twins. In a limited way they demonstrate this themselves. Louis finds himself under strong compulsion every now and again to ring his brother, only to find that Donald has been positively willing him to do so.

While this is obviously a useful way for Donald to save on phone bills, they would prefer to be able to use what they recognise as a far more important form of telepathy – shared thoughts. Even this skill, however, cannot be harnessed at will, but it does emerge from many documented cases. Ruth and Nancy Grover, for instance, were identical twins who both went to school in New York. When they came to take external examinations where they could choose to write on any one of six topics, Dr Sarah Roody their invigilator found that they had not only chosen the same topic but written word for word the very same story – yet they were seated in opposite corners of the room.

Tim and Greg Hildebrant, who executed the art work for the film, *Star Wars*, found a similar matching of minds on the job. Painting together and working side by side, one or other would occasionally stop work to take a rest or even a sleep, leaving the other to carry on. On waking the results never offended, worried or even surprised either of them. 'It's like magic,' Greg admitted. 'When Tim paints, it's as if I'm painting.'

The real question is why twins who can exhibit such powers on occasions cannot use them when they want to do so. Aldous Huxley in *The Doors of Perception* suggested that the brain is a kind of 'reducing valve', with its main function to screen incoming messages and admit only those of importance, so maybe a similar screen only allows conscious telepathy where unusual or dangerous events are concerned. One such case occurred with identical twins, Mary Brooks and Selina Strong. Mary was undergoing surgery when Selina suddenly seemed to see her twin and distinctly heard her say 'Liney, I'm leaving now.' Not unnaturally, Selina thought at first the worst had happened and Mary had died on the operating table. But she survived, though medical records showed that her heart had stopped at 2.30 for a short period and she had been rescusitated. That was the time Mary had received the message.

Operative pain itself can also be shared according to Tel Wolfner in *Parallels – A Look At Twins*. There he describes how one young twin was found rolling on the floor in agony when the family came to tell her that her sister had been taken into hospital with appendicitis. Later in the waiting room at the hospital, the same girl claimed to know exactly when surgery started and when it finished, reacting to perhaps a form of sympathetic shock.

In his studies Dr Keith records a twin who suddenly felt her body enveloped in intense heat and pain, later finding that at precisely the same moment her twin sister died in a fire as two jets collided on the ground in the Canary Islands.

The problem with ESP is that it has never, as far as we know, been proven scientifically. That is, proclaimed experts in ESP have not shown under strictly controlled conditions that they can accurately transmit thoughts to others in a different place, at will. More than that, so many who have claimed extra-sensory powers have been exposed as frauds.

The claims of Uri Geller for his 'telepathy' and ability to bend metal from a distance were exposed when he was a stage illusionist in Israel, before he left to pass his 'message' to the world.

Typical of a Geller trick was his experience reported in *Psychic* magazine in June 1973. He described an 'out–of–body' experience, when he successfully transported himself to Brazil on the request of a colleague and psychic researcher Andrija Puharich. Finding himself in a city, he was told by a passer-by that he was in Rio de Janeiro. He then, remarkably was pressed by a man to accept a brand-new 1,000-cruzeiro note to prove his 'journey'. On his re-awakening on the couch in America this note was found in his hand.

If true, the story is conclusive. However, a São Paulo resident, G. L. Playfair, was – to say the least – doubtful about it. For a start, no 1,000-cruzeiro notes were being used in Brazil in 1973, as they had been withdrawn or overprinted with higher values in 1967. Puharich replied by giving the note's serial number to Playfair, who, on checking, found that it was one of a batch of notes printed in April 1963 – it was therefore very unlikely to appear new in the streets of Rio in 1973.

Playfair followed the story farther. As the finger-prints of every Brazilian are recorded, and prints are easily recognised from new notes, he asked for permission to 'dust' the note. If Geller's story were true it might well be an easy matter to trace the generous (very generous by Rio standards) person who had donated the note. Despite repeated requests, neither Puharich nor *Psychic* communicated further with Playfair.

Playfair gave his account of the affair in a letter to the *New Scientist* on 14 November 1974; he left readers to draw their own conclusions. It may be of interest to add further facts. Puharich was in Brazil in 1963, when a 1,000-cruzeiro note could be bought for 50 American cents. Secondly, Puharich subsequently wrote a book praising Geller, a book which did not mention the note story.

One apparent fraud does not mean that all ESP practitioners are tricksters, but it makes it imperative that the others are investigated thoroughly. We believe that this means they should willingly submit to scientific trials and controls. Unhappily few do so, and even fewer, when they do, can reproduce what they claim to be able to do without such scrutiny.

Attempts have been made to prove telepathy for many years by J. B. Rhine, who invented in the 1930s a set of *Zener* cards. The pack, similar in size to playing cards, comprises twenty-five cards in five sets of symbols; a cross, a square, a circle, a star and three wavy lines. Each person reveals a card in turn and tries to project the symbol mentally to the recipient in another room. The average score is five correct out of the twenty-five. People who claim telepathic powers do not guess the cards, nor do they 'project' them any more than 'non-telepathic' subjects. In the almost fifty years since the tests were started only two people have scored twenty-five out of twenty-five, and no one has been able to repeat high scores regularly.

Telepathists discount such tests as irrelevant, saying that ESP is related to human feelings and emotions, and not to the boredom or lifelessness of Rhine's cards. That is as may be, but it still proves impossible to check their ESP claims without resorting in the end to the sort of faith that, say, a chemist, physicist or biologist would reject without independent evidence. At times the pressure to produce results has led the most respectable researcher to falsify the records of tests similar to Rhine's. It happened in 1974 to Dr W. J. Levy, of the Institute of Parapsychology; his fraud was exposed by others, and his reputation lost (See J. B. Rhine, 'A New Case of Experimenter Unreliability' – *Journal of Parapsychology*, 1974, Vol 38).

One man who has ripped away much of the trickery surrounding ESP, yet who still believes in its existence, is Stan Gooch, a professional psychologist who has himself experienced, apparently quite by accident, telepathic messages. His first was at a lecture by Marcel Vogel, who is not only a devout Catholic and a senior chemist at IBM, California, but a powerful 'psychic'. Gooch described what happened in his book *The Paranormal*. About ten minutes after the start of the lecture, Vogel announced that he was going to try to transfer an image telepathically to the audience.

Gooch determined not to 'receive' the message as he knew of no one who could produce results to order, yet he 'saw' in his mind's eye a triangle, which was first blue, then changed to red. Fifty people in the audience raised their hands when asked if they had perceived an image. Gooch did not bother to raise his. When he heard that Vogel had started to project a yellow triangle in a circle, then changed it to a red triangle, Gooch 'almost literally fell off his seat'.

There are no other concrete examples of telepathy in Gooch's detailed study of the paranormal, but he cites many cases of apparent telepathy in animals, including mice which could apparently find ways of evading shocks delivered to them in a random pattern and timing; rats whose behaviour changed when chosen for sacrifice, and goldfish which became more active in their bowls when their owners decided to lift them out of the water. The most remarkable story was that of Mrs Brenda Marshall, who decided with her husband to spare a cockroach's life. Thereafter, the cockroach would climb up the arm of her husband's chair, to sit there throughout the evenings.

There are many stories of animals 'homing' after their abandonment many miles away, or after families have moved. They can be explained by the same direction-finding power as pigeons appear to use. But how does one explain the successful search of an animal for its master hundreds of miles away from home? Prince, an Irish terrier, somehow travelled across the Channel in World War I to reach his master in the front line. There have been reports of animals which have brought their young out of a building which soon afterwards caught fire. Are these forms of extra-sensory perception?

If so, how do they link with the amazing brain of Emanuel Swedenborg, the eighteenth-century Swedish man of science and a philosopher? One Saturday afternoon in 1759, Swedenborg was at a party in Göteborg on the west coast of Sweden, when he became shocked and pale. He announced to the party that a serious fire had broken out in Stockholm (on the other side of the country), that a friend's house had burned down, and his own was threatened. Two hours later he cheered up. He knew that the fire had halted three houses from his own.

Swedenborg was so sure of his facts, and the populace trusted him so much that the governor of Göteborg demanded a full report from him – which he gave in detail. The news from Stockholm, confirming in every detail what he had 'seen', did not arrive until the Monday morning. The fire had started and finished exactly when he sensed it.

This story has come down to us from Immanuel Kant who never met Swedenborg. If it is true, then our puny efforts to prove telepathy by today's scientific methods are failing not because ESP does not exist, but because we have no real means yet to measure it.

Gooch believes that ESP does exist, but probably is stronger the longer the distance between 'transmitter' and 'receiver'. We are programmed, he says, to have ESP powers, using the part of the brain we call the cerebellum. The programme, however, is not for today's stage in our development. ESP, Gooch believes, will be the main means of communication, instantaneous and faster than light, when man reaches space. It will be interesting when the first telepath arrives on the surface of the moon!

It is fair to say that orthodox doctors and scientists do not hold with Gooch's views. We prefer to keep an open mind: after all, nearly every great advancer of medical or scientific thinking has had to fight orthodoxy, and usually against savage and bitter opposition.

Although there seems little scientific basis and even less scientific evidence for what we term telepathy or ESP, it may be that the very circumstances and controls necessary for proper test conditions, in some way affect or nullify powers which anecdotal material suggests emanate from the subconscious usually in a quite arbitrary fashion.

There is certainly a wealth of testimony, at least some of which cannot be dismissed, that some people have strange precognitive experience. The cynics among us may mutter about coincidence or argue that all the best prophecies are perceived only in retrospect, but the fact remains these things do happen and are recounted. They often take the form of precognitive dreams, which would be flimsy evidence indeed if they were only reported later after the events they foretold had taken place. Often these dreams are so vivid that the dreamer recounts them at the time and to more than one witness, so that there is corroborative testimony later when, to everyone's amazement, the dream comes true and the factor of prevision is recognised.

Our incredulous minds, so conditioned in a scientific and technological age only to accept the logical and explicable, will find some such stories difficult to credit, but at least they have to be seriously considered when they involve people of known integrity. Such a man was Abraham Lincoln, who on at least two occasions had precognitive dreams, both well documented. The first was a dream in which he correctly foresaw the imminent victory of Union troops and the surrender of the Confederate General, Robert E. Lee. If the cynics argue that wishful thinking and coincidence together might be enough to explain that dream, at least they cannot explain the other and far more disconcerting dream he reported very graphically ten days before his death. He told people that in a dream he had heard the sound of sobbing, and wandered from room to room in the White House. All were empty until he came to the East Room, where he saw his own body lying in state in a coffin. He was told by one of the soldiers standing ceremonial guard that the President had been killed by an assassin.

It is interesting to wonder that if Lincoln's gift of precognition had extended to details of the actual murder, whether he would have been able to avoid his fate. There have been instances of a prevision of the future seeming to change events. The Hon. J. Cannon Middleton was booked on the *Titanic* for her maiden voyage. With no reason for apprehension about sailing on what was considered then 'the safest ship afloat', he still dreamed on two successive nights about a week before the sailing that he saw the ship sinking and people struggling in the water. Two nights running would seem to eliminate the usual possibility of mere coincidence and clearly this cautious gentleman thought so too. He hastily invoked business reasons to postpone his departure and the decision may well have saved his life. As everyone knows, the *Titanic* was sunk on that very first voyage with the loss of 1,500 passengers and crew.

An even more striking example of precognition allowing successful intervention to avoid tragedy was recorded by Dr Louisa E. Rhine in the *American Journal of Parapsychology*. She recounted how when her son was only a little boy she had dreamed the family were camping on the shores of an inlet. In her dream she left the child happily throwing handfuls of pebbles into the water while she went back to the tent to get some soap to wash out some clothes. When she got back the boy was lying face down in the water and when she pulled him out he was dead. At that point she woke sobbing, with the agony turning to joy as she realised it was only a dream and her child was safe. Eventually the dream was forgotten. Later that summer she was camping again on a shore with friends and sitting happily talking to them on the beach while they watched the children play. Suddenly she decided to do some washing and picked her son up carrying him back to the creek and putting him down by the water. As she went back towards the tent to get some soap she suddenly saw the child throwing pebbles into the water and in that instant the whole dream flooded back. In her own words:

> It was like a moving picture. He stood just as he had in my dream – white dress, yellow curls, shining sun. For a moment I almost collapsed. Then I caught him up and went back to the beach and my friends. When I composed myself I told them about it. They just laughed and said I imagined it. That is such a simple answer when one cannot give a good explanation. I am not given to imagining wild things.

If Dr Rhine really saw the future in her dream, it was a future she was able to change by her recall and reaction. Another instance of precognition which allowed useful action was recalled by Sir Stephen King-Hall, the well-known and highly respected British writer and broadcaster. This was a vivid premonition in broad daylight when he was wide awake, and indeed had to be for he was officer of the watch on the *Southampton*, steaming towards Scapa Flow. Ahead of him he could see a small island about a mile distant. Quite suddenly he knew without any shadow of doubt that as they passed the island a man would fall overboard. The feeling grew so strong as they got nearer the island that he gave orders to put out the lifebelts and muster the sea boat crew. Not surprisingly these were challenged by the Commodore who in strong naval vernacular demanded to know what the hell he thought he was doing! As the poor junior officer struggled for any sort of explanation which would not make him seem totally mad, the cry went up 'man overboard'. It came not from his own ship but from the *Nottingham*, the next ship in line, and thirty seconds later also from the *Birmingham*, third in line, both times exactly as the ships came abreast of the island. 'We went full speed astern,' Sir Stephen recalled, 'our sea boat was in the water almost at once and we picked up both men. I was then able to explain to a startled bridge why I had behaved as I had done.'

Commander Stephen King-Hall, as he was to become, recounted this story for a contribution by another well-known British writer, J. B. Priestley, to the book *Man and Time*. Priestley recorded this and many other examples of precognition and ESP, examining them and testing them both for authenticity and for their relationship to his own unconventional views on 'time', in which he conceives of what might be termed 'time slips' or to use the sci-fi jargon, 'time warps', in which some people for no apparent reason suddenly tune in, as it were, to a different time, usually in the future. His careful analysis of hundreds of cases reported to him following a BBC television programme he did on the subject in the very sober 'Monitor' series, allowed him to conclude that although a few premonitions allow action to be taken to avoid catastrophe, these are few and such previsions rarely concern the useful middle-ground of our lives to help solve practical problems. Most are concerned with the terrible or the trivial, the one usually unavoidable and the other usually unimportant. One exception was the case of a medical photographer who after moving into a new building and ordering a lot of new equipment found two large developing tanks were completely missing. After searching everywhere he presumed they had been stolen. One night soon afterwards he dreamed that he visited one of the new rooms, still not in general use but where various items were stored. In his dream he found a cupboard labelled FJA 39 and in it found the missing tanks.

Later on the next day he remembered the dream and looking through the key box found one labelled FJA 39. He also found the cupboard and the tanks – the same grey colour as the shelves, they had been missed first time round.

It would be extremely useful if precognition or ESP could be initiated at will, but it seems entirely arbitrary, which suggests little hope of expanding this particular potential. For just a few people, the psychic revelation of past events on demand appears to be possible. Almost every day, newspapers record instances of psychic powers used in this way to aid criminal investigations. One such recent case in Nevada involved a psychic, Kay Rhea, who correctly advised the police that the body of a murdered girl would be found in a shallow grave in one specific spot beside the highway outside Reno.

Although officialdom does not accept the evidence of psychics in court, it is often happy to act on such information. In this case it led to the murderer, John Mavaan, being convicted and sentenced to death.

Initial belief in ESP grew largely from the work on 'magnetism' by the Marquis de Puységur, a retired French doctor, in 1784, coincidentally the year that his mentor, Mesmer, was driven out of France by an official Commission of Investigation into 'Mesmerism' and 'Animal Magnetism'. Puységur's patients, who were in what is now known as hypnotic trance states, were claimed to be able to read papers held behind them, and to perform other tricks similar to those exhibited more recently by Uri Geller and other stage magicians. Hypnotised subjects are certainly particularly open to suggestion, and their ESP abilities may only have been due to a heightened sensitivity to the movement and actions of the people around them. In fact, Puységur's claims cannot be repeated under modern hypnosis: close investigation of claims of thought reading under hypnosis has never confirmed them.

If Mesmer's invention did nothing for ESP, it certainly established hypnosis as a reality. His theory was wrong, but his practice could not be faulted. In 1766, when he was thirty-two, he established 'animal magnetism' as the basis on which he built his treatments. He capitalised on a much older idea that the human body was in some way dependent on magnetic forces. Mesmer's disciples and patients believed that some curative fluid magnetic impulse flowed from the great man into them.

Naturally this upset the medical establishment in Vienna, where he first practised – very successfully, then later in Paris. He worked for the rest of his life in Constance in Germany, but his influence there was so great that a professorship of Mesmerism was set at Berlin University.

Mesmer's effects were spectacular; cure, he thought, lay in the production of convulsions, and the highly emotionally charged atmosphere in which he conducted his multiple treatments, mostly in women, ensured that in most cases he succeeded. He also succeeded in convincing the Commissioners of the French Royal Society of Medicine that the practice might cause habitual convulsions in some patients and lay suggestible women open to sexual 'outrages'. The damage, they said, might even be transmitted to future generations and affect public morality. References to orgasmic reactions in women and the similarity to the cases of 'demonic possession' in nuns in convents reinforced their feelings. Two of the eight signatories of the report were Benjamin Franklin and Lavoisier, the chemist who discovered oxygen and was later to die on the guillotine.

Trance states were not a part of Mesmer's treatment, but they were central to Puységur's. He sat patients on stone benches round a 'magnetised' tree. They held hands, closed their eyes, and submitted themselves to Puységur's 'magnetic force' for up to four hours. Only Puységur could waken them from this state, of which they later remembered nothing. Even at this early stage in what was later to be termed hypnosis, the warning signs were recognised. Puységur stressed that only the 'magnetiser' should touch the patient, and recognised that the patient, in his or her extremely suggestible state, could become extremely dependent on him. Freud, a century later, re-discovered the phenomenon, and called it 'transference'.

By 1913, mesmerists recognised that the one essential for successful hypnosis was the subject's complete faith in the 'magnetiser'. It was not magnetism that produced the results, but the willingness of the subject to put himself totally under the control of another. The world 'hypnotism' was coined in 1843 by Dr James Braid, but it was not until the turn of the century that doctors practising it became respectable.

Now, hypnosis is an accepted form of treatment – but not for the severely mentally ill. Ordinary, psychologically normal people are the best hypnotic subjects: few psychiatric illnesses respond to hypnosis. The technique is used as an aid to pain relief, as in dental surgery or childbirth, or perhaps to discover the underlying cause of the symptoms of stress. In the first case hypnosis is used to suppress the normal pathways of pain in the nervous system, in the second to lift the suppression of painful, or stressful memories. Deep trance states are not necessary for the first; the patient remembers everything, and is conscious and co-operative, but feels no pain. They are essential for the second. During trance the subject remembers, indeed relives, long-forgotten episodes from the past, then, when reawakened, forgets them again. Stage hypnotists often take adults back to a birthday in childhood, when they delight, or embarrass, depending on taste, the audience with the exhibition of a child, in an adult's body, going through the joys and sadness of presents and tantrums of many years before.

Such shows only scratch the surface of the real meaning of hypnosis. Every detail of every minute of our lives is recorded, as if on tape, within the brain. Almost all of it is hidden beyond conscious recall, and can only be brought to the surface by techniques such as hypnosis, in which all inhibition of brain function is removed.

The authors were recently involved in the case of a middle-aged man who all his adult life had suffered attacks of choking, mainly at night, and so severe that he tore at his throat, making it bleed, and provoking vomiting. There was no known physical cure, and the clue to its psychological basis lay in the fact that this distressing symptom could threaten in any enclosed space such as an aircraft or lift. As a highly successful businessman who had to travel widely, the condition was intolerable and growing worse with age.

He sought the help of a medically qualified hypnotist, who after several sessions regressed him to childhood, during which he relived an agonising choking attack of croup, and in doing so was greatly reassured by the hypnotist! His adult problems, which had clearly stemmed from this forgotten childhood illness, have not returned in the twelve months since the treatment.

Some drugs, such as the anaesthetic Pentothal, have similar inhibition-releasing effects, although their reputation as 'truth drugs' has been grossly exaggerated. Their sedative effects are more likely to produce a garbled confusion than any recognisable 'truth'. More effective in tapping into the brain's memory tape is surgery.

Patients may undergo brain surgery under local anaesthesia. This is not so horrific as it sounds, and is often absolutely essential if such problems as tumours, blood clots, or convulsion-producing scars are to be isolated and removed. The procedure sometimes, of necessity, involves electrical stimulation of the grey matter on the surface of the brain and the reaction depends on the stimulation site. It can give rise to movement of a limb, or the sensation of smell or hearing, or it may switch in to the 'memory tape'. On the table the patient begins to relive some past event, just as he might when hypnotised.

The possibilities, of course, are enormous. Given the correct trigger, it may eventually be possible to have total voluntary recall of everything which we have experienced in life. The value of this to our knowledge and experience, if we could use it all without going crazy, is immeasurable. However, there is a drawback. Once out of the hypnotic trance, or freed from the influence of the drugs or the direct electrical stimulation, the experience is totally forgotten.

There is almost certainly good reason for this. If we were able to bring everything to our conscious recall we would be confused into a state beyond sanity. It would be impossible to sort out the relevant from the irrelevant in order to make decisions or judgements. With a brain flooded with a mass of memories and experiences would come insanity. Indeed it could be argued that this is precisely what has happened in patients suffering from mania, once one of the most difficult psychiatric diseases to treat, and now usually quite satisfactorily controlled by modern suppressant drugs. The dividing line between genius and madness may well be as narrow as popularly supposed. The difference between them may only be in the ability of the conscious brain to control its relationship with the subconscious memory bank.

Hypnotists can only awaken the subconscious by first making the subject very much more submissive and open to suggestion, and then to lead him the way the hypnotist wishes him to go. Although few of us in our lives are taken into the deep trance state, there are plenty of people willing and eager to take all of us some way along that line. Political or religious leaders use the same tricks to whip up enthusiasm for their causes – and when the two are combined in one person the result has always been catastrophic. The first stage is a willingness to believe, to subjugate one's will and reason to that of the leader: the second is the suspension of logical thought, to be replaced by complete acceptance of what under normal circumstances would appear ludicrous. There is no real difference in the persuasive powers of Hitler and Mussolini, of the Moonies and the Jones suicide cult, of Amin, Pol Pot or the Ayatollah Khomeini. It is not confined to the rabble-rousers or the evangelists: pop entertainers are powerful manipulators of the mass mind, and so, to some extent, are advertisers. It may not be called hypnosis, but their methods are designed to manipulate our minds and reactions.

William Sargant, until recently physician in charge of the psychological medicine department in London's St Thomas's Hospital, takes this much further. When we let others manipulate the control of the mind, whether under hypnosis, or under the emotional sway of one of these manipulators, he believes the limits we set upon our minds are stretched, and even broken. We go beyond the bounds of normal reason, and act in a way which may be interpreted as heroism by some, or as idiocy by others.

The screaming of teenagers at pop concerts, the raging of students at besieged embassies, the whole nightmare of mob mentality, the sudden conversion of people to religions, the 'possession' of bodies by devils or gods, or of soldiers rushing, careless of the danger to themselves, against the enemy, are all examples, says Sargant, of this sort of release from inhibition. The influence is insidious and dangerous even to those who would be expected, by their position, to be immune. Father Surin, a Jesuit priest who was called in to exorcise the devils thought to be possessing the nuns of Loudun in 1635, eventually became himself possessed. He felt two spirits within him, fighting one against the other.

They prevented him saying Mass or feeding himself, made him forget his sins before confession, and diverted him from his prayers. Through the mouth of one nun the devil in him boasted that Father Surin was under his domination. Small wonder that the poor priest became severely depressed for twenty years thereafter, recovering enough to write his account of the possessed nuns and his own ordeal only as an old man. He remained a devout Jesuit and a believer in demoniac possession – his own and the nuns – until his death. Even in his day, however, there were thinkers who knew better, but in the religious climate of the time could only speak out anonymously.

One still unknown pamphleteer of that time wrote the following of the nuns:

> Granted that there is no cheat in the matter, does it follow that the nuns were possessed? May it not be that in their folly and mistaken imagination, they believe themselves to be possessed, when in fact they are not? It may happen in three ways. First, as a result of faith, watchings and meditations on hell and Satan. Second, in consequence of some remark made by their confessor – something which makes them think they are tempted by devils. And, thirdly, the confessor, seeing them act strangely, may imagine in his ignorance that they are possessed or bewitched, and may afterwards persuade them of the fact by the influence he exercises over their mind.

Aldous Huxley, who made a special study of the Loudun nuns, was certain that their disastrous affliction was due to the last cause, and had been produced and fostered by the very physicians who were supposed to be restoring the patients to health.

It is not a great jump from such examples to the conversion of St Paul or the effect of the preaching of John Wesley or Billy Graham on their audiences – or congregations, depending on one's point of view. But how does this relate to yoga or the antics of oriental fakirs?

Simply, they are all manifestations of the same process of release from inhibition of the mind – or brain, again depending on one's viewpoint. Except that in these cases, the subject releases himself or herself from the inhibiting forces. Whether this is a good or bad thing is not for argument here, but that it happens is undoubted.

The basis of yoga is that the mind, if completely dedicated to the task, can control all the bodily functions. The simplest of its aims is to help one to relax both body and mind. Some of the claims made by its devotees may be excessive, and the advantages of some of the poses which are struck by adepts are obscure, to say the least, but there is no doubt as to the physical effects it can have. Yogis can, and frequently do, lower their blood pressures and pulse rates merely by thinking about them in an abstract way. The technique has been adapted in medicine, mainly in the United States, to help people control high blood pressure without drugs. Indeed it has gone much further.

No one can have any idea of the pattern of the electrical currents produced in his own brain and traced by electroencephalograph pens on a recording paper. The waves have been classified by doctors into several groups, depending on their frequency, which appear relatively more or less often when the emotions change, or the eyes open, or under the influence of drugs. Epilepsy and brain tumours are some of the conditions which can be diagnosed from their pattern. Nevertheless they are very crude representations of what really goes on inside the brain, telling us no more about it than the naked eye can tell us about the complexities of the universe.

Nevertheless, subjects experienced in 'feedback' exercises can alter the pattern and frequency of these waves at will, even though no one is conscious of producing them, and no one understands where or how they are produced! It appears that we can control the deeper mechanisms in our body, just by thinking about them in an abstract way, and with no conscious understanding of how we do it.

It is probable that the 'feedback' mechanism touches on the same brain areas as hypnosis. In 1959, L. F. Chapman, H. Goodell and H. G. Wolff performed experiments on thirteen good hypnotic subjects. Under hypnosis, the subjects were told that one arm was either 'normal' or 'anaesthetic', 'numb' or 'wooden' and devoid of any sensation. The other, it was suggested, was 'painful', 'burning', 'damaged' and exceedingly sensitive or 'vulnerable'. Then it was suggested to the subjects that the arms were going to be injured. A standard painful stimulation was then delivered in turn to the arms, and the reactions judged by photography. To avoid bias, the experiment was repeated several times in each subject on different days, switching the suggestions for the arms each time.

In almost every case, the so-called 'vulnerable' arms became much more influenced than arms declared normal. Even more interesting, the arms the subjects believed were anaesthetised or without feeling did not react to the burn even with the normal reaction.

The only conclusion that can be drawn is that the brain not only controls the reception of pain, but may also be persuaded to control the reaction of the body to damaging stimulations or at least to the one stimulus used in the Chapman experiments, heat. It certainly explains the ability of the African and Indian showmen to walk on hot stones without apparently burning themselves. They first attune their minds into a self-hypnotic state, force their bodies to ignore the danger, and make sure they walk on before the burning heat breaks through the mental barrier they have created.

René Cutforth, the British broadcaster, war correspondent and author, has actually seen this. He told us, 'There's no possibility of deception. They can clearly not only block pain signals but somehow the normal physical responses. Their feet show no sign of burning. The answer lies in their faces and eyes – they are totally blank and withdrawn, indicating a trance-like state which ordinary nerve signals cannot penetrate.' The wonder of the fire-walkers is not that they can do what they do, but that the scientists have not found the way to progress beyond this relatively simple ability to push beyond these limits of our powers of mind over matter. At last, this whole area of man's mental power over his physical state is taken more seriously by researchers.

They have before them daily in medical practice two striking examples of the power of the mind to influence the ill effects of disease. The first is the 'physician effect' – the benefit a patient gains from confidence in the doctor himself. The second is the 'placebo effect' – the benefit gained, including actual elimination of symptoms, from a substance which the patient (and at times the doctor) erroneously believes to be an active drug. The old bottles of coloured tonics beloved of generations of patients and doctors were really only placebos.

Everyone has had experience of the placebo effect, if only because a headache has disappeared within five minutes of taking an aspirin, when in fact the drug cannot act within twenty. The placebo story is an amazing one – yellow capsules work better, for example, than grey tablets. Drug trials comparing placebo and active drugs have shown initial benefit from the placebo in 30 per cent of all patients; in some disorders, in up to 70 per cent.

The placebo effect does not last, because it does not alter the progress of the disease. It has been successful for thousands of years because patients become better, coincidentally, despite the treatment. Nevertheless it clearly demonstrates the ability of the mind when strongly motivated to exercise its powers beyond the normal limits. How far they will lead us along the path to complete mental control over every symptom of illness is impossible to guess. Meanwhile the power of mind and of mental attitudes in influencing sensitivity to pain and affecting endurance and even survival are being constantly demonstrated.

7

Pain, Tolerance and Resistance

It cannot have been pleasant to have a leg blown off by grapeshot in the middle of a battle. The shock from loss of blood, the agonising pain of torn muscles and splintered bone, the realisation that a major part of one's body was gone for ever would surely put the soldier at extreme peril of his life. Yet, when it happened to one of Wellington's aides in the heat of the Battle of Waterloo, all he said was: 'I say, my damn leg's gorn' – and rode on into the fray.

Perhaps his behaviour was a little extreme, but similar reactions to severe injury in such conditions are not uncommon. This sort of incident was confirmed many times over by René Cutforth, who experienced battle in Spain and Abyssinia in the 1930s, fought in the desert in World War II, and covered the Korean, Congo and Algerian conflicts.

The essential ingredient for bravery and heroism, and for tolerance to pain which under other circumstances would be overwhelming was excitement. And that excitement was born out of fear. To be a hero, says Cutforth, you need to be frightened. In battle, men, though deeply fearful, set out not to show themselves as cowards: the excitement of the moment helps them tolerate the intolerable and cancels out fear.

One Battle of Britain Hurricane pilot said: 'Success in the game is the great incentive to subdue fear. Once you've shot down two or three the effect is terrific and you'll go on till you're killed. It's love of the sport rather than sense of duty that makes you go on.'

Cutforth told us of an Indian soldier in the Eighth Army who walked through desert minefields ahead of the British tanks for sixteen hours. In that time he was blown over by one mine, but struggled up to carry on. The second blast stopped him by blowing his foot off, yet he didn't complain. He thoroughly deserved his subsequent decoration.

Mr Cutforth, who was no mean boxer in his youth, sees boxing and battle as similar:

> In the excitement of the fight or battle, pain is often not felt as pain at all. A boxer reacts to it with a slowing down and weakening, but only later when the fight is over will it really register as pain, and then more severely if he has lost. Some old boxers are almost impervious to pain,

and so are some good soldiers in the heat of battle. But it's not deliberate bravery. Your VC is rarely the sort of *Boys' Own* hero positively welcoming risks and suffering in the great cause. He's more often a man who is sensitive enough to be very afraid, but uses that fear to provide the spur to action. Fear and physical action together can blank out his immediate reaction to pain, but later in the field dressing station when the action is over, then he is an ordinary suffering mortal like the others.

These 'ordinary suffering mortals' in the field dressing stations were not, however, so ordinary. H. K. Beecher, an army surgeon in World War II was astounded to discover that only 1 in 3 of the soldiers severely wounded in battle required morphine for their pain. Most denied having pain, or said they had so little that they needed no pain killers. As they were not in shock, the lack of pain could not be explained by nervous-system failure. Indeed they could still feel inflicted pain, as they complained as much as any other people when the doctor bungled a vein puncture for blood sampling!

After the war Beecher questioned a number of ordinary civilian hospital patients immediately after surgery had left them with wounds like those of his soldier patients. This time 4 out of five were in such severe pain that they asked for morphine.

Beecher's experiences (*Measurement of Subjective Responses*, Oxford University Press, 1959, p.165) convinced him that there was no simple, direct relationship between the wound itself and the pain experienced. He wrote:

> The pain is in very large part determined by other factors, and the significance of the wound is of great importance. In the wounded soldier the response to injury was relief, thankfulness for his escape alive from the battlefield, even euphoria, at a wound which would send him home. To the civilian his major surgery was a depressing, calamitous event!

This effect of emotion on pain is surely recognised by everyone who has visited a dentist. The toothache which keeps us awake all night often disappears in the dentist's waiting room the next morning. In a minor way, facing the dentist's chair may well resemble the excitement of battle!

The appreciation of pain can be altered by emotions in the other direction. Anxiety in the face of an expected pain increases its intensity. In 1945 K. R. L. Hall and D. I. B. Kerr showed that, just by adding the word 'pain' to a set of instructions relating to an experiment in healthy but anxious volunteers, electric shocks previously regarded as innocuous became painful. Other experiments have shown that dispelling anxiety in volunteers exposed to shocks or burning heat stopped the complaints of pain.

The part emotion plays in pain perception is clearly shown in ethnic differences. R. A. Sternbach and B. Tursky showed in 1965 that, regardless of cultural background, the sensitivity of the nerves to non-painful sensations upon the skin is the same. They subjected housewives of Italian, Jewish, Irish and longstanding American stock to increasing small electric shocks. The strength at which they became perceptible was the same for them all. As the shocks increased in strength the women of Italian descent were the first to call a halt. The Jewish and 'Old American' women held out considerably longer.

Such differences derive almost certainly from cultural variations in attitudes to pain instilled from early childhood. Italians, perhaps, are more vocal in their complaints and less disciplined as children, whereas the 'Old Americans', with their strong puritan ethos, suffer more in silence. Whether they feel as much, but just complain less is a matter of dispute. There is strong evidence of geographical differences in pain perception. In 1952 J. D. Hardy, H. G. Wolff and H. Goodell (*Pain Sensations and Reactions*, Williams and Wilkins), subjected a series of women volunteers to different intensities of heat. Strangely, levels of heat described as 'warm' but not unpleasant by women from Northern Europe were 'painful' in women from the Mediterranean. The latter included both Italians and Israelis, whose characters are popularly supposed to be poles apart.

It appears, therefore, that people differ not necessarily in their reception of pain, but in how their brains interpret it. This interpretation varies according to their previous mental and social conditioning, and to the state of their emotions and expectations at the time. The woman looking forward to childbirth suffers less than the one who is anxious and fearful. The patient who thinks, rightly or wrongly, that he is recovering from illness can bear pain better than the pessimist.

Pain can even, apparently, be transferred from one person to another. The anthropologist A. L. Kroeber described in 1948 various cultures in which pregnant women work in the fields until their babies are born. Meanwhile their husbands lie down and groan, as if in labour. When their ordeal is particularly severe, the exhausted men rest in bed with the baby, recovering, while their wives return to their farming duties. Women in our culture may suspect that the father's pain is more imaginary than real, and no more than an excuse for a day or two in bed!

The worst pain of all must be that deliberately inflicted by one human being on another. Corporal punishment, torture and execution have, sadly, been prominent throughout our history. Ian Donald, Emeritus Professor of Midwifery at Glasgow University, was no stranger to having pain inflicted on him by his fellow surgeons, after three heart operations in the 1960s and 1970s, the last two being complicated valve replacements. Professor Donald described his experience as a patient to his fellow doctors in two prominent medical journals.

> There are many things that make pain worse, such as the spirit in which it is inflicted. This makes a great difference to a patient's acceptance or struggling against it. It makes a difference to know that everyone is supporting you. It is also a help to know something about what you are in for, because the operation does not then come as quite such a surprise as my first operation, when I had not foreseen how disagreeable thoractomy (opening the chest) can be – far worse than laparotomy (opening the abdomen).
>
> The absence of sympathy from attendants whether it be in the form of silence, reticence, off-handedness or even frank callousness, must make torture or capital punishment for the criminal on his way to the gallows a particularly ugly and painful experience.

This was well recognised in the days of public executions, when it was commonplace for the relatives of the condemned to bribe the executioners to ensure a quick death. Those being tied to the stake would be grateful to be strangled unobtrusively before the flame was lit, and when on the scaffold take what little comfort they could from the person in the pit below paid to pull on their legs.

For some, however, to die for a cause appears to have been the ultimate in satisfaction rather than pain. Heretics burning in the Middle Ages, are described as dying with looks of pleasure and passion on their faces, as they went with absolute certainty to meet their God. Bishop Hugh Latimer's last words to his fellow Protestant on the way to the stake in 1555 make emotional reading even today. 'Be of good comfort, Master Ridley,' he said, 'and play the man. We shall this day light such a candle by God's grace in England as I trust shall never be put out.' By contemporary accounts their faiths pulled them through their horrifying final ordeal.

Odette Hallowes, to use her present name, was also sustained by faith during her ordeal of capture, torture and imprisonment by the enemy during World War II. A Frenchwoman and a Catholic, she was married to an Englishman and already living in England with her three little daughters when the war started. She described herself then (as she still does now when you talk to her) as just an 'ordinary' woman. But under the spur of intense patriotism she was to prove a very 'extraordinary' one.

The seeds of her motivation had been sown early. She explained:

> I was brought up in Picardy near the old battlefields of the First War and my own father had been killed at Verdun just thirty days before the Armistice in 1918. I remember as a child going each week to his grave and being taught that freedom was something you had to be prepared to fight for and if necessary to die for.

Odette had come to love her adopted country of England, but after the fall of France she felt increasingly ashamed to be living there in relative safety while the French people and her own family were suffering the horrors of the Occupation.

It was an urgent request from London for anyone having pictures of certain parts of the French coast that first took Odette to British Intelligence. The pictures were useful but someone decided Odette might be even more so. She was French born and they sensed in her extraordinary qualities of strength and purpose. After the usual security checks, she was asked if she would consider joining the French Section and working as a secret agent in occupied France.

It was a greal deal to ask of the mother of three young children.

> I went through four months agony trying to decide,' Odette confessed, 'I really wanted to keep out of it. I dreaded leaving my children and I also doubted if I was up to the job. But in the end I decided I must at least do the training. Really I was convinced I would fail and end up doing some nice safe translating job.'

Odette did not fail then or later. By the time she had finished training and passed her course she knew she must agree to go to France. She admitted:

> I'd learned a great deal by then. How desperately French-speaking agents were needed, how terrible the conditions were in France, how vital it was to get support to the resistance movement and to get information back to England. I'd also learned the dangers. I knew that I'd probably not see my children again. I accepted then that death would be the likely outcome. Once you have accepted death, you accept everything else.

Everything else for Odette was capture, torture, solitary confinement and finally the extermination camp of Auschwitz, all the time under sentence of death which could be carried out at any time.

Somehow this 'ordinary' woman found the strength not merely to endure but to fight back, never submitting and never breaking even when one toenail after another was dragged out in an attempt to make her reveal details about her work. In addition to her faith and her patriotism, Odette now also had love to sustain her, and throughout all interrogations she sought to protect Captain Peter Churchill, captured with her, the man with whom she had worked so closely and whom she was later to marry.

Kept in appalling conditions of cold and damp which led to serious TB, Odette continued to defy survival odds. With no medical attention and on only starvation rations, she typically chose to remember one Belgian doctor's theory that tuberculosis could be cured by starvation.

> I thought at least I was in the right place for that treatment, and maybe it worked because at least I didn't die. Also in those years I developed a special way of escaping out of my body and out of suffering. I found I could summon a sort of grey screen in front of me and then by hard concentration I could project onto it pictures of my children, people or places I loved, or re–run happy scenes from the past. I would do that for hours at a time.

By this method and by having a certain time each day when she and Peter Churchill had agreed to direct their thoughts towards each other, Odette used the power of the human mind and spirit to triumph over physical misery and restraint. Her body was imprisoned and ill-treated; her mind remained free and unscarred. She told us:

> After my release doctors who examined me were amazed that I suffered no nightmares or breakdown. I never have since though I am often ill in my body. But then I use the lesson I learned. I abandon my body, remove my mind from it so that that does not get sick – and the enemy goes away.

The monopoly of such striking resistance to fear and pain is not held by Christians, with their certainty of eternal salvation. Thomas Henry Huxley, the contemporary of Charles Darwin, and the first self-styled 'agnostic', was able, when dying in pain, to bid his family 'farewell, for ever' without complaint.

Kitty Hart was just one of the millions of Jews persecuted, captured, tortured, beaten and held in Nazi death camps. But Kitty didn't die and recently her film *Return to Auschwitz* had tremendous impact on British television, showing her revisiting the scene of her suffering with her doctor son.

It seemed important to us for this chapter and this whole book to know how Kitty and her mother had survived and what Kitty felt was the secret of bearing pain and indeed the secret of survival. She herself had received 25 strokes with a leather whip made up of 25 thongs, 625 lashes in all. No amount of time could dim such memories, and the return there only a short time before we talked to her had in some ways perhaps sharpened them.

Kitty recalled:

> The only way to endure pain was to try and pretend it wasn't happening to you – not being inflicted on *your* body. I had already been toughened by those years on the run from August 1939, lived with terror, starvation and hardship, and after capture known what it was like to be put against a wall and told I was going to be shot. So for my mother and I, being herded into Auschwitz in April 1943 was just going from bad to worse. For those who were sent to the camps straight from home and a degree of comfort and civilisation, the trauma was too great, the contrast too appalling and extreme. Often they were physically strong, nothing wrong with them, but within two days they were often dead from the sheer shock of the conditions.
>
> But we were in a sense acclimatised and also we had each other – not often able to be physically close but giving moral support and sometimes even practical help. My mother was wonderful and not just to me. She worked in the camp hospital block, if you could call it that – with no drugs, no dressings, no bedding and no attempt at treatment. All my mother could do was strive to give people the will to live, to survive another hour, another day. This was another of the secrets – not to look back or look forward – just to get through each moment of each day.
>
> You could always recognise those who had given up – their eyes were vacant – they made no effort to get food, the very basis for survival. Sometimes my mother could give them the will to live as she gave it to me. But there was a point beyond which this process, not of physical but of personal disintegration, could not be reversed. Even if you gave them food they didn't eat it. The Germans themselves recognised these people and for some obscure reason called them the *Mussulmans*; we all knew they would die – already they were the walking dead.

To survive at all you had to take risks. Survival depended on getting food, on somehow getting extra clothing, on having something you could trade for access to water, and above all to secure shelter and somewhere to sleep.

Every extra layer of clothing gave you a better chance of survival. We were only issued with one layer and once in winter even this was taken from us for de-lousing. We were three days with no clothes, completely naked. People were shivering and moaning with cold but I remember telling myself 'It isn't happening to you. You are not cold. You are not cold – it is not your body that is frozen' – it was a form of self-hypnosis.

So those who survived were those who could do this and also who could take the calculated risk for the extra bit of bread, the extra layer of clothing. I smuggled all sorts of things through the main gates – you died if you were caught, but then you died if you didn't do it. I smuggled in bits of bread, once a whole tin of meat held somehow between my legs as I shuffled through. My beating was simply for breaking curfew to try and find some bits of wood for the small stove, the one bit of heating in our hut. I was caught in a searchlight and chased by an SS woman, who fortunately did not carry a gun or I would have been shot on sight. I gave her the slip and managed to run back to my hut but she followed me and reported it all. We were told we would all be sent to the gas chambers if the one who had been out after curfew didn't own up. Collective punishment and collective death was commonplace. So I had to own up and maybe because I did so quickly I got off lightly by their standards – just that 25 lashes with the 25-thonged whip. I remember again telling myself that this was not happening to me. I wouldn't let myself believe it was my body. At the end I was unconscious and just left lying outside in pools of water in the penal compound. My mother saved my life. She couldn't get to me but she knew about my beating and she arranged for someone to pick me up and get me into shelter.

Of course the weals were open and many were infected; most wounds became infected but we never really saw our injuries because we never undressed. If you dared to take off your clothes and put them down, they would have disappeared. It was the same with bread. If you had an extra bit you hid it in your filthy clothing, because there was nowhere else to hide it and if you put it down someone took it.

You had to trade your way with precious bread or clothing to get access to the one tap that had to serve hundreds in any compound. The dirt, the smell, living and sleeping in excrement, these were the things that newcomers to the camp could not stomach. But we learned to live with filth and with terror. If disease didn't get you, if you could still walk and work, then there was a chance that Mengele might point his baton the right way – that you might be allowed to live a little longer.

It was all a question of determination and motivation. Determination not to be brainwashed, to break the rules, do the opposite to what was expected but without being caught. Above all to learn to become invisible and develop a sixth sense for danger, anticipate it – be like an animal, like a fox, able to sniff it out. You needed to be alert to everything that was going on – to anything unusual – any strange happening, any unusual commotion – they could all mean danger, then you needed to take avoiding action. But you had to take positive action too – always the driving need to somehow get hold of something to trade, even by stealing, so that you could buy somewhere to sleep or somewhere to hide. It was the most determined, really I suppose the most selfish who came through, and the great motivation apart from your own survival was to live long enough to see justice done. For this, someone had to tell the world what had happened.

Kitty Hart lived and so did her mother, both liberated by the Americans. Her one obsession was to kill a German to get revenge for all her companions who had died. Yet strangely when she had the chance, when she had a knife in her hand and with other escaped concentration-camp victims had a German family cowering in front of her, holed up in the cellar where they had been hiding, she found she could not after all use it. As she put it: 'I suddenly knew there had been enough killing, that these people were as frightened and helpless as we had been only a few hours previously. Above all I saw the terror in the children's eyes.'

Kitty Hart and her mother eventually escaped from the cause of their pain and torment, but there are many who have to live with constant pain due to disease or injury, and some whose pain comes both as physical agony and mental anguish.

This particularly applies to disfiguring injuries and burns, and one group of men in particular became famous for their ability to endure and survive. These were Sir Archibald McIndoe's so-called Guinea Pigs, pilots and aircrew, mostly from the Battle of Britain, young men whose dreadful injuries – in particular, burns – he treated at this special unit at East Grinstead.

Looking at their individual stories, many of which are recounted in the book *McIndoe's Army*, two factors apart from mere courage seem to be involved in the long but usually successful process of recovery and rehabilitation. These were comradeship and motivation. The Guinea Pigs were, and still are, a club. They sustained and supported each other throughout the periods of intense pain, inward despair and desperate embarrassment when with reconstructed bodies and faces they forced themselves out again into the world. Pity or commiseration was not part of their vocabulary or their thinking.

Bertram Owen Smith, today a plastic surgeon himself working on the black and white wounded in Rhodesia, uses the understanding he gained as one of McIndoe's patients to help others. As he puts it:

> It's what goes on inside a man's head that matters more than anything else. Very early on, while he's still grieving over what's happened to him, he's got to make a decision. Is he going to make the best of things, in other words is he going to utilise to the full what remains? Or is he going through the rest of his life bemoaning what has happened to him, becoming a burden to himself and to all whom he meets?

Owen Smith was only eighteen when he had to kick out a window to emerge in flames from his burning aircraft. He had two pieces of luck. He was wearing gloves which helped to save his hands and by chance he ran in the right direction, past the tail of the aircraft and straight into a river, where the water put out the flames and the bank protected him from the explosion when the crashed Whitley blew up. But his burns were appalling and there were to be twenty-six operations on his face and hands in the years that followed.

What sustained him during that time apart from the comradeship he found, was a growing interest in the complexities of the surgery being used on him. Soon he let it be known he wanted to be a doctor. No one really believed it would ever be possible. Before joining the RAF at seventeen there had been only a brief time to fill in and that was spent in an insurance office; not even the routine school-leaving examinations had been taken. All the same he was supplied with books and encouragement because it was recognised that here was the motivation needed for recovery.

In the end he proved them all wrong. He matriculated, qualified as a doctor, became a Fellow of the Royal College of Surgeons and returned to East Grinstead, where McIndoe encouraged him to specialise in plastic surgery.

Face-saving for McIndoe meant far more than just saving the exterior physical face – it meant saving self-respect and creating self-sufficiency.

Jimmy Wright, another of the group, was at the start of a career in films before he joined the RAF as an aerial photographer and film cameraman. His plane crash left him blinded and it took McIndoe four years of extensive plastic surgery to rebuild his face and eyelids. He never regained his sight though seven attempts were made to give him a new cornea in the left eye. Each time there were complications. In all he endured between seventy and eighty operations and while he waited between each one he learned braille. Determination, hope each time of regaining sight, and again comradeship helped him through the pain and despair. 'Sharing was very largely the driving force,' he explained. 'One always met someone who was that much worse off and perhaps in more pain than oneself and this was the reason why everyone just pressed on. You simply couldn't give up . . .'

When he finally left hospital in 1951 Jimmy Wright was given the chance to join a small film production company just starting up. It meant he had to learn a completely new job, no longer behind the camera but behind the organisation of film making. His drive, determination and excellent memory combined with a good braille filing system and braille shorthand machine mean that today he is a highly successful producer of both commercial and documentary films. A blind film producer would seem impossible, but not for Jimmy Wright remembering Sir Archibald McIndoe's maxim for instilling vital confidence in his Guinea Pigs – 'Nothing is impossible,' he used to tell them, 'it simply takes just a little longer.'

If motivation was always vital it was also almost always different. For many it was just to get back to flying. In the case of Geoffrey Page, who was 'fried' as they casually called being burned alive, he was also determined to shoot down an enemy aircraft for every operation he had to endure. There were fifteen in all, but when he got back into ops he shot down seventeen more German planes. At the airborne attack on Arnhem, Page was shot down for the second time and for the second time became a Guinea Pig back at East Grinstead, one of only two men to qualify twice. His lust for revenge was burnt out but he still used flying as his motivation for recovery and got back not to operational flying but flying with an air training calibration unit. He is now a successful businessman, married to the daughter of the British actor, Nigel Bruce. Sir Archibald McIndoe was godfather to one of their children.

Donald Melzack, Professor of Psychology, McGill University, who with P. D. Wall formulated the theory of pain on which much of modern medical and surgical treatment of it is based, has described it in his book *The Puzzle of Pain.*

Melzack dismisses the view of pain as a simple sensation produced by injury – a cut, a burn, a stone in the bladder, a boil – which will stop when the cause is removed. There are types of pain which continue and increase after the first stimulus has gone, so that the pain becomes an illness in its own right. These pains are almost always very difficult to treat, can be agonising to the point of making the sufferer consider and even commit suicide, and may persist for many years. One of the worst is the pain of a 'phantom limb'.

'Phantom limb' pain was first described in battle veterans by Ambroise Pare, the founder of modern surgical techniques and a French army surgeon, in 1552. (G. Keynes, *The Apologie and Treatise of Ambroise Pare*, Chicago University Press, 1952). Pare wrote:

> Verily it is a thing wondrous strange and prodigious, and which will scarce be credited, unless by such as have seen with their eyes, and heard with their ears, the patients who have many months after the cutting away of the leg, grievously complain that they yet felt exceeding great pain of that leg so cut off.

Most amputees feel a 'phantom limb' immediately after the operation, but only about a third of them report pain in it. It at first feels so normal that patients sometimes forget it has been removed, and try to stand on it! Arm amputees have been known to try to stretch out a non-existent hand for cutlery or a pen. As time passes, however, the limb usually 'shrinks' and the sensation slowly subsides.

For 1 in 20 amputees, however, the story is very different. They have severe pain, which worsens over the years. It has been variously described as cramping, shooting, burning or crushing. Imagine the torment of a patient whose sensation of a severe continuous cramp in a clenched non-existent fist or a curled-up non-existent foot cannot be relieved by the usual easy remedy of stretching the spasm-afflicted muscles!

'Phantom limb' pain can be stimulated by such mundane things as urinating or defecating, or by the merest touch of 'trigger zones' in other, distant parts of the body. In 1943, W. K. Livingston (*Pain Mechanisms*, Macmillan) described the classic case of 'phantom limb'. The patient was a doctor, a close friend of Livingston's who had lost his left arm after a gas-gangrene infection. (A syringe had broken and cut him when injecting the germs into a guinea pig).

His arm was amputated in 1926: he suffered his subsequent symptoms for several years before seeking help. His lost hand was, according to his brain, still there, but clenched in a tight ball with the fingers closely pressed over the thumb, and the wrist sharply flexed. In the subsequent six years his brain was unable to persuade the hand to unflex. The tension in it was worsened when the stump was cold or had been bumped, and at times was unbearable. Worse still, he often felt that a sharp knife was being driven repeatedly into the site of the original syringe puncture wound.

Between the worst bouts of pain, his 'phantom hand' persistently 'burned': as this was more bearable than the pain, it was almost welcome.

Livingston asked him once why he complained so much about the cramping, tense sensations. He was told to hold his own hand high up in the same position: at the end of five minutes Livingston was sweating freely and, finding the position no longer bearable, stopped.

'But you can take your hand down,' said his friend.

It was not until 1932 that a solution was found. In that year, during a particularly bad attack of pain, he was given by Livingston an injection of novocaine, a local anaesthetic similar to those now given by dentists, into the plexus in the neck, from which the network of nerves controlling the circulation of the arm originate. The result was sensational. The pain disappeared, and to his amazement, he could move his 'phantom fingers' for the first time in six years.

Not all 'phantom limb' pain is, in the end, so completely relieved by anaesthetising the nerves to the amputated limb. Indeed in 1968 S. Sunderland (*Nerves and Nerve Injuries*, E. and S. Livingstone) wrote that even cutting the appropriate nerves as they leave the spine fails to stop the pain. The case was reported in 1969 of an arm amputee, identified by the doctors as Henry B., who after such surgery, was completely without any feeling from shoulder to navel on the side of his amputated arm, yet still felt excruciating pain in the 'phantom fingers' (J. C. White and W. H. Sweet, *Pain and the Neurosurgeons*, C. C. Thomas, 1969).

The same doctors reported one man with a painful splinter of wood under a fingernail, whose hand was suddenly accidentally crushed. The splinter continued to cause severe pain in his subsequent 'phantom hand'!

Yet another patient lost a leg at the same time as fracturing his spine. Although paralysed and without any feeling from the waist down, he still had pain in his 'phantom limb' which did not abate when the only possible nerve connection between his legs and his brain, the sympathetic chain lying outside his spinal column, was removed by his surgeon.

From these examples it is evident that pain may be remembered and reproduced in nerve circuits within the brain, long after the connections with the rest of the body are lost or cut. The possibilities that this raises are at the same time fascinating and frightening. Fascinating because it opens up the possibility that the brain itself may be trained, if only we knew how, to cut out the sensation. Frightening because the nerve impulse, whatever or whether it is in the brain, which creates the sensation, once learned, may recur at any time.

There are some people, who have been trained to ignore their chronic pain, purely by changing their mental attitudes. W. K. Livingston showed that the pain of causalgia, an excruciating chronic pain which sometimes follows slight injuries, can be abolished if patients suffering from it were encouraged to tolerate it.

Dietrich Bonhoeffer, the German pastor tortured, then finally murdered, by the Nazis in World War II, took this to extremes. Under the most foul torture he found he was able to project himself outside his body, and to convince himself that he was only an onlooker at the terrible acts perpetrated upon it.

Perhaps it was the ability of people like Bonhoeffer and Kitty Hart, and others, like Odette Hallowes who suffered intensely at the hands of Gestapo torturers without revealing the names of her Resistance colleagues, that altered the techniques of torture in the 1970s. Now, the infliction of pain has given way to the deprivation of senses. The placing in complete darkness, without any sound or other form of communication, is calculated to make people dedicated to a cause break down faster than exposing them to pain. Even then, determined people can resist by actively thinking of something which will exercise the brain. Mathematics, music, jokes, games can all be replayed in the mind time and time again – as long as the subject keeps off his immediate predicament or the effect his capture may be having on his family. Hostages and kidnap victims kept under such circumstances must eventually find some way of communicating with their captors if they are not eventually to break down.

One of the surprising things about kidnap victims, especially those who have spent long periods in captivity, is the rapport often reached between them and their kidnappers, particularly if the kidnapping is a political one and the victim a symbolic, if not specific choice. Obviously there was no such rapport between the tragic Aldo Moro and Hans-Martin Schleyer and their abductors. However, the Dutch hostages taken by the Moluccan nationalists in 1976–7, and many of the hostages taken by other political activists in the last decade, have emerged from their ordeals with views extraordinarily influenced by their captors. The extreme example, of course, was Patti Hearst. The victims are always profoundly and permanently affected by their experience; few of them wish to take up their careers again, shunning positions of responsibility or further promotion, and most change to simpler and less demanding life styles.

The mental effort needed to control pain or, for that matter, to tolerate sensory deprivation, appears to be a considerable one. Perhaps it needs training from early childhood, or the stimulus of extraordinary motivation to produce it.

The rest of us have to make do with painkillers, or analgesics, to do the work for us. The relief of pain by drugs has been known for thousands of years. The opiates, originally made from the seed of the white poppy, have been used to kill pain and offer sleep since the time of Hippocrates. Aspirin, discovered in the late nineteenth century, was at the end of a long line of drugs with origins in preparations made from the bark of willow trees in medieval times.

That these drugs are effective is proven by their long history of use. Indeed more aspirin is swallowed the world over than any other medicine. Yet it is only in the last ten years that medical scientists have known how they, and the opiates, abolish pain.

There are two places at which drugs can attack pain – at the site of the injury or disease causing it, or where the sensation is interpreted as pain, in the brain. Aspirin and similar drugs such as paracetamol and the new drugs against the pain of rheumatism and arthritis act mainly 'on site', by neutralising the chemicals produced there by the injury and which stimulate the nerve endings thought to carry the pain sensation to the brain. With high doses, however, they start to influence the brain in various ways. The opiates, which include morphine and heroin, alter the brain's interpretation of pain. They make no difference to the impulses running along the nerves to the brain, but in some way change the perception of them when they arrive at the cells responsible for consciousness. Indeed, the brain itself has recently been found to produce opiate-like substances, called endorphins.

It may be that people like Odette, Pastor Bonhoeffer, Kitty Hart and the Christian martyrs who died so bravely in the face of terrible pain were able to do so by the quite unconscious production of their own endorphin painkillers. Indeed the euphoria and even ecstasy they exhibited in their times of trial could well also be produced by them. Could it be that the only difference between the heroes and all the others is that their brains produce different amounts of these and other, as yet unidentified, chemicals in response to their predicament? Some physiologists would hold to precisely that view, but we have drawn up short of such an extremely mechanistic view of the human character.

If tolerance to pain can be controlled by the will, is the same thing possible for other threats to life, such as poison or disease? The ancient Romans certainly learned much about extending the human tolerance to poison. They had to, for the number of Caesars who died of old age in their beds was very small indeed. Prospective Caesars were given small doses of various vegetable poisons from an early age, gradually increasing them as they grew older, so that any attempt at deliberate poisoning later might fail. The theory would certainly be correct for some poisons, but was disastrous for others, such as arsenic, which act cumulatively, and would certainly kill them. One theory, in fact, for the eventual collapse of the Roman Empire, was that the wealthy ruling classes, whose household water was delivered in lead-lined pipes, died in early adult life from lead poisoning, while the plebeians, who had to draw water from wells, survived. The resultant imbalance in the population destroyed the social structure and was a major reason for the chaos of later years.

There is evidence that Napoleon was poisoned by arsenic while on St Helena, but whether by his British captors or fellow Frenchmen with some grudge against him will probably never be known. Arsenic could have given him the stomach problems from which he certainly suffered. Maybe that's why he was almost always painted with his right hand inside his waistcoat!

Tolerance to poisons in recent times has led to 'super-rats', animals immune to doses of the poison Warfarin hundreds of times those which were lethal when it was first introduced. Warfarin is used in people with disorders of excessive blood clotting, such as thrombosis, but there is no news in the medical press, as yet, of 'super-people'. All the same, there are other drugs to which people rapidly become tolerant. The most common are those which affect mood, such as the opiates and the tranquillisers. One of the dangers of such drugs is that the dose needed to continue providing the desired effect has to be stepped up almost daily. In one author's experience of the treatment, in 1962, of a man of thirty with inoperable bone cancer, the dose of heroin needed to control his pain was, at the beginning of treatment, one-twelfth of a grain three times daily. Within three weeks, he needed twelve grains two-hourly, a 500-fold rise.

Today the work of Cicely Saunders and her colleagues with dying patients at St Christopher's Hospice in London and the newer, less addictive, drugs has made such massive treatment unnecessary, but the lesson is there for the drug abusers, who are on a one-way road to ever increasing doses and expense, with awful reactions if they miss a dose.

Opiates have been largely replaced by the tranquillisers for less serious disorders, but patients become quickly tolerant to them, too. Another patient known to the authors was obtaining Valium capsules – the name is now such a household word it is not even necessary to explain what they do – from several sources, and swallowing between twenty-five and fifty every day. For anyone unused to them, such a dose would certainly produce coma and possibly death. This patient continued to run his business – he was an electrician – as if he was totally normal. He proved that he was not, unhappily, by wiring up a kitchen chair to the mains and skilfully electrocuting himself. The depression during which he took his life may well have been deepened by the drug, which is not, as some people believe, a mood lifter, but a tranquilliser.

It is not only drugs to which the body can be trained to become tolerant. The mechanism of tolerance could hardly have arisen in nature because of the need to resist the effect of drugs – it was specifically designed for the fight against disease. Once infected by a germ, the body's defences produce substances called antibodies which neutralise any future attack by the same germ before it can multiply enough to cause the same disease a second time. This is why we usually only fall foul of the childhood diseases such as measles or chickenpox once. We catch more than one cold because there are more than 500 different viruses which are known to cause the common cold, and we have to produce separate antibodies to each one before we are immune to them all.

Over the last few thousand years, it appears that the communities in Europe and the mainland of Asia must have, by the process of natural selection, become relatively resistant to the childhood infections. By this, it is meant that although children still catch them, they are rarely a threat to life.

It was another story when the same diseases were spread to areas where they had been unknown. Whole communities died from measles when this disease first reached the Plains Indians and the Eskimos from Europe. There were many deaths on St Helena after a visiting boat in the nineteenth century brought a child suffering a mild attack of measles to its shores.

The greatest killer of the infectious epidemic diseases, however, may be a surprising one. In the four months between October 1918 and mid-February 1919 this illness killed more than 21 million people in the worst epidemic the world has ever known. This was almost three times the number of soldiers killed in the four years of World War I. The disease? Influenza. It is now thought that the influenza virus, which was not discovered until 1933, changed so completely in the summer of 1918 that no one anywhere in the world possessed any immunity to it. There is some evidence that it may change as drastically again: enough small changes occur every few years to ensure that people have repeated influenza illnesses, but with today's medical knowledge, horrifying death rates such as those in 1918 should never be repeated.

By 1980 the World Health Organisation officially declared smallpox eradicated – yet the event was hardly noticed by the mass of people in the developed countries. This was because they saw very little of the disease in their lifetimes. How many of them appreciate the real significance of the news, or indeed of the nursery rhymes that their children still enjoy?

Why was it, for example, that poets wrote of shepherdesses and dairymaids as the epitome of health and beauty? The French ideal of female beauty is enshrined for ever in the Folies Bergère – the Shepherdess. The reason was not just the rustic charm of these girls, but the fact that in the past they were the only women in the whole community not pock-marked by the ravages of the smallpox virus.

Their protection came from mild localised infections with similar viruses – that of orf in lambs and cowpox in cattle, which they caught when children, and the realisation of this led to the development of the whole process of vaccinations which has not only stamped out smallpox but vastly reduced the risks of catching polio, typhoid, yellow fever, and more recently german measles (rubella) – so dangerous to the developing foetus.

The worry now is that people have become complacent in the mistaken belief that, with things patently under control, there is less need for vaccination. This is simply not true, as has been shown by the recent outbreaks of fatal and paralytic polio in Dutch religious groups opposed to vaccination. Smallpox will not come back, as the virus is now extinct, but the diphtheria, whooping cough and polio germs are another matter. The recent whooping cough vaccine scare, when acceptance rates in the UK dropped from over 80 per cent to 39 per cent, led in 1978 to the worst whooping cough epidemic in many years and ten deaths. A related retreat from the rubella vaccination programme seems to be leading to a similar rise in german measles and the resultant damaged babies.

Populations as a whole become resistant to diseases, but only because a majority of people have become individually immune. Their bone marrow is producing the white blood cells which ensure speedy destruction of any invading germs, and other systems produce the antibiotics to coat the germ surface, thereby making it impossible for them to infect or reproduce.

Before the recent establishment of specialised hospital units to care for them, babies born without the ability to make white blood cells or to manufacture antibodies died very quickly in infancy from overwhelming infection, and often the infections were caused by germs quite innocuous to normal people.

For some of these tragic cases the technique of bone marrow transplants from healthy people can reverse their deficiency and help them to lead a normal life. Unhappily, this was not possible for young Anthony Nolan who died, aged eight and a half, in 1979 after having spent all of his short life isolated from close contact with all other people. His death was not in vain. His courageous mother inspired a fund to establish an international system for typing bone marrow, which should give a better chance of survival in the future for children like Anthony.

The publicity on transplants, whether of the marrow, kidney, liver or heart, has been such that people have begun to wonder how far we can do without these organs, previously thought to be vital to life.

It is true that there are now many thousands of people living without any kidneys at all. They are the patients on kidney dialysis machines, awaiting transplants, whose own failed kidneys have been surgically removed. This is very much a last resort: it is possible to function well, and to remove all the waste matter produced each day, on less than half of one kidney. The giving of a kidney by a living donor to a sick relative still leaves the donor with plenty of reserve kidney power.

The liver, too, has plenty of spare capacity. Patients with chronic liver disease can lose as much as three-quarters of all their cells before there are any signs of disease, such as jaundice or itch. The same can be said of the lungs. There are many people still living who in the 1940s and early 1950s had a tuberculous lung deliberately collapsed by surgery, leaving them with much less than one lung with which to breathe. The world-wide epidemic of smoking-induced lung cancer has left hundreds of thousands of victims with a lung removed, yet who can conduct normal everyday life without a hint of breathlessness. It is possible, indeed, to survive quite happily on half a lung, although its possessor will hardly be an athlete.

Modern surgery in people with serious and widespread bowel disease has allowed the removal of all but one and a half feet of the normal thirty feet of gut, yet still allows the patient to survive, albeit on a very special diet which contains all the basic foodstuffs in a state which allows immediate use by the body without the need for digestion. Organs such as the stomach, the spleen, the pancreas, the ovaries, the womb, the testicles, the prostate gland, the thyroid, can all be done without, now that there is detailed knowledge and experience of how to guide people in coping without them. The hormone and chemical substances which are given in their place are virtually chemical 'transplants'.

The heart, of course, may be replaced by another or even, in the future, by a machine – after all, it *is* only a pump, although a much more efficient one than ever was devised by a human engineer. Christiaan Barnard, the first heart transplant surgeon, no longer simply replaces one heart with another – he adds the donor heart to half the patient's diseased heart, as a 'booster' of the circulation.

The one organ which it is generally thought will never be transplanted is the brain. As the accepted seat of knowledge and character – not to mention the soul – it would be difficult to determine, it seems, the identity of the transplant recipient after the event. Would he be simply the original recipient with a new computer, or the original donor in a different body? The question, of course, is a ridiculous one, for no one believes that even if the transfer of new brain and intact blood supply were feasible – a brain without blood develops some irreversible damage within two minutes and dies in four – the many millions of microscopic connections of nerve fibres between the new brain and the recipient's spinal cord could never be made.

The case against brain transplants seems watertight, yet there is a small sign that it might not be. In 1979, researchers into the distressing Parkinson's disease, which is caused by degeneration of cells in an area of the brain called the basal ganglia, were working on monkeys. They first produced in adult monkeys the same symptoms as human Parkinson's disease by damaging their basal ganglia. Then they took fresh basal ganglia cells from foetuses taken from the wombs of pregnant monkeys and transplanted them into the affected adults. The transplanted cells 'took', and remained healthy, even multiplying in their new host, and cured the symptoms of the disease.

The monkey experiments are a long step from the use of such techniques in humans, particularly as surgeons would need to obtain the donor brain cells from living human aborted foetuses. By the time a baby is born its immune systems have developed to such an extent that its tissues would be rejected by a recipient. It is difficult to see how donor material obtained in this way would be generally accepted, at least in the near future. Ethics have changed so much in the last twenty years, however, we would not like to predict that such techniques will not be commonplace before the end of the century. And if it can be done for the basal ganglia cells, why not for others – say the lateral cerebral cortex for new cells to co-ordinate sensation and movement in stroke cases; or even the frontal cortex, the seat, we believe, of thought, to increase the intelligence in the subnormal? Where do the concepts of 'character' and 'soul' enter into such deliberations?

As it is, we can survive, though with difficulty, with half a brain. Many have to, as the number of 'strokes' rise in our Western, developed society. But what about half a *body*?

In 1977 doctors in Britain were shown, in one of their weekly newspapers, the photograph of an American patient apparently sitting up in bed, smiling wanly at the camera. The caption below it explained that the poor man had literally been halved, horizontally, in a line just below his umbilicus. His weight was taken on the stump of his spine. He had lost everything from below his waist – his legs, pelvis, genitalia and hips. His bodily functions were performed through small holes in what remained of his abdomen.

The operation had been performed for an incurable cancer of the pelvic bones which had spread to fill the whole of his lower abdomen. He had been in great pain and discomfort, and the heroic operation was his surgeon's answer to his problems. The alternative was to give powerful, opiate painkillers and keep him as comfortable as possible until his death.

Faced with such a disease as a patient, or with such a choice as a surgeon, we feel we know how we would have viewed such treatment. But we were *not* in the patient's position: life even in such a state can seem precious. We leave it to others to form their own opinions on the case, and whether it has indeed gone beyond the limit.

8

Ageing– Towards the Ultimate Limit

Sophocles more than 2,000 years ago wrote 'the gods alone have neither age nor death'. Since then, over much of the world belief in the gods has become a little shaky, but our belief in the mortality of man, in that ultimate limit, has been all too consistently reinforced.

It is this very knowledge, the fact that alone among the animals man can comprehend his own ageing and his own death, that has driven him to try and postpone the inevitable, achieve the impossible, hold back time and conjure dreams of immortality, if not of the flesh then at least of the spirit. It forms an understandable and instinctive defence mechanism against the unknown or the void.

In his long and desperate search for eternal youth and to extend the limits of vigorous life, man has certainly tried everything – spells, incantations, pacts with gods and devils, mythical fountains of youth, quite unmythical maidens popped into old men's beds, the breath of virgins, the touch of kings, the sex organs of animals, the 'new' electricity, blood serum, foetal cells, sex hormones, drugs and transplants.

Yet contrary to popular misconception human life-span has not been greatly extended. Through better living conditions, better hygiene and better medicine, we have certainly eliminated many of the causes of early death and even defeated the infections which in old age once carried so many off. The result is just more and more people living to reach their Biblical three-score years and ten. In fact, ironically, we are simply achieving more and more old age.

And to be truthful the situation, unless we begin to tackle quality as well as quantity of life, is hardly enviable. Age carries with it today not only the traditional burdens of stiffening joints, reduced mobility, failing sight, loss of hearing, but also relatively new burdens in the form of loss of prestige, involvement and dignity. In a world which worships youth, the old are increasingly diminished, de-valued and shunted off too often – in our culture at any rate – into the antiseptic segregation of special Homes.

However good these are, however well run, well equipped and well intentioned, they rarely manage to engender the very factors which experts now recognise as vital if at least psychological ageing is to be kept at bay – a sense of purpose, of being needed, of identity, involvement and belonging: these are the real elixirs of life.

As it is in our culture, social and psychological ageing is positively thrust upon us with enforced retirement at sixty-five, however fit, capable and anxious to work a man may be. Forced to accept society's verdict that he is too old to be any longer useful and cost effective, the result is that before long he actually ceases to be either. Trade unions currently campaigning for earlier retirement need to think again, unless people are better equipped to use and constructively enjoy their leisure, replacing the stimulus of work with hobbies and interests that provide some sort of challenge.

Age is not in itself a disease and though it is a time when diseases can accumulate, they are still capable of treatment. The ageing are too ready to accept philosophically the assertion some doctors make that aches and pains are just due to age. One elderly man, told the pain in his left knee was due to his age, replied, 'Well, doctor, why isn't my other knee sore – it's ninety-two years old as well?'

There are far too many people who achieve superbly late in life for any norms or limits to be set. Sixty-five may be the accepted retirement age in our society, but long past that age Michelangelo painted 'The Last Judgement' and he was working on the St Paul in his eighties. Titian was painting a 'pieta' at the age of ninety-nine when he died, not of old age but of the plague. So perhaps there is some truth after all in the saucy limerick which records:

When Titian was mixing rose madder
With his model perched on a ladder,
The model's position,
Suggested coition,
So he ran up the ladder and 'ad her.

Blondin, the French acrobat, was still turning somersaults on stilts on a tightrope when aged over sixty-five, and Jean Borotra was playing tennis for France at Queen's Club. Catherine the Great took a new lover, Haydn composed 'The Creation', Sir Winston Churchill led Britain throughout World War II and Charlie Chaplin not only won a peace prize in East Berlin but fathered his fifth (and not his last) child!

The examples of vigorous creative life going on well into the normally accepted period of old age are endless. Sir Arthur Rubenstein was still giving concerts at ninety-seven, and Sybil Thorndike still acting at ninety-three. Plato was eighty-seven when death interrupted his writing and Bernard Shaw, Bertrand Russell, Voltaire, Goethe, Tolstoy, Ruskin, Victor Hugo and Thomas Mann are just a few other writers who produced top-class work in their seventies and eighties.

Pavlov, the physiologist, was at the height of his powers at eighty-six when he died of pneumonia, Sir Christopher Wren was ninety-one when he died, Carl Jung eighty-six, John Wesley eighty-eight and Sibelius ninety-two. The thing they all had in common was interest, involvement and recognition. They remained persons not just 'old people'. For the same reason statesmen tend to live long – Cato, Gladstone, Jefferson, Benjamin Franklin, Clemenceau, Petain, Hoover, Lady Astor, Adenauer and Truman all lived into their eighties or nineties, and today Manny Shinwell at ninety-five can still vitalise the Labour Party Conference.

Dr Irene Gore, a British expert on ageing, fervently believes that to keep the body working *well*, you must keep it working – that activity and movement create the energy the body needs and that the worst thing a person can do is to take things easy. One impressive Russian experiment took a group of sixty-year-olds and put them through a quite tough gym programme each week. Ten years later, they were, on every physiological count, actually younger than they had been at sixty. What we take to be normal ageing is in their view pathological ageing and older people do not have to be weak or decrepit physically or mentally.

The large numbers of musical conductors who were still going strong in their eighties seems to bear this out, for theirs is a strenuous occupation physically and stimulating mentally. They include Arturo Toscanini, Pierre Monteux, Tullio Serafini, Sir Thomas Beecham, Leopold Stokowski, Bruno Walter, Otto Klemperer, and Vittoria Gui.

Paul Paray, the French orchestral conductor, who died aged ninety-three in October 1979, was conducting only a few months earlier at the opening by Prince Rainier of a new auditorium in Monte Carlo. The soloist was Yehudi Menuhin. This was more than half a century since he had first conducted Menuhin as an eleven-year-old child prodigy in his Paris debut in 1929. They played the same piece, Mendelssohn's Violin Concerto. After the 1979 concert, however, Paray flew off the following morning to give fifteen concerts in Israel, followed by a tour of Sweden . . . real proof that active life can be extended far beyond the traditional three-score years and ten.

The genetic factor in ageing, which would suggest that one of the best bets for a long life, would be to choose if it were possible the right parents, is well borne out by the Amati family, the famous violin makers. Three brothers, and the son of one of them, all lived and continued active work until they were between eighty-four and eighty-eight years of age.

So it is not really *normal* to become 'old' in the accepted sense of apathy, aches and pains and problems that cannot be treated. What does happen is that we become more prone to disease as certain changes take place. But what happens and why does it happen? The enormous increase in the ratio of elderly to young in the populations of the developed world has stimulated a surge of research to try and answer these questions. In 1974 when one of the authors was in the US looking at research into ageing going on at the cellular level, 11½ million dollars had been earmarked for that year alone for this work. The EEC are spending £1,833,000 on a somewhat less ambitious programme, both sides of the Atlantic recognising that 'the cost of living' has a very real meaning when social services cost three times as much for those over sixty-five as for the rest of the population.

As the mysterious mechanisms of biological ageing begin to yield up their secrets, it becomes clear that there is no one single process but many working together.

In the past, of course, it was thought that we quite simply wore out, and that God or evolution (or maybe both in conspiracy) had designed us that way. It was too simplistic a view but it contained truths which the latest research is confirming. Our life span does appear to be programmed, genetically determined and fixed for each different species. Humans generally live not longer than 90 years, horses 30 years, dogs 15, mice 3, fruit flies only 30 days and the Galapagos tortoise 150 years.

From the evolutionary point of view, it was really only ever important for the individual to survive long enough to propagate and rear the next generation. After that, death in a way was essential, providing the door through which the long slow procession must pass, in order to permit natural selection to breed out weaknesses, breed in favourable adaptations, and all the time continue to improve the species to meet and match changing competition and conditions.

It is clear from this that while adverse factors had to be eliminated as far as possible in early life to allow the reproductive phase, there was no special reason to worry about them creeping in later. In fact it is the gradual accumulation of such faults and failings right down at the cellular level, which results in what we call ageing and death.

Only at the single-cell level, with an organism as simple as the amoeba, can there be anything like real immortality. There, reproduction by simple cell division ensures that each time the whole parent survives as part of the offspring. But it also permits no improvement or development of the species.

With the human and higher animals the penalty we have had to pay, at least until now, for our very complexity and adaptability is our mortality. Only the germ cell itself, the small genetic package that contains the inherited characteristics, survives. This is passed intact from generation to generation, but then the two sets of genes are shuffled as they come together, like packs of cards, to produce an infinite variety of new combinations and new individuals, instead of a series of carbon copies, which would give natural selection no scope.

The sophisticated view of ageing which sees us as 'programmed to die' is gaining wide support. According to men like Dr Bernard Strehler, whose brilliant researches at the University of Southern California back in 1974 were already beginning to unlock the secrets of cell behaviour, we are programmed to die in the basic blueprint carried in every one of our trillion cells. Evolution keeps a firm hand on the vital switches, so that at maturity a process of degeneration is brought into operation, by deliberately turning off essential cell behaviour, which until then has been designed to renew life.

Without getting too technical, it is helpful to understand a little about normal cell mechanism. To start with, although each cell carries the whole blueprint, it uses only part of it, translating only the instructions that are in its own special code. This individualised interpretation allows differentiation, so that liver cells for example are produced and in the normal way go on receiving instructions to produce new liver cells, exactly like the old, so that youth continues.

But eventually, Dr Strehler argues, the process is *made* to go wrong. At maturity a switch comes into play which deliberately 'turns off' the ability of cells to read certain instructions, so that the coded messages become incomplete and the body fails to make the essential materials it needs to stay vital and regenerate.

And it goes beyond theory. Work done on plants and dogs has shown that ageing tissues do lack the genes responsible for the manufacture of substances vital to formation of new proteins, without which a cell can neither divide nor survive.

It all sounds doomy and gloomy, but Dr Strehler believes it is not as frightening as it appears. 'My theory actually holds out the best hope of some day being able to prevent ageing,' he insists. 'We hope eventually to develop techniques of cellular engineering which will allow the instructions which operate the maturity switch to be cancelled, and so permit the cells to behave and go on renewing as they do in youth.'

Twenty miles across the urban sprawl of Los Angeles, working in 1974 at the rival University of California, was Dr Roy Walford. He also believes ageing is a built-in programmed process, but he ties it in firmly with the body's auto-immune system. Roy Walford insists the body becomes progressively disorganised to the point at which cells do not merely fail to reproduce themselves, but actively destroy themselves as they no longer recognise each other as kin. He compares it roughly to the way in which the body rejects heart or kidney transplants, but with ageing the body is rejecting its own faulty cells not foreign ones.

His own experimental work on this has produced some fascinating results. If Walford's theory is true, everything which suppressed the auto-immune system ought to increase life span. With this in mind, the drug Immuran, normally used to suppress immune responses in transplant operations, was fed to healthy mice. They showed a ten week mean life-span increase over a group of control mice.

Unfortunately what works for mice kept in germ-free laboratory conditions would not in practice work for humans, who with impaired immunity would simply succumb sooner than they might otherwise do to some form of infection.

The disorganisation and failure of cells to copy correctly is now widely accepted among scientists as a basic cause of ageing. At the National Institute for Medical Research in London, Robin Holliday's team have found a 5 per cent error in a certain enzyme in normal cells in culture. The percentage rises as the cell culture ages. Cells from patients with Werner's syndrome, a disease which causes patients to age at twice the normal rate, also show a higher level of the defective enzyme. Eventually the accumulation of such errors reaches 'catastrophe' level.

The question on which scientists do not agree, is whether such errors are programmed, as Strehler believes, or are the result of radiation or even chemicals, both of which are known to cause cells to mutate, producing more and more errors in their continuous copying process.

Quite apart from these cells which normally renew themselves but with age fail to do so correctly, there are other non-multiplying cells. The fact that these make up such key organs as heart and brain must confirm the strong suspicion that nature clearly intended us to die. After the initial period of growth, these do not divide again, and so in time become subject to loss and injury.

This further cause of ageing brings us right back to the old wear and tear theory, with the body like an old motor car gradually running down, as one part after another begins to fail. Between the ages of thirty and seventy-five, for example, heart function declines 33 per cent, lungs 40 per cent, kidneys 44 per cent but the liver only 10 per cent. This variation in rate of decline for the different organs strongly confirms the idea that more than one deadly biological time clock is slowly running down. As always, however, the body gallantly strives to cope with its own built-in obsolescence. Liver function is reduced by only 10 per cent, simply because it manages to compensate in complicated ways for the fact that blood flows through it less efficiently. Effects of declining kidney function would be immediate and far worse, if the body did not compensate by producing more anti-diuretic hormone to protect against dehydration as the kidneys fail and start to store urine. The increasing success of transplant surgery with development of better drugs to prevent rejection and the promise implicit in Interferon, the newest development in protection against virus invasion and some cancers, will offer a better and better spare-parts service – already new corneas, hearts, kidneys, bone marrow and livers are possible, but even so the time must come when too many systems fail and further salvage becomes impractical.

Looking far into the future, of course, if biologists like Bernard Strehler do succeed in tampering with the biological time switches, they may find it possible to stimulate a controlled second growth of organs such as heart and brain, but Dr Strehler pointed out that there would be problems. 'The brain would be the most difficult,' he explained, 'because memory is stored in connections between brain cells. If it were made to produce new cells, the old would have to be sloughed off and with them would go whatever knowledge had been stored there.'

As well as combating the ageing mechanisms at work in the cellular material of the body, in attempts to postpone the 'ultimate limit' there is another process which has to be taken into account. This involves the body's non-cellular materials making up important things like blood-vessel walls and elastic fibres. These also suffer an age change by a chemical process similar to the tanning of leather. This so-called 'colloid ageing' results in the sort of change of structure and texture which makes an old boiler fowl tough while a young chicken is tender.

Ironically this chemical change appears to be brought about over the years by the rogue action of the one substance essential to life – oxygen. Experiments have been going on to see if anti-oxidants can be found to prevent the adverse side effects of the oxygen circulating in our blood. Vitamin E was at one time a candidate but more recently it has been a substance called BHT, used oddly enough to preserve potato chips. This has been shown to considerably postpone age changes in mice and if ever the potato-chip makers latch on to the idea, the mind boggles at the sort of names and slogans they might be tempted to use: 'Young and spry on Methuselah Fry' perhaps?

Whatever wonders future cellular biologists may come up with, in their attempts to slow down the various ageing clocks now known to be ticking inexorably away, there will almost certainly be a limit to life. The old theory of the 'immortality of the cell' for which rather ironically Alexis Carrel was awarded the Nobel Prize, is now known to be wrong. He believed he had kept chicken cells dividing in tissue indefinitely, but it is now accepted that he was inadvertently introducing fresh cells in the embryo extract he was using as a medium. Later work has shown that chicken and human cells kept in culture actually die after about fifty to sixty doublings, and the older the human donor of the cells the fewer doublings they make. In fact the only truly immortal cells achieved in laboratories are mutant cells, transformed by virus action into what we call cancer. As an interesting sidelight on this, there is the case in the 1950s of an American woman, named either Helen Lane or Henrietta Larkin – scientists strangely still argue about these alternative names in learned journals – who had breast cancer. The growth was removed by surgery and some of its cancer cells kept alive in the laboratory with nutrient fluid and oxygen. They were found to be useful to researchers because they provided a very good medium for the growth of viruses. Indeed so useful were they that cultures of what are now known as HeLa Cells (after her initials) are to be found in laboratories all over the world. In fact Mrs Lane or Larkin's tumour is now estimated to weigh several tons! Yet nothing is known of what happened to her or, indeed, whether she ever knew or knows of her 'massive'contribution to science.

Although work is going on with normal cells to see if their lifespan can be manipulated by changing conditions such as temperature or locating the switch mechanisms, any beneficial spin-offs from this sort of work still lie far in the future. So what is available now on the scientific and medical level and what can we ourselves do – if not to add years to our life, at least to add life to our years?

A technique, once very much for the rich but more recently taken up even by medium-income people, is cell therapy. This was developed by the famous Dr Niehans and was reputed to have worked wonders for people like Adenauer, De Gaulle, Churchill, Eisenhower, Pope Pius XII, Marlene Dietrich, Somerset Maugham, Charlie Chaplin, Noel Coward and the Windsors.

The rich and leisured once had to travel to Niehans' special clinic in Switzerland for treatment with extracts of foetal lamb tissue, supposed to regenerate the ageing human tissues. The therapy has now become available round the world as methods were devised to dry the embryonic cells and reconstitute them before use. Niehans believed the dried cells not only equally effective but more gentle in action than live cells and he preferred them for older patients.

In England the great exponent of cell therapy is Dr Peter Stephans (the degree is in homeopathic medicine). In his Welbeck Street consulting room where he sees some 300 new patients a year, he explained to one of the authors exactly how it is supposed to work. He insisted:

> It's not a question of replacing human cells with animal cells. What we do is use embryonic cells taken from unborn lambs and use these to stimulate the human cells by setting up antibody antigen reaction. All our cells are constantly dying and being replaced during the whole of a lifetime. The rate of reproduction and dying of these cells governs your health. By analysing each individual patient, using blood and urine tests, we can find out which parts of the system are under- or over-functioning and what the results of these misfunctions are. Having done that, we then set out to re-balance the whole system by injecting new cells corresponding to the deficiencies.

There is in the Niehans–Stephans logic faint echoes of work such as Dr Strehler's, which has shown ageing tissues to lack substances vital to normal regenerative processes. If there should prove to be substances, perhaps in the form of nucleic acids, common to all vigorous young cells in whatever species, it would strengthen the cell therapy concept.

Peter Stephans is emphatic it is not 'rejuvenation', but what he calls a 'preventive servicing routine' for the body. 'I can't make people any younger,' he insists, 'but I can make them look and feel younger by bringing them into healthy metabolic balance. I have had men of sixty and seventy, who had become totally inactive, once again playing golf and enjoying life.'

A course of treatment, which may be by injection or suppository, today costs about £500, and Alex Comfort is on record as stating that all it will do is 'rejuvenate someone else's bank balance'.

Most doctors reject the concept completely, largely because it uses animal tissue to regenerate human tissue which they insist is biologically impossible. While cell therapists point out that it is foetal tissue they use and that this provokes no allergic response, this is a very dubious argument. Certainly foreign tissues transplanted into a foetus may not produce a reaction, because the foetal immune systems are not mature enough to recognise the intruder and react against it, but the converse is not logical. The mature immune system will reject or be allergic to a foreign protein whether it comes from a foetus or an adult of its own or other species.

Cell therapists are in fact looking for results at the wrong end of life, except that from their point of view it is the end where the profits are to be made. But in reality it is the infantile patient who may one day benefit from injections which will, if given early enough before the rejection mechanism begins to operate, possibly be able to prevent all the allergies it could become prone to after birth – these include eczema, asthma and the diseases doctors now call the 'auto-immune diseases', which include forms of arthritis, pernicious anaemia and some thyroid disorders. Some researchers believe that in this way such diseases could be eliminated and that it could work for virus infections and perhaps for cancer which many feel also stems from abnormal immune responses. There is an outside possibility that ageing could be susceptible to this approach too, if that also proves to involve the same immune mechanism.

Equally suspect with most doctors in the West is the 'Procaine' treatment developed by Dr Ana Aslan of Rumania, who is head of the Bucharest Geriatric Institute. Dr Aslan claims the drug has cured a wide variety of age-related complaints, including arthritis, baldness, grey hair, angina and impotence. In addition she insists it has extended the life of patients by as much as 30 per cent and infused the late years with vigour and good humour.

The weakness of the 'procaine' case is that controlled trials have failed to reproduce these results anywhere outside of Rumania, and although it is available there as part of state medical benefits, it remains in other countries both controversial and luxury medicine. In America, with a recommended three injections a week, doctors were cashing in to the tune of more than 10 and 15 dollars a shot for ampoules that cost less than 10 cents each to make. In the face of this it is small wonder that it was banned to prevent such exploitation.

In oral tablet form, however, it is widely sold in Europe as Gerovital or KH3 and in England as CH3. What cannot be denied is that it does seem to improve both mental and physical conditions of elderly patients. Dr Ana Aslan would claim this is achieved by the drug working on the central nervous system and stimulating cell vitality. The sceptical (including the authors) suspect there is a placebo auto-suggestion effect. Dr Alex Comfort concedes only that it functions chiefly as an anti-depressant.

George Hamilton, the actor, talking recently on British radio, albeit in humorous vein, didn't seem to have found this treatment gave him much uplift. After 'procaine' from Ana Aslan he said his hair remained grey and after foetal lamb cells he merely grew 'a good coat of wool'!

While much rejuvenation hopes today are based on the idea of renewing cell vitality, there are other doctors who believe you are as young as your blood. Their system involves either transfusions of young blood into elderly patients, or removal of old blood and replacement by salt solutions, which in turn force the body to replace the lost blood serum with fresh new blood, self-manufactured. In this way they claim age-accelerating factors are removed from the blood. Experts like Strehler and Comfort do not entirely discount this method, but it is extremely expensive and experimental and in our view a non-starter simply because the effect would not last. The red cells which carry the oxygen to the tissues last only about three months in the circulation but much less than this after transfusion. The white cells function for only a few days – if at all – after transfusion, while the platelets so important for clotting are virtually non-existent. Consequently to be of any value, and there is nothing to suggest that people's blood cells even in extreme age are grossly inefficient, such exchange transfusions would have to be performed at least monthly if not more often. Clearly that would be ridiculously wasteful of time and finances, but most of all of blood desperately needed for more important purposes.

Having made this reservation, there does appear to be something circulating in the blood of the old which is a powerful cause of ageing. Doctors in the know were shaken in the late 1960s when the true cause of the death of Dr Barnard's second heart transplant case, the dental surgeon Dr Blaiberg, became known.

The recipient of someone else's heart faces enormous odds in his battle to stay alive. His own body is geared to reject this foreign material, and to prevent this fatal response the patient must be given high doses of drugs to suppress this immune response. This leaves him at the mercy of any germ that happens to be passing – not just the ones which cause illness in other people, but those which are normally thrown off without causing any symptoms and which are always in our environment.

Consequently the transplant patient is walking a tightrope, with the risk of rejection on one side and overwhelming infection on the other. Anyone would have expected Blaiberg to have died of one or the other. He didn't. He died because his heart, the new one from a young donor aged only twenty, passed within one year in his chest through a lifetime of ageing. Dr Blaiberg died of advanced degenerative heart disease. At the post-mortem the transplanted heart and the section of main artery which was donated with it were, if anything, in a worse state of senile degeneration than Dr Blaiberg's own heart one year before. Who said something about new wine in old bottles?

Heart transplants are no longer performed in the elderly or for degenerative heart disease. After the Blaiberg case, they have been reserved for younger people with very specific diseases of the organ unrelated to the ageing process.

The publicity around transplants has led naturally to speculation on the possibility of extending life's limits by this and other 'spare part' surgery. The Blaiberg experience strongly suggests that this approach will lead to a dead end in more senses than one. However, the outlook is much better for the younger patient dying of diseases of other organs. Kidney machines and transplants are already postponing early death for almost 10,000 Britons every year, and our rapidly increasing knowledge of the control of rejection and infection means that their life expectancy is continually rising. Patients with liver disease who face transplants or death can also be given hope: survival for some liver transplant patients is now measured in years rather than months. Marrow transplants have transformed the lives of children who are born without, or lose, the ability to make their own white or red blood cells. Lung transplants may not be far off.

In terms of extending the limits of life, however, it has to be faced that transplants are not likely to be the answer, except for the unfortunate few whose diseases are ending their lives many years before the expected span. Even if they were successful in the older patient, they take up enormous resources, not only in money but in the training and time of skilled staff and the use of hospitals and theatres. The money spent on each transplant patient could substantially help the care of hundreds of the elderly sick, and no community of whatever political colour, no matter how wealthy, will ever be able to afford to give transplants to everyone who needs them.

There has, however, been one magnificent spin-off from transplant research, and this is in international co-operation. For the best results the tissues of the donor and recipient have to match very closely in many different ways. Matches are less difficult to find the larger the population from which to locate donors. Consequently there is a computerised kidney transplant service covering the whole of Europe which even penetrates the Iron Curtain, and recently this has extended across the Atlantic. Concorde's saving of several hours' flying time is much more important for the success of a kidney transplant than for the tycoon.

Another spin-off from transplant research may prove even more important for ageing people and surprisingly it may involve nothing more sophisticated than those old familiar standbys aspirin and cod liver oil, both of which have been found to help prevent blood clotting, one of the first stages of transplant rejection as well as a hazard in ageing, narrowed arteries. A prospective survey is under way in Britain in which

5,000 family doctors are taking aspirin three times a day for the rest of their lives. Their age at death and its causes will then be compared with a similar number who have agreed not to ever use the drug. The result should clearly define the place of aspirin in preventing this aspect of ageing, but it is likely to take at least ten years before even a trend clearly emerges. It was exactly such a trial involving British doctors of an earlier generation which proved the link between smoking and cancer.

The greatest advances in the extension of life will come from measures to prevent illness much as those outlined above. This is not to say that treatment of established diseases will not play a part. In the last decades the outlook for many fatal diseases has improved enormously. New drugs very successfully control high blood pressure, antibiotics have wiped out deaths from tuberculosis and meningitis and prevent bronchitis from progressing into pneumonia. Other drugs have vastly reduced the deaths from stomach ulcers, childhood leukaemia is no longer a death sentence, and women can be thankful for the enormous advances in the treatment of cervical cancer which is 100 per cent curable if caught early. An even more staggering advance is the transition from a 100 per cent death rate to a near 100 per cent cure rate of cancer of the placenta.

Even if all cancer were conquered tomorrow, it has been estimated that the average lifespan would be increased by only two years. Slowing down the ageing process must be the aim if we wish to really extend the limits, but in doing so quality of life gained is more important than mere quantity. One way this is achieved today for many women is by hormone replacement therapy. Women are programmed for their ovaries to shut down in mid-life and loss of the female sex hormones involves more than loss of reproductive capacity. For many women it can lead to degenerative changes of which one of the most serious is brittle bones (osteoporosis). Replacing the lost hormones prevents bone loss and diminishes the risk of broken femurs, a common cause of death in older women. This revolutionary treatment for post-menopausal problems is dealt with in detail in *No Change* by one of the authors.

One of the saddest aspects of ageing and one that most depletes the quality of life is the mental confusion, loss of memory and general deterioration of brain function, so insensitively termed 'senile dementia'. Although all of us lose cells from the brain's frontal lobes and the temporal lobes (the ones involved with memory) and by the age of eighty 40 per cent of these have been lost, only a quarter of people over that age suffer from this problem. So clearly it depends on more than cell loss or even the clogging of remaining cells with protein debris. Recently new work in Scotland, Sweden and America, suggests not only a cause but the possibility of preventing or at least treating the condition. Modern understanding of brain function has shown something of the complicated electro-chemical systems at work. For connections to be made from one cell to another an electrical impulse has to be flashed from one cell to the next. It must be eased across the cell junction by what are called neurone transmitters, like acetylcholine. In sufferers from senile dementia, there is up to 70 per cent less of this chemical, and their brain cells simply cannot connect. Work is going on to see if supplies of precursors of the chemical – that is, substances from which it is derived – can be increased to the brain, or if breakdown of the existing stocks of acetylcholine can be prevented by what are termed 'inhibitors'. Already this has been done with striking restoration of memory by using a drip to feed an appropriate 'inhibitor' into the bloodstream. While the drip is working so is the brain. But the effect does not last once the drip is stopped, as the brain cannot store the compound. So hopes may lie in more positive introduction of acetylcholine and one of the most fascinating things to emerge from this latest research is that diet may play a part. The very foods – liver, eggs and particularly fish – legendary for helping the brain are rich in cholines, the substances now known to be involved. Modern scientific discovery is only confirming ancient and presumably instinctive wisdom.

Another interesting and perhaps significant fact to emerge, which again may eventually help us to extend the limits of brain function, is that senile dementia seems to be a disease of Western society. In the undeveloped countries it is much less of a problem and not only because people generally do not live as long. They also live free from contamination by certain salts, heavy metals, lead, aluminium and some viruses, which have been shown experimentally in animals to have effect on the acetylcholine system.

Leaving aside both present and future medical advances there remains a great deal we can do to help ourselves extend the limits of useful and satisfying life. The importance of mental and physical activity has already been stressed but sensible care of the body dictates a few obvious do's and don'ts. Among the don'ts the most important is DON'T SMOKE.

People associate such warning with lung cancer but the truth is that while some will undoubtedly die an early and nasty death from this disease, every smoker develops bronchitis and has circulating in the blood nicotine (which accelerates the ageing of blood vessels) and carbon monoxide (which poisons the muscles of the heart and deprives the brain of oxygen). Small wonder then that we are witnessing a world-wide epidemic of deaths from heart disease, stroke and circulatory disorders. These diseases are no respecter of persons. The last four British kings, all very heavy smokers and all giving royal warrants to cigarette companies, paid with their lives. Edward VII was so crippled by chronic bronchitis in his last years that he had to be driven to his butt (grouse shooting not fag end) and shot the birds from the comfort of his car seat. George V had repeated attacks of lung failure throughout the last fifteen years of his life, to the last of which he succumbed. George VI was unfortunate enough to have three smoking-related diseases, all of which contributed to his death . . . lung cancer, Buerger's disease and coronary thrombosis. Edward VIII died of cancer of the throat. Although the Queen herself no longer smokes and Prince Charles and his father object strongly to the habit, those incongruous royal warrants have never been withdrawn – indeed the Queen Mother, who after losing her husband so tragically might have been expected to have most reason to condemn smoking, incredibly added her warrant to a cigarette company as recently as 1974, despite the fact that 50,000 of the Queen's subjects in the UK die each year from smoking.

There are signs that the lesson is being learned – 5 million Britons over the last ten years have stopped smoking and whereas at one time half of all doctors used cigarettes, only 1 in 5 now does so.

Drinking to excess is almost too obvious to mention if it were not that alcoholism is on the increase, particularly in the young. As a result deaths from liver disease, once rare in Britain, have multiplied twenty-fold in the last fifteen years.

Eating to excess in our prosperous third of the world is so common that a weight we regard as normal shortens our lifespan and is in fact overweight by at least 10 per cent. The proof of this is to be found in the actuarial tables of the life insurance companies. Alex Comfort proved with rats that diet works. He told us that he could slow the rat's ageing clock by a simple limitation of calorie intake.

> Just by alternate full-feeding and fasting one day in three, or by simple calorie limitation to 60 per cent of the control diet, rodent life span has been increased by 20 per cent to 40 per cent. All causes of death which multiply with age were postponed, tumours included, and the animals were content, active, underweight and still young when the controls died. It is virtually certain, with adjustment to our own diet, that a similar result could be obtained in man.
>
> A 20 to 40 per cent longer natural life span is possible now if we have the foresight to work out the optimum eating pattern and the

> self-control to use it. The trouble is, to judge from cigarette smoking, public concern for longevity does not extend to making itself uncomfortable. So, if calorie restriction does prove to be the answer, it may have to wait for the development of a blocking agent, already under test, which will neutralise the harmful effects of overeating but leave our intake unchanged.
>
> At any rate, providing funds are made available for continued research, I predict that by 1990 we will probably know more than one proven way of extending vigorous life by about 20 per cent at least, and the likely agents will be simple, cheap and used extensively.

However cheap, to us the concept of medically condoning overeating in a starving world is immoral, even if it should prove possible.

While a boy at birth today in the developed world can still only expect to live sixty-nine years and a girl seventy-five, these may be the maximum unless there is the sort of shift in living habits that the experts suggest. In the US the trend for men is downwards, with American men dying on average almost a year younger than they did ten years ago.

As always there are exceptions. The Guinness Book of Records reports that the greatest authenticated age to which a human has ever lived is 113 years 214 days and this was a woman, a Mrs Delina Filkins who died in 1928. In 1979 the Japanese fêted Shigechiyo Izumi, of the island of Tokuno-Shima, when he reached 114. Japan takes age so seriously that 15 September is set aside as the National Day of Respect for the Aged.

There is no doubt the number of centenarians is rising. In Britain in 1951 there were only 140 recorded but the 1971 census showed 2,430. Miss Alice Stevens dying at 112 in 1973 almost took the record from her American rival.

The widespread belief that people in Russia and South America, living stress-free lives at high altitudes, commonly achieve extraordinary longevity is no longer given credence. Apart from almost total lack of birth registrations and reliance only on hearsay, it is known that many quite deliberately took on an older man's identity to avoid military service . . . Where there has been close scrutiny of birth and death rates, no one has ever been found to reach the age of 115. In Sweden the limit is 110. Even more interesting are the records of the British peerage which have been closely documented for over 1,000 years. In that time only two of these privileged people reached a century, one of them actually making 101. The Russian claims were even denounced by one of their own gerontologists, admittedly only after his expulsion. Stalin was a Georgian and encouraged the idea that Georgians were more long lived than others. Consequently the locals tried to please him by excessive claims.

Few of us who really know the score would envy most of the really aged today. Once, the really old were the really healthy. Because of modern drugs and resuscitation old age too often now is just a prolongation of the process of dying, the slow humiliating deterioration of the body and the mind. But is this really the end – the ultimate limit?

9
Death – the Ultimate Limit

The Reverend Philips was just fifty-two when he first fell ill. It didn't seem serious to him at the time – just some form of indigestion. Still, he had never had such problems before, so he approached his doctor for 'some medicine to settle his tummy'. A few questions and a gentle palpation of the minister's thin abdomen quickly revealed the cause of his pain and constipation, but making the diagnosis gave his doctor no sense of achievement. It was obvious that his was a growth of the bowel wall, and highly probable that it had spread too far to be checked.

Suspecting that his patient and friend was facing death within months at the most, the doctor sent him to the surgeons, explaining, as was the fashion in those early 1960s, that there was probably 'an abscess' that might need removing.

The surgeon discovered the worst. Not only was the growth highly malignant, it had spread to the liver and there was no hope of saving the minister's life. It was decided to start him on the usual morphine-based painkillers, and send him home to die, peacefully, in the care of his wife.

She, of course, was told the truth. But what about the minister himself? After a long discussion, just between the two of them, the family doctor and surgeon decided to continue with the white lie about the abscess. The minister's wife, a very strict, one might say puritanical, Christian, agreed to co-operate, but only after considerable misgivings. She believed the truth always to be better, no matter how unpalatable.

His illness led to the usual downhill course, but his spirits were kept high by the daily visits of his doctor and friend, and the district nurse's thrice-daily injections. All was well, and his life reasonably content, when his wife, anxious for him to prepare to meet his Maker, blurted out the truth.

The poor man was unable to face it: full of guilt and doubts, his character changed. Far from thanking his wife he cursed her: he could no longer trust his medical and nursing help, he raged at the unfairness of it all. He lived for only three more days, in pain, fear, and anger at what had happened to him. His doctor and surgeon estimated that without the sudden blow, he would have lived several months longer. Without hope, he had crumbled, both in mind and body.

No one doubts that the dying person, deprived of hope and feeling, unable to continue the fight against disease, may accelerate his or her own death.

When it comes to hastening one's own death by any sort of mental influence or motivation, the story of the rich elderly Mr Bond just might come under this heading. An enthusiastic amateur actor he hired Covent Garden to stage Voltaire's play *Zaire*, himself acting the part of the nobly born old father doomed to die dramatically upon the stage. On the night he threw himself into the part with such fervour that he actually expired at the appropriate moment, one must hope to thunderous applause as he would certainly have been unable to take the curtain call. When it was reported to Voltaire he is said to have been 'very touched by this display of sensibility', accepting it as a fitting tribute to the power of his writing.

If death can be accelerated, is the converse possible? Can the moment of death, the ultimate limit, be postponed by an effort of will?

It is the stuff of all fiction – the dying hero or heroine, managing to keep alive against all the odds until the arrival of a loved one, so that death can come while cradled in the lover's arms. Unhappily real life rarely bears this out. For every person whose life seems to hang by a thread for an inordinate time, there are many, many more whose deaths occur either unexpectedly, or as predicted by the doctors caring for them. And it matters not whether the patient has all the will-power in the world. There are also elderly people, alone, depressed and inactive, who admit to being ready to die, to wish to meet again their dead family, and who live on, in spite of themselves, for many years.

Perhaps it is the subconscious wish of all of us that somehow we can control that final limit, to fix our deaths at a convenient time for ourselves – and usually as far ahead as possible – that makes many of us believe in life after death. The number of writers trying to persuade us that there is scientific evidence for this – that death indeed is no limit at all to human potential – has multiplied in recent years.

Before we declare our own opinions on that, we feel it is only fair to review the evidence. If we had defined death, say, two decades ago, it would have been easy: it was the time when the heart stops beating, the last breath is taken and the brain ceases to function. The change should be, and usually is, obvious. Death greatly alters the appearance. The blood drains from the skin, giving a grey, waxy look. As the muscles of the face die, all trace of expression goes. Those thriller writers who describe the faces or eyes of their murder victims as 'still twisted with horror' – and even doctors like Conan Doyle did so – are writing rubbish. No matter how death comes, it leaves the face without trace of emotion.

This isn't to say that mistakes have not been made. The founder of modern anatomy, Andreas Vesalius, who should have known better, had demonstrated the art of dissection to his students on hundreds of bodies before he set to work on a Spanish nobleman who came back to 'life' on the table. This was in the sixteenth century, at the height of the Inquisition. The Spaniard survived, but Vesalius was sentenced to death. Strangely, the Grand Inquisitor was himself, shortly afterwards, the subject of dissection. He, too, briefly 'came alive', but the shock of finding himself in such a disagreeable position must have finished him, for he quickly returned to his 'dead' state.

The premature diagnosis of death has worried people in every civilisation. Ancient Roman writers certainly described it, and Victorians and Edwardians positively wallowed in it. In 1905, W. R. Hadwen wrote a book *Premature Burial* in which he suggested that 2,700 of the half million or so people 'dying' each year in England and Wales were, in fact, buried alive.

At that time there was plenty of reason to fear mistakes. In 1896, the *London Echo* reported the strange affair of the Greek Orthodox Bishop of Lesbos, who after lying for two days on a ceremonial bier in his church, suddenly sat up and complained at the people filing reverently past. Hadwen tells of a missionary to India, the Reverend Schwartz, whose flock, singing a hymn at his funeral, were surprised, to say the least, to hear the good pastor join in from his coffin.

Another Victorian with an interest in the morbid was G. E. MacKay, who wrote about premature burials in *Popular Science* in 1880. He related how Francesco Petrarch, the poet, 'woke up' just four hours before the time for his burial, apparently stimulated back to life by a sudden draught of cold air about which he bitterly complained. He lived for thirty more years. A fellow Italian, Luigi Vittori, carried for many years the stigma of his 'death', in the form of a burnt nose, after a doctor, doubting a first doctor's dismal diagnosis, held a candle to it.

Probably the most grisly of the books warning of the dangers of precipitate burial was M. R. Fletcher's, printed in Boston in 1890, entitled *One Thousand Buried Alive By Their Best Friends*.

The British can't be left out: medical schools paid money for fresh corpses dug from graveyards in the 1820s. The anatomists could not have been too happy with the publicity in 1824 which followed the waking up of John MacIntyre, raised illegally from a local churchyard, who complained loudly when the dissector's knife entered his chest. The demonstration had to change quickly to life-saving repair.

Lyall Watson, in *The Romeo Error*, describes the exhumation of a young pregnant woman in 1893 from whose coffin noises had been heard. The horrifying conclusion was that she had obviously struggled to free herself, and at the same time given birth to her baby; both had then suffocated.

Small wonder, then, that many Victorians and Edwardians left specific instructions on what was to be done if they were found, presumed dead. Wilkie Collins always kept them by his bedside: Hans Andersen carried them about with him. A US army doctor, Edward Vollum, suggested that every coffin containing a non-embalmed corpse should also contain a bottle of chloroform for use in the unfortunate event of revival.

More popular, but perhaps more expensive, should have been the mechanism proposed by a chamberlain to the Tsar, Count Karnice-Karnicki, in which a tube from the coffin led to a closed container above the ground. In theory, any evidence of life within the coffin would cause the lid of the container to open, supplying air, and at the same time a flagpole would rise, complete with flag, bell and flashing light. It is not known whether the humane Count produced or sold any of his machines, but he intended to sell them to cemetery authorities for rent to the departed for a fortnight after burial.

Of course, today one would think that with all the equipment of modern medicine and the skill of our doctors such precautions are unnecessary and even ludicrous. Or are they? Readers of London's *Daily Telegraph* were presented in 1963 with the story of Elsie Waring, a woman in her thirties who was certified dead by no fewer than three hospital doctors. She began to show signs of life only when being encoffined in a North London public mortuary.

A year later, according to Lyall Watson, a 'corpse' in a New York mortuary leaped from the slab and grabbed the pathologist, who had just started his post-mortem, by the throat. The patient survived, but the pathologist didn't! The Germans have always done things more efficiently: they have waiting rooms in their mortuaries, just in case. Indeed for centuries the dead of Munich were laid out in rows, in a great Gothic hall, all attached to a line which, if pulled, rang bells in the caretaker's office. We don't know if he was regularly disturbed by their ringing!

With such doubts about the diagnosis of death still lingering, it is not surprising that people still write into their wills that their veins be opened or their hearts incised before their remains are dispatched to the crematorium or graveyard. Mistakes should be much rarer than they were, now that electrocardiograph tracings, recording the electrical activity of the heart muscle, are widely used to determine death. It was a salutary lesson to the doctors using for the first time, a new, very sensitive, instrument in the Sheffield, UK, mortuary in 1970 when it showed that a twenty-three-year-old girl, thought to have died from a drug overdose, was still alive!

Even the cardiograph can make errors. Keith Mant, the famous British forensic pathologist, skilled as he is in the diagnosis of death, was at a loss to explain the case of one badly wounded American GI in Vietnam in 1967. After three-quarters of an hour of intensive efforts to revive him, he was declared dead by the doctors because both the electrocardiograph and the electroencephalograph (which traces brain electrical activity) gave completely flat tracings. Four hours after arriving in the mortuary he recovered – and at the time of writing he is presumably still alive in his home state of Illinois.

There can be only two explanations of these reports. The first is that the vital functions still continued, the heart beating and the lungs expanding just enough to supply the brain with oxygen to allow it to continue to tick over until normal function was resumed. The brain is the important area: it dies irretrievably within about six minutes of the heart stopping, and much sooner if the patient has been very active or has had a high fever just before death. The other organs are not so important – they can last much longer, even hours, without being irreversibly damaged. It is just within the bounds of feasibility, therefore, that with the amount of residual oxygen in the lungs and with a system which just, and no more, keeps up the circulation specifically to the brain, a patient can continue to live and be apparently dead.

The second explanation goes much deeper. Could these people in states of apparent 'suspended animation' really have died, then later become alive again? If so, where was the energy, or life force, or soul, or whatever we like to call the thing that differentiates the living from the inanimate?

Orthodox doctors have little doubt. They dismiss this death-like state as one in which the nervous system is temporarily in a state of inhibition – of shock, in lay language. If it continues, it leads inevitably to true death. If it can be broken, then the victim may return to normal bodily function. The teachers of forensic (legal) medicine in most British medical schools include a short description of suspended animation in their courses for students. They don't dwell upon it, remarking that it is a rare curiosity, and even when recovered from has usually caused so much damage to the vital organs that true death quickly follows.

C. J. Polson, until recently Professor of Forensic Medicine at Leeds University, describes recoveries from apparent death from drowning after over an hour of resuscitation attempts, and after submersion for half an hour. Electrocution, too, leads to 'suspended animation', and Polson records recoveries after two hours of continuous resuscitation attempts. Nowhere, however, does he consider that during this state true death has occurred.

To Polson, and most of his colleagues, death presents in two phases: firstly, the extinction of personality, or somatic death, which is our usual idea of death; and secondly, the disintegration of the body tissues, or molecular death. Many have tried to determine exactly what happens to the body at the end of the first phase, even going as far as placing dying patients on weighing-machine beds. In the 1920s Zaalberg van Zelst in the Hague and Duncan McDougall in Britain independently reported that the body lost exactly 2·45oz (69·5g) at the precise time of death. Suggestions that this might be the weight of the soul were rejected when later researchers were unable to repeat their findings.

The inevitable approach of the first phase, but the possible avoidance of the second is what has led a few Americans to follow Dr James H. Bedford of California.

Dr Bedford paid £1,500 to enable his body to be permanently stored in liquid nitrogen at a temperature of −321°F (−196°C) and another £70,000 for research into the deep freezing of bodies. At least ten Americans have followed him into the deep-freeze tubes, and thousands have joined the cryonics societies in the hope of future revival and cure from their, until now, fatal diseases. There are forty tubes in the first cryotorium awaiting those unable to face what they think is total oblivion with death. They will set future scientists bent on their resurrection enormous problems, for apart from their diseases, the massive destruction of their cells by ice crystals will have to be reversed.

There are people, however, who appear to have already experienced death, and have returned to this side of the barrier. The cryotorium is not for them. For if their experience is to be believed, almost all of them found their time on the other side so enjoyable as to be 'blissful' or even ecstatic. Many resented being 'brought back' to life.

Such an admission from two authors who are very definitely committed to a humanistic approach to life, and whose attitude to religion is at least sceptical, if not opposed, might be surprising, if it were not for recent advances in the care of people who in past decades would certainly have died. The resuscitation of heart-attack victims, of road-accident victims, in hospital intensive-care units; the long-term survival of patients dying of kidney disease on dialysis machines and with transplants; the revival of patients dying from cancers and blood diseases, all have prolonged lives by periods unthinkable to a doctor whose career started, say, in the early 1960s.

Even where cure is not possible, the multitude of new drugs, particularly for heart and blood-pressure problems and cancer, have extended people's lives for years. It has to be admitted that people still die, usually, in their seventies, but many more of our generation will reach three-score and ten than in any previous population.

This quiet revolution in medicine has meant two major changes in the relationships between doctors and patients. First, because doctors are better able to treat diseases, even the most serious, they are better able to tell their patients the truth. At the time of the Reverend Philips' death, over 9 doctors in every 10 never admitted to their patients that their illness was likely to be fatal. His medical men were only following the fashion of their time. It may, with hindsight, have been wrong, at least for him. If he had been told earlier, perhaps his anger would have settled and he would have adjusted himself to his fate. On the other hand, it may merely have meant that his breakdown was precipitated several months earlier. No one can tell.

The doctors of the 1980s would, almost to a man (or woman), tell patients like the minister the truth. It would be tempered, perhaps, by more optimism about the treatment than could have been offered twenty years before. And he would be helped by specialist attention to the process of dying, the substance of which has accrued from the magnificent work done by Dr Cicely Saunders and those like her who pioneered and still run the hospices for the terminally ill which have grown up in Britain in the intervening years.

American doctors, too, have changed their approach to the dying, but partly for different reasons. It is difficult not to tell the total truth to patients in an atmosphere where malpractice suits against the doctor are now a national pastime. Many patients (in some hospitals 15–20 per cent) dying from chronic diseases are included in research trials in which the law says that the patient must be told all the facts about his case, and sign a document which shows that he knows them. It will soon be impossible to present some of the truth kindly and shield the patient from the worst, a development that many doctors and nurses fear. For there must surely be patients for whom it is better not to know.

The second change is that patients are now talking to their doctors. The modern patient no longer shrouds medicine with mystery and his relationship with his doctor has improved, at least from the patient's point of view, as a consequence. The doctor can now be asked questions, and may even answer them! He is no longer on an academic or mystical pedestal: his diagnosis and treatment may be challenged, and he is seen as an ordinary man, fallible and human. And, if it has done nothing for his ego, the change has taught him that the patient may have something useful to contribute himself to the management of his case.

Nowhere has this been better demonstrated than in the case of the resuscitated dying or dead. Every day apparently 'dead' patients are 'shocked' back to life by electrodes placed on their chests, or heart massage, and the cardiologists or anaesthetists who perform this service are not always faced afterwards with a grateful patient. After years of work in this field, doctors have collected remarkable case histories from patients who have 'died'. They are remarkable not just for their content, but for the series of similarities they present, which, if given as evidence in any field of human experience apart from this last one, would be accepted as well beyond the possibility of coincidence.

People have talked of what has happened after revival from their apparent deaths for thousands of years. The reaction of others, who have not shared their experience, has usually been to declare them mad or to ignore them. Such recoveries occurred too rarely then for any critical assessment or comparison with others even by a few educated people who might believe them. Enough, however, have come down to us to suggest that they have happened in every century.

One example appears in Bede's *History of the English Church and People*, written in AD 731. It is remarkable in that it names the man to whom the crisis occurred, a family name still well known today. He was a Cunningham of Northumbria, who died in the early hours of one morning after a gradually worsening illness. At dawn, with all his family and friends grieving round his corpse, he suddenly sat up. Everyone but his wife ran away. He explained to her that he had been guided in death by a man in a shining robe to a broad, deep, dark valley of infinite length. From there they entered an atmosphere of bright light, and crossed a high wall beyond which was a broad and pleasant meadow. His guide then told him he must return to live among men again. Although most reluctant to leave such a pleasant, beautiful place he had no choice but to do it, and he suddenly found himself back in his body, alive.

A similar reluctance to return from death was apparently expressed by two small tenth-century Irish boys, who, revived from death by drowning by the Celtic Saint Senan, protested to their mother that they wished to return immediately to the land which they had seen during their time 'dead'. They were allowed to 'die' again shortly afterwards.

Similar stories are told in cultures as far apart as the American Indians and the Hindus, the Maoris and the Western Europeans, and they have many characteristics in common – including dark valleys or long tunnels, a 'being of light' full of love and compassion to welcome the recently dead to their new existence, and often a dead relative or friend to put them at their ease.

None of this was known, however, to Elisabeth Kubler-Ross, or Raymond A. Moody, or Maurice Rawlins, all now doctors of medicine, or Ian Currie, a doctor of sociology, when they separately started to probe the limits of dying and death in the 1960s.

Dr Kubler-Ross, of Illinois, has devoted over twenty years to the care of the dying. She was forced to the conclusion that, after the pronouncement of clinical death, when all orthodox physicians believe that all consciousness has irreversibly been lost, people remain aware of their surroundings. They 'float out' of their physical bodies, and find the experience peaceful and very pleasant. They are aware of another being there to help them, and often meet loved ones who have died before them. And when they are brought back by modern medical procedures, they resent the interference, at least in the first few hours. Later they are glad of the second chance of life, and often permanently change their lifestyles to ones of serenity, confidence and religious activity with all fear of death removed. Dr Kubler-Ross now has hundreds of patient records which follow this pattern.

Raymond Moody admits from the outset that he is biased. He grew up in the Presbyterian faith, but looked on it as a code to live by, of spiritual and ethical guidelines, rather than a set of fixed doctrines. He was a philosophy student at the University of Virginia in 1965 when he first met a man who had been revived from death. The man, a Professor of Psychiatry in the School of Medicine, had 'died' twice. His memory of what happened during his two periods of 'death' was concise but to quote him 'quite fantastic'. He was in every other way a normal person, but Moody dismissed his story at the time, consigning the talk to his stock of taped notes. Years later, as a university teacher himself, and after giving a lecture on the attitudes of Plato to life and death, Moody was approached by one of his students. The student's grandmother had 'died' during surgery, and on her returning to consciousness described an experience almost exactly like that of the Professor's, whose story had not been mentioned in the lecture.

From then on Moody discussed with successive groups of philosophy students the subject of survival of biological death, carefully avoiding any mention of his two cases. He was astonished to find that in almost every class of about thirty, one student could tell a similar story.

Moody, partly because of his growing interest in the phenomenon of death, turned from philosophy to medicine in 1972. He now has 150 cases of death or 'near-death' experiences on his files. They comprise three groups. The first are all people who have recovered after being judged clinically dead by doctors; the second includes people who were very close to death because of accidents or illness; in the third are the statements of people who, as they died, told witnesses what was happening to them. All correlate well, but not exactly, which drives Dr Moody to conclude that they form a continuum with each other. In his book *Life After Life*, which describes many of the death experiences, he has attempted to pick out their commonest elements. There are about fifteen which recur repeatedly.

A typical hospital intensive care 'death' has the following pattern. At the height of the patient's physical distress, when he feels his worst, suddenly all physical agony disappears. Then he clearly hears the doctor talk of the death. This is followed by an uncomfortable ringing or roaring noise and he feels as if he is moving rapidly along a black tunnel. Suddenly he is outside his body, in another one which can float and transport him effortlessly. Usually he is still near his old body, which he can see, along with the staff working to revive him, but with whom he cannot communicate.

People come to meet him, to help him on his next step – sometimes a 'being of light', full of compassion and love, and radiating a brilliant but not blinding light. At this point he may be presented with a series of 'playbacks' of the major events his life, good and bad, not in any way a judgement, but apparently to make him think about the value of his life.

At the last the new arrival is presented with a barrier. It may be a wall, a stretch of water, a bank of mist, or even a line on the ground. It seems to symbolise the border between this life and the next. Crossing it clearly means that return is impossible. As all the patients interviewed returned, what is beyond that barrier is unknown to them, but about one thing Dr Moody is clear. All those who reached this far on the road after death would have preferred to go on than to come back. They were overwhelmed by feelings of joy, love and peace. Re-entry into their usually sick bodies was a painful, unpleasant reverse for them.

Moody is the first to emphasise that these events are only related by a small number of those who return from apparent death. The vast majority remember nothing of what happened during the critical time.

Maurice Rawlings, an American specialist in heart diseases, used to be an atheist, but is now a devout, even evangelising Christian. His sudden conversion started not in church or after listening to a hot-gospeller, but in his own consulting room. During an investigation of a forty-eight-year old postman for suspected heart disease, the patient's heart suddenly stopped. Rawlings immediately initiated the usual emergency procedures. A nurse started mouth-to-mouth breathing, he began heart massage, and the patient began to 'come round'. Unfortunately, the heart could not keep up a beat strong enough to sustain the circulation, and Rawlings had to break off his resuscitation efforts to insert a pacemaker device into one of the veins. This takes time, and meant several intervals of a few seconds from the heart massage.

The patient's reaction to his stopping the massage was remarkable. Fully conscious and aware of the pain of severe and repeated pressure on the chest wall – to the extent that ribs might be broken – the usual reaction of a patient is to protest loudly and ask to be left alone. This man screamed for the doctor to continue, because he was in hell! He 'died' several more times in the next hour, and each time he apparently returned to hell, and the terror and distress he experienced was worse than anything in Rawlings' long associations with the dying.

In the end the patient asked Rawlings, the unbeliever, how he could stay out of hell. The doctor had no alternative but to pray with him, foolish as it felt at the time.

The postman recovered, and two days later had forgotten his brush with the infernal regions. Rawlings had not. It was the start of his collection of similar cases and for his book *Beyond Death's Door*.

Rawlings' conclusions about the process of death are the same as those of Moody and Kubler-Ross, with one major difference. He alone of the three was with most of his patients during their death experience and spoke to them in the seconds immediately after the crisis. The others based their reports on interviews conducted at least a week after the event, and were only informed of good after-death experiences. There is no trace of a hell in their books.

Rawlings explains this very simply. The hell-bound patients have such a terrifying time during their out-of-life period that on return their consciousness could not retain the memory without making them insane. The memory is therefore suppressed deep into the subconscious, from which only hypnosis, perhaps, could make it emerge. Attempts to hypnotise such patients, Rawlings believes, might not only put the patient at serious risk of losing sanity or life, but could precipitate him back into hell. He will not do it.

Interestingly the postman became, after the hell episode, a strong Christian. He also had another cardiac arrest months later. This time the experience reflected those described by Moody and Kubler-Ross, and did not fade with time.

Rawlings has encountered the 'bad' death experiences as often as the 'good' ones. The 'being of light', identified by patients of the other doctors with Christ or, in those of other religions, with Krishna, Buddha or Mahomet, and the meeting with departed relatives are very much part of the 'good' episodes, but some return talking of lakes of fire, moaning wretched people, and tormenting devils.

Now a fundementalist Christian, yet still very much a practising heart specialist, Rawlings finds no difficulty in explaining such experiences. He quotes the many New Testament references to Jesus as the light of the world, the conversion of Saul of Tarsus to Paul by the blinding light as a similar phenomenon. All the authors remark on the similarity of the deathly valley or tunnel to the valley of the shadow of death of the 23rd Psalm. Rawlings explains the hell-like states as only to be expected from the Book of Revelation.

But what about non-Christians and atheists, who have also reported meetings with the loving and compassionate 'being of light' and felt soothed and welcomed by him? Moody and Kubler-Ross have no doubts that all are welcomed in death, irrespective of religion or their behaviour in life. Rawlings is not so sure. He considers this initial awesome encounter as a first sorting ground. To Rawlings and to other evangelists such as Billy Graham or Stephen Board, it could even be Satan in disguise, deceiving the returning person into a security and complacency which will prevent him changing his life.

This assumption shows the lengths to which fundamentalists will go in preserving their own beliefs. Judgements or conclusions about death experiences, even by these doctors and psychologists who presumably have some scientific training and knowledge, are still apparently highly coloured by their particular religious leanings.

Take Ian Currie, for example, a Canadian sociologist who for thirteen years was an academic at the University of California. Now he is a full-time psychic researcher and lecturer on death and dying. In his book *You Cannot Die* he states that 'we are the 2,000th human generation to be haunted by the most fundamental of all the questions that man can ask himself. Why am I here? Why do I exist? Where do I come from, and what will become of me?' He continues, 'We will be the last generation, though, not to know the answer.'

That is as may be. He is certainly very persuasive. His chapters on out-of-the-body experiences, deathbed visions and resuscitations are virtually identical to those of Kubler-Ross and Moody, and to the 'good' experiences of Rawlings. But he adds something else: a series of after-death paradises through which the person's spirit must ascend by enlightenment to a seventh and final stage in which it becomes merged in 'God'. He also presents many cases which appear to 'prove' reincarnation. The Hindu and Buddhist influence is obvious, and independent, particularly scientific, observers could claim that this must prejudice his judgement.

To be fair, Currie's case histories appear to be well researched; he gives names of people, places and dates which are easily verified, and many of the people he interviewed are still living. The tunnel, the out-of-the-body feeling, the dead relatives and the 'being of light' are all again described. The usual descriptions by the resuscitated 'dead' of details of what happened, including remarks and actions by doctors and nurses during the time of their 'death', are given, as are the feelings of joy and peace. His additions to the Moody, Kubler-Ross evidence, however, are as disturbing as those of Rawlings. For Currie appears to be a committed spiritualist.

Many of the people he interviewed after 'death' experiences talked of hosts of 'earthbound' dead who have never moved on from the immediate time and place of their deaths. There was no loving relative or 'being of light' to welcome them and guide them to the next stage of their existence. Currie sees in them the ghosts and 'spirit contacts' of the world of the dead – the entities who answer those who play with ouija boards; and even those who 'possess' the living.

Birth, to Currie, is not a beginning, just as death is not a limit. How else, he asks, could the behaviour of Robert, a six-year-old boy, be explained? Robert was born in Britain in the 1920s of a Belgian father and English mother. He met his paternal grandmother on a visit from Belgium for the first time at the age of two, and struck up a very close friendship with her. He stayed with her for long periods after that. At three, a visitor to the house started filming with a ciné camera, the handle of which produced a rapid clicking noise. Robert screamed in terror for him to stop: that he had been killed like that last time.

The noise was reminiscent of machine-gun fire – his father's older brother had been killed by a German machine gun in 1915. The links between Robert and his dead uncle multiplied: the grandmother was called pet names only known to the dead man; his photograph was claimed by the boy as of himself; in character and petty likes and dislikes the dead uncle and living nephew were identical.

It is easy to interpret Robert's story as one of wish fulfilment by a mother grieving for a lost favourite son; the grandson's behaviour could have developed subconsciously or even consciously along the path she desired. But how to explain the first behaviour of the child, which started before he knew her, and in apparent ignorance of his dead uncle and his death?

Robert's case could be dismissed as coincidence if it was a rarity. Ian Stevenson, Professor of Psychiatry at the University of Virginia, is certain that it is not. He has 1,700 case histories of people who remember previous lives, many of which are so detailed that their former selves have been identified. Almost every former life concerned an ordinary person whose existence was unknown until after the checking of the statements of the subject. People who dismiss the claims as rubbish might care to read Stevenson's *Twenty Cases Suggestive of Reincarnation*, and the sequel *Cases of the Reincarnation Type, Volume I*, published by the University Press of Virginia.

The very small number of people who remember previous lives, follow, according to Stevenson, a common pattern. As soon as they can talk they persist in claiming that they have been someone else. The parents, shocked by the 'mental instability' in so young a child, usually try to suppress such statements, but the toddler persists, despite the opposition and even punishment. Names and addresses may be given which can be verified, the home surroundings of the former life recognised and changes remarked upon. Meetings with the former family produce bizarre scenes of the child greeting the former 'wife' with husbandly affection, and former sons and daughters with paternal advice.

This inexplicable behaviour gradually recedes, rarely persisting past the age of ten, so that the new personality emerges unscathed and suitably integrated into the present existence. Often the teenager has no memory of the disturbance – although it certainly leaves its mark on those around him.

Stevenson finds conscious remembrances of previous lives an extreme rarity. Ian Currie believes that far from being rare it is universal! According to him anyone can be placed under hypnosis and 'regressed' to previous lives. He claims that subjects under hypnosis typically display highly accurate details of the times and places of their previous lives, details that few of them know in their present existence. They may even speak in archaic dialects of languages other than their own which, taped, are recognised by specialised linguists. The one person in ten who is a poor hypnotic subject, says Currie, has almost certainly died a violent death in a recent past life, and his subconscious is frightened to relive it. If the hypnotist reassures him or her of protection and safety at the beginning of the session the hypnosis is usually successful.

Arnall Bloxham, a British hypnotherapist, has collected tapes of over 400 previous lives revealed under hypnosis. Most are run of the mill, and many are without historical verification. One, however, sticks out. He took a Welsh woman, Jane Evans, with no psychiatric or medical problems, back to the twelfth century, when she was apparently a Jewish woman living in York. Unhappily, it was the year of the English anti-Jewish atrocities – and Mrs Evans, now Rebecca, was trapped, with her small daughter, in the crypt of a church by the mob. After detailed descriptions of the town and the church, she relived the full horror, first of her daughter's, then her own murder.

The tapes of Jane Evan's hypnotic session were given to the University of York's Professor of History, Barrie Dobson, who found in them a very accurate representation of twelfth-century life and events, some of the details of which could only have been known by a professional historian. Professor Dobson, however, had a problem. He was able to identify the church in which Rebecca met her death but, like all the old churches in York, apart from the Minster itself, it did not possess a crypt. Rebecca denied that she was in the Minster. It was inevitable that the story had to be wrong: and if that aspect of it was inaccurate, then the rest, no matter how authentic it sounded, was thrown into doubt.

In 1975, with the Rebecca story forgotten, the church Professor Dobson had pinpointed, St Mary's in Castlegate, was turned into a museum. The missing crypt was found under the altar, where it had been blocked off and forgotten for centuries. Those who dismiss the story as coincidence or contrivance would do well to read Jeffery Iverson's book on the Bloxham tapes, *More Lives Than One?*, published by Warner Books in 1977.

Individual experiences of reincarnation may not convince the rational, scientific, twentieth-century man. They did, however, lead Dr Helen Wambach, an orthodox New Jersey psychologist, to set up in 1965 a unique scientific study to test them. She reasoned that if she could take hundreds of people back to their previous lives, she would hear of many aspects of everyday life that would be common to them all, and certainly unknown to the ordinary people of the twentieth century.

Her results are astonishing. She has over 1,100 'regressions' in her files from 1,000 people. Only one described a life from the history books – that of James Buchanan, President of the United States from 1857 to 1861, and that includes details which corroborate the truth of the claim, rather than suggests a reference to already known aspects of his life.

Much more important are the answers Dr Wambach received about the food being eaten, the clothes worn, or the coins used to buy them by people under regression hypnosis. People back in the same geographical area and the same historical period described the same details for them all. There are many short lives, obviously from people dying in infancy. She also refuted one of the major arguments against reincarnation. This depends on the vast increase of the human population in the last century. As most of the human lives that have been lived since we first appeared on this earth relate to the last 100 years, how could we all have lived in the past?

Dr Wambach showed that the population was reflected in the lives of her subjects! They described few lives before the first century AD. The numbers doubled in the following fourteen centuries, again in the next four, then quadrupled in the last century. Not only does her answer confound the critics, it has strongly encouraged the supporters of repeated human rebirth in another. She suggests that the answer to the question, 'How long does death last?', is not an eternity, but fifty-four years!

Where do we stand? We have to admit to starting this chapter as total sceptics. In the fashion of twentieth-century scientific man and woman we believed that after death there is dust and no more – except perhaps, and hopefully, happy memories in the minds of our closest family and friends.

Even after reading the evidence and speaking to various believers, Christian and otherwise, we remained unconvinced, mainly because their own experiences were so at variance with ours. We have never knowingly been in the presence of 'earthbound spirits' or heard revelations from the resuscitated 'nearly dead' or 'dead' which remotely resembled those described in the books, and one of us, having been a hospital doctor and general practitioner, certainly had many opportunities to hear them. Nor had either of us heard of or experienced out-of-body experiences. As for reincarnation, despite the obvious sincerity of its believers, it still seemed a nonsense to both of us.

Determined, however, to keep an open mind and not to allow scientific logic – which cried out against everything we had heard and read – or plain prejudice to obscure our judgements, we decided to probe a little further, and into our own family circle. The result was discomforting to say the least.

When walking in London in the summer of 1976, the Smith family – Tom, his wife Mary, and children Catriona and Alasdair were communally knocked down on a zebra crossing by a speeding bus, the brakes of which had failed. Tom and the children were relatively unhurt, apart from the shock of seeing Mary, hit full in the stomach, flying through the air, to land on the pavement. As it turned out, she was relatively lucky, getting off with a few internal bruises and no broken bones. After a night spent in a hospital casualty department we were all allowed home.

Now three years later, for the first time, and only after reading the first draft of this book, Mary admitted that during those first moments after the crash she knew she was dead. She was not unhappy about it because we were all, as far as she knew, dead with her, and it was not unpleasant. She was not in any pain, indeed she could not feel her body at all. On reflection, she felt that she was probably not in her body for those few seconds, but did not feel that at all unusual.

It was only when she found herself lying on the pavement, attempting to get up, that the pain started, and she was back with us again. She had never thought to mention this experience before, because she did not think anyone would understand, and she might appear 'odd'. To her it was a unique experience.

Most scientists and doctors might pass this off as just an episode of fleeting unconsciousness or momentary confusion, and Tom Smith is no exception. But his knowledge of his wife, and her reasons for not revealing her feelings at the time suggest otherwise. As a doctor it seems possible to him that the sudden blow caused her heart to stop for the short time in which she had this experience, which is not described after mere fainting or loss of consciousness.

The same evening Tom's father, one year a widower, read the same first draft. His account of the long vigil with his wife, dying after several strokes, hovering between semi-consciousness and coma, and her apparent rational conversations with long-dead brothers and sisters, corresponded almost exactly with those described by Kubler-Ross and Moody in the 'near-death' experiences of their parents. Tom's father had never mentioned them to anyone, partly because he might be thought to be a foolish old man (which he patently was not, and still is not), and partly because of their highly personal and emotional nature.

So, on the first day that the possibility of life after death was seriously raised in this otherwise close family – surely it is odd in itself that such a fundamental subject should not be discussed – two members admitted for the first time to experiences of the sort described by the pioneering Kubler-Ross and Moody.

To add to these coincidences – consider this exchange, which took place on a train on the following day. Chatting sociably with three speech therapists on the way to a conference, the subject of 'near-death' experiences arose. Two of the ladies expressed interest, but the third remained quiet and thoughtful. Before there was a chance to describe Dr Moody's researches in full detail, she interrupted the conversation with an experience of her own. Three years before she had undergone gynaecological surgery. As she was being anaesthetised, she felt a fleeting sensation that there was panic in the operating room. Then came the rushing noise, the tunnel, the out-of-body experience, and the flooding with light, and a feeling of great joy and peace. The next sensation was wakening in the hospital bed after her operation. Her anaesthetist later admitted that she had had a brief period of cardiac arrest during the operation. All this the lady volunteered without any knowledge of other people's similar experiences. Indeed she had mentioned it to no one for fear of being laughed at, although the experience was so real to her that she now has absolutely no fear of death. Imagine her amazement, and that of her two companions, when they were given the first draft of this chapter of the book to read!

A similar coincidence awaited the other author when discussing the subject for the first time with her family. One of them, Dr John Harrison, a thirty-seven-year-old plant biologist, described a strikingly similar experience without being told any details other than that some strange stories had emerged when researching for this chapter. He described how at the age of seventeen with a ruptured appendix, complicated by peritonitis and pneumonia, he underwent an emergency operation performed by Mr Wilson Harlow, an eminent surgeon.

Hardly expected to survive the operation he surprised everyone by hanging on, but lay for days semi-conscious and still expected to die. For ten days he was fed intravenously. His weight dropped to only five stones, and temporarily paralysed from the waist down he had no control of functions. It was becoming increasingly difficult to find a vein for the drip and in pain, with his tongue peeling from dehydration, he felt his will to live weakening. In desperation John Harrison pleaded with his special nurse for just a little fluid by mouth. Perhaps because at that stage there seemed nothing to lose as he was so clearly dying, she gave in and offered a drop of milk. When he immediately vomited it back, he clearly remembers taking the decision to give up the fight and seek peace in death. Immediately the pain left him and he was outside his body looking down on himself; then he was floating through what seemed like a long, cool, green valley; at the far end was a bright light like a stretch of glistening water, and all around he was aware of people, many of them strangers but some whom he sensed were dead relatives, in particular his maternal grandfather whom he had loved very much in life.

His story is particularly interesting because at this point he knew that he had a choice – either to stay with them all in peace which would be death, or go back and fight on which would be life. His decision to go back was made reluctantly and simply because he didn't want to let down the nurse who had tried to help him. In retrospect he feels this was a strange reason as there was no more than the usual nurse-patient bond between them, but he feels now that she represented – in some way perhaps because she was the last person he had seen – *all* the others on earth who had cared about him and cared for him.

Once his conscious decision was made, he was back in his body and again dimly aware of the ward and the nurse crying because she had considered he was dead.

The fight back to normality and health after that took five months and over the years that followed he told the story to no one except his mother as he felt embarrassed about it. In some ways the experience had an unexpected effect, turning him from a religious young man not into an atheist but at least into an agnostic, questioning established beliefs and certain that far from being controlled by outside forces we actually control our own destiny. It also left him afraid neither of death nor any other experience.

There's no better way to finish this book than with the true story of Durdana Khan, a young Pakistani girl, now living in London with her doctor father. In November 1968, when she was two and a half years old, Durdana had been taken very ill. She was thought to have encephalitis: her attacks of vomiting, episodes of blindness, clumsiness and finally paralysis were extremely distressing, and both her parents knew she was dying.

One morning, while Dr Khan was in the nearby Army Medical Unit – the family were posted to a station in the Himalayan foothills at the time – his wife called him urgently to Durdana's cot. The child was dead. Mrs Khan took the still, small body gently into the bedroom, and laid her on her husband's bed, a bed with which Durdana was almost completely unfamiliar. Dr Khan half-heartedly, knowing that it was useless, carried out the mandatory army resuscitation procedures, while repeating, silently, in his mind, 'Come back, my child, come back.'

There was still no sign of life. Mrs Khan handed him a phial of nikethamide, a heart stimulant, which he trickled into Durdana's mouth. To the Khans' astonishment, she woke up, complaining about the medicine's bitterness. Although she slept again for a while, she then began to recover slowly. She had been 'dead' for at least a quarter of an hour.

A day or two later, Durdana told her mother where she had been while 'dead'. 'Far, far away, to the stars,' she said 'where there were gardens with apples, grapes and pomegranates, and streams.'

'What else?' asked her mother.

'My grandfather was there, and his mother and another lady who looked liked you,' she told her mother. 'Grandpa said he was glad to see me, and his mother took me in her lap and kissed me.'

'Then what happened?'

'I heard Daddy calling me, "Come back, my child, come back." I said to Grandpa, "I must go now; Daddy is calling me." He said we would have to ask God. Holding his hand we went to God, and Grandpa told Him that I wanted to go back. "Do you want to go back?" asked God. "Yes," I said, "Daddy is calling me." "All right," said God, "Go." I said "bye bye" and down, down, down I fell from the stars onto Daddy's bed.'

'And what was God like?'

'Blue.'

'Blue?'

'Yes, blue.'

'But what did He look like?'

'Blue.'

Try as she could, Mrs Khan could get nothing more than 'blue' from the child.

Durdana's suffering was not yet over. The 'encephalitis' turned out to be a brain tumour, which needed extensive surgery. The neurosurgeon Dr O.V. Jooma, of the Jinnah Post Graduate Centre in Karachi, said about the Khans – 'They brought me a dead child, but somehow against all the odds, she survived.'

Before leaving the city after the operation, Durdana was taken by her mother for the first visit to her great uncle's home. While stumbling about the living room, she suddenly pointed with great excitement to a photograph on a table.

'Mummy,' she said, 'this is my grandfather's mother. She was up in the stars and she took me in her lap and kissed me.'

Durdana's great grandmother had died long before the little girl's birth and this, the only photograph of the old lady, had never been shown to her before that day. Nor indeed had she seen pictures of her grandfather, who had also died before she was born.

Dr Khan's story is all the more remarkable on several points. His wife knew nothing about the 'Come back, my child, come back' plea, nor had Durdana been conscious enough to be aware that she was on her father's bed when she 'came back'. The couple were sure that she had never heard stories from them or anyone else about heaven or any place such as the one she described. The 'blue' of God Dr Khan can only believe expresses His infinite nature, without the form or shape of finite things.

The sequel is bitter-sweet. Durdana is now thirteen, very talented in art and music. Her mother died in 1979. She and her father picture her in the gardens Durdana visited those years ago, with grapes and apples and pomegranates, by the beautiful streams . . .

Of course, scientists believe they can explain everything that has been described. As the brain dies, or is severely shocked by sudden injury, the tape-recording within may unwind and replay old memories or produce bizarre hallucinations which have a chemical or electrical, but purely material, basis. We don't ask any reader to take all, or even any part, of what is written here as proving that death is not the ultimate limit. Judge that for yourselves. It is not difficult to do so. Just ask a few close friends or relatives some leading questions. It is not a scientific thing to do: scientists are only supposed to believe volunteered statements given 'blind' to the background information.

But then no one volunteers information about events that are so personal. The taboo about death and dying is the strongest one in our society. The fact that doctors have taken the lead in telling what they now see as the truth to the dying patient may be the first step in destroying it. If it is, it may be the beginning of an enormous expansion of our understanding of life, death and their purpose. There may be a vast reservoir of knowledge hidden under the inhibitions of the ordinary, average man and woman, which once tapped will not easily be dammed up again. Or there may be nothing at all.

Are we ready to take the risk and open the flood gates?

Epilogue

Determining normal human potential has been the easiest part of the book. Structure, fuel intake, capacity, power, mechanical defects, wear and tear, all these are the rational limiting factors proscribing man's possible achievements and endurance. Competently driven, we should then all be able to go just so far and just so fast, but never beyond that without a breakdown.

In man, however, it does not work like that. Machine he may be, but he is also something more. There is another factor, a quality of mind and spirit which enables him to reach out far beyond the normal physical and mental limits to defy the mere mechanical rules.

This book inevitably leaves many questions unanswered, but at least one powerful influence emerges clearly. It is difficult to define. Perhaps the nearest we can get to it in a single word is 'motivation' and it comes in many forms – for Odette it was patriotism and love, for Kitty Hart a burning desire for justice, for Mawson and the Robertsons it was basically the urge to survive. Athletic achievers find their motivation in their ambition to be the best or the greatest. Habeler and Messner aiming for the top of the world just wanted to do what no one else had done unaided. Another famous mountaineer, Chris Bonnington, summed up for us the vital role of motivation. 'One of the key requirements to survival is being accustomed to the environment in which you are to survive. If an experienced mountaineer is caught halfway up the North Wall of the Eiger or on the South West Face of Everest by a savage storm he is in a situation which he has met on many occasions before and, therefore, he is equipped to deal with it. The completely inexperienced mountaineer would be psyched out by the situation before even the cold, the wind and the snow had made any effect. The experienced climber, on the other hand knows how to keep himself warm and dry and can be comparatively comfortable in a situation which would kill the inexperienced. It is, therefore, very much in the mind built up by experience, that the individual survives these kinds of incidents.

The remarkable thing, perhaps, is where an individual, such as the pilot of an aircraft, is landed in a wild situation which is completely outside his experience and then manages to survive. This probably is caused by his adaptability, his coolness and his determination to live.'

Individually and collectively human potential could be unlimited if spirit and will worked together to this end. The old elements of aggression so strongly built into human genes as basic equipment for survival need to be modified by a new spirit. The obscene expenditure on fuelling our own destruction could, if we set a different course, clear poverty, disease and famine from the earth.

If this book shows anything at all it is that the motivation and will-power inherent in the ordinary human being should enable us as a species to do just that.

Bibliography

The Guinness Book of Records — Ross and Norris McWhirter
The Body in Question — Jonathan Miller
The Body — Anthony Smith
Man – Hot & Cold — Otto Edholm
Supernature — Lyall Watson
The Fearful Void — Geoffrey Moorhouse
Wind Sand and Stars — Antoine de Saint Exupéry
The Home of the Blizzard — Douglas Mawson
This Accursed Land — Leonard Bicknell
Alive!: Story of the Andes Survivors — Piers Paul Read
Dolly Dimples — Celesta Geye
Survive the Savage Sea — Dougal Robertson
The Gathering Storm — Winston Churchill
Sleep: The Gentle Tyrant — Wilse B. Webb
Functions of Sleep — Ernest Hartman
Modern Track & Field — Kenneth Doherty
The Complete Book of Running — James F. Fixx
The Remedial Therapist — Mike Tetley
The Stages of Human Life — J. Lionel Taylor
Four Million Footsteps — Bruce Tulloh
Heart Attack? Counterattack! — Ted Kavanagh
Touching — Ashley Montague
Hilary — Dorothy Clarke Wilson
Lessons from Childhood — R. S. and C. M. Illingworth
Know Your Own I.Q. — H. J. Eysenck
Memory — Prof. Ian Hunter
Parallels – A Look at Twins — Tel Wolfner
The Doors of Perception — Aldous Huxley
The Paranormal — Stan Gooch
Odette — Jerrard Tickell
Pain – Sensations & Reactions — Williams & Wilkins
The Puzzle of Pain — Ronald Melzack
McIndoe's Army — Peter Williams
Apologie and Treatise — Ambroise Pare
Pain Mechanisms — W. K. Livingstone
Nerves and Nerve Injuries — E. & S. Livingstone
Pain and the Neurosurgeons — J. C. White and W. H. Sweet
No Change — Wendy Cooper
A Good Age — Alex Comfort
Beyond Death's Door — Maurice Rawlings
Life After Life — Raymond Moody
You Cannot Die — Ian Currie
Twenty Cases Suggestive of Reincarnation — Ian Stevenson
More Lives Than One? — Jeffrey Iverson
Premature Burial — W. R. Hawden
The Romeo Error — Lyall Watson